The Mystery of the Great Zimbabwe

A NEW SOLUTION

Wilfrid Mallows

W.W. NORTON & COMPANY · NEW YORK · LONDON

The text of this book is composed in Caledonia, with
display type set in Weiss Italic. Composition by the Vail-Ballou Press, Inc.
Manufacturing by the Murray Printing Company.
Book design by Nancy Dale Muldoon.

First Edition

Library of Congress Cataloging in Publication Data

Mallows, E.W.N. (Edward Wilfrid Nassau), 1905–
    The Mystery of the Great Zimbabwe: a new solution

    Bibliography: p.
    Includes index.
    1. Great Zimbabwe (City)   I. Title.
DT962.9.G73M34   1984   968.91   83–8189

ISBN 0-393-01789-3

W. W. Norton & Company, Inc., 500 Fifth Avenue, New York, N.Y. 10110
W. W. Norton & Company Ltd., 37 Great Russell Street, London WC1B 3NU

1 2 3 4 5 6 7 8 9 0

To
DIDA GAYK TONY CECCA
For whom this book was in danger of becoming
more of a myth than a mystery

I love to lose myself in a mystery.
—*Sir Thomas Browne*

Contents

LIST OF PLATES

LIST OF FIGURES

Preface

EVERY building, every structure, every town or city made by humans, has a code, or if you like, a signature tune. This code or tune is its plan, which grew directly out of its function, out of the job it was designed to do for those who made it, or caused it to be made. In the normal way of building or planning, a program is first made setting out this job—a "brief", a "schedule of accommodation"—and after that a process of planning and design starts that eventually, after many mishaps, false starts, and backfires, ends up somehow with the final product, the completed building or town. This connected sequence of Program-Process-Product is the well-worn track down which every architect, designer, or planner has to travel every day of his working life, and with the internal linkings, cross-currents, and continual harassments she or he is all too familiar.

In the case of ancient structures whose origins, nature, constructors, and designers (if any) all remain unknown or at very best uncertain, this sequence of Program-Process-Product can be reversed into Product-Process-Program. One can start with the Product, which lies there on the ground for all to see, and then by a careful study of the plan and its siting retrace the linkage through the Process back to the Program and so indicate possible profiles of authors and instigators. By doing this one can break the secret code of the building and uncover the blunt truth of its purpose and origin.

The Great Zimbabwe ruins in Southern Africa can be put through this reversed process of analysis. Theories of their purpose, origin, and most particularly their potential authors, have provoked intense controversy out of all proportion to their probable proximity to any truth, and from which streams of theory but very few facts have emerged; so that still today, well over one hundred years since their first discovery by the hunter Adam Renders in 1867, they remain almost as much a mystery as when he first set eyes on them.

The ruins lie on the ground, some mixed with improbable, surrealistic rocks on a hill for all to see and touch. They have their own definite physical pattern and inter-relationship, yet no one—despite many books by experts and not-so-experts—has yet attempted to analyse the plans, uncover their program, and so break their code.

This book is such an attempt, but also tries to go further. Having broken the code of the building, it then examines a series of historical contexts that might provide a "fit" to the program uncovered by the breaking of the code. With some surprise, after fairly extensive enquiries from a great variety of historical and other sources, a possible historical "fit" was found for the program. What had been required was some history mixed with planning analysis.

The result of that mixture, based on logic and common sense, is surprising enough to make a good story, although it takes a

Western reader into somewhat uncharted seas of history—the little-known byways of that most ancient East, the monsoon world of the Indian Ocean lands, the cradle of civilised humanity.

The result is very contrary to most current explanations, but if seen in its total context it becomes one way of giving a coherent meaning to what has remained so long and so obstinately an intriguing mystery. It can only be left to the reader, expert in any field, or just plain commonsense person, to judge the result.

Acknowledgments

Thanks are first due to two friends: Mr. John Barkham of New York, who had the kindness and foresight to introduce me to my publishers; and Mr. George Brockway of W. W. Norton, who gave severe but sympathetic criticism throughout. To these two I owe the birth of the book.

To four others special thanks are due: Julian Kraft, who originally explored the ruins and their setting with me in detail and took part in the early discussions and data collection; Mr. C. K. Cooke, of the National Museums and Monuments of Zimbabwe, who gave good advice about the ruins on the spot, made accessible all the records and maps in the museum at Bulawayo, and gave permission for the reproduction of his photograph of the entrance to the Khami ruins (plate 28); Hugh McNeil, who made available photographs of the ruins taken by his father, H. H. McNeil, in 1914 (plates 4 and 7), as well as the astonishing metallic object found in the ruins at the same time (see Appendix); and John Minnery, who took a keen interest in the project while in Bulawayo and later in Australia pointed out the possibility of Indonesian and Melanesian influences.

Grateful acknowledgment is due many others who gave information, answered queries, or provided material: Wilhelm Dolgner, for translating long sections of the *Mohit* dealing with the navigation of the Red Sea and the African East Coast; Mr. A. C. Campbell, director of the National Museum and Art Gallery, Gaborone, who gave data on prehistoric ruins and mines in Botswana, as well as the astonishing hollow wooden buffalo; Mr. Hassan Ahmed Maniku, director, Department of Information and Broadcasting, Male, Republic of Maldives, for historical and navigational material; Dr. D. N. Beach, University of Zimbabwe, and Mr. J.R.D. Cobbing, Rhodes University, for comments on the legend of "bullet-proof" medicines; Mr. A. J. Dieperink of Potgietersrus, for detailed siting of the rock painting near the Salt Pan (see Appendix); Mr. R. W. Dickenson, University of Zimbabwe, for information on Sofala and the routes to the interior; Mr. Michael Law, and Mr. Alan Tyler of the Planning Department, Shrewsbury, for information on the hill forts of Old Owestry and the Wrekin; Mrs. N. H. Wilson and the University of the Witwatersrand Press for permission to quote passages from João de Barros, *Da Asia*, vol. 1 (Lisbon, 1778), quoted on p. 142 in E. Axelson, *Portuguese in South-East Africa, 1488–1660* (Cape Town; copyright University of the Witwatersrand, Johannesburg, Ernest Oppenheimer Institute of Portuguese Studies, 1973); Little Brown and Company of Boston, publishers of *The African Past*, by Basil Davidson; and the staff of the Inter Library Loan section of the Library of the University of the Witwatersrand for their continuous assistance.

Acknowledgments are also due for permission to quote from the following books: to the Pathfinder Press of New York and

W.E.B. du Bois for the quotation at the head of the Prologue; to the University of London Press and Professor George Kay for the quotation at the head of Chapter 4; and to the Oxford University Press and G.S.P. Freeman-Grenville for the quotation at the head of Chapter 8.

Equally grateful acknowledgment is due to the staff of three official agencies in Zimbabwe for providing illustrations. The Tourist Board provided the fine photographs for plates 1, 2, 12, and 27; the National Archives, the now critical photographs for plates 5, 6, 17, and 19 showing the state of the walls and entrances before "restoration"; and especially the Surveyor-General, Harare, for the air photographs of the Marhumbini dock, specially enlarged for this book and making clear for the first time its real nature and extent. The National Museums and Monuments also gave much advice on the source of possible illustrations.

Other organizations gave permission for illustrations: Ms. Barbara A. Shattuck on behalf of *National Geographic* magazine, for the drawings of dhows (plate 24); Mr. P. L. Shinnie of the University of Calgary and his publishers Thames and Hudson of London for the figures from his book *Meroe: A Civilisation of the Sudan* (figures 24, 25, and 26); Mr. N. J. Van Warmelo and the Government Printer, Pretoria, for the portraits from *Ethnological Publication*, vol. 8, "The Copper Mines of Musina and the Early History of the Soutpansberg", reproduced under Government Printer's copyright Authority 7890 of 12–11–1982 (plates 21, 22, and 23); the Hydrographer of the Navy, United Kingdom, for the diagrams from *Africa Pilot*, vol. 3 (figures 19 and 20); the Argus-Africa News Service for plate 11; City Lab (Pty.) Ltd for plate 29 (in Appendix); and Engineering Reproduction Services (Pty.) Ltd for the photo reduction of most of the figures.

Personal friends lent their own photographs or drawings: Glynton le Roux, plates 3, 8, 9, 10, 13, 15, 16, 18, 26, and the sketch of the stone door (figure 29); Rudy Erasmus, plate 14; and Johann Louw, the plan of the East Ruins.

My most sincere thanks to Mrs. Ann Bell, who typed the text, notes, and references several times, with a dedicated commitment that was equalled only by the illegibility of my manuscript; and to Ms. Pat Raybould, who made all the fine drawings for the figures.

Finally, my thanks are due above all to my wife, who urged me to complete the book and willingly gave up, over several years, many hours and days of scarce leisure time.

The Mystery of the
Great Zimbabwe

PROLOGUE

Ancient Africa

Africa, Mother of Man.
—*W.E.B. Du Bois*

AFRICA is still the oldest and darkest continent. It has, still surviving, relics of the world's remotest past, and it holds like closely guarded secrets many puzzles and problems lying still unsolved. Its image is of something strange and wild, very strong and very old: a place of hard, unconquerable deserts; of deep and tangled forests; of endless plains with scattered bush, unremitting sunshine, and many more animals than humans—an older and prehuman continent in which man for millenia was always an intruder.

This ancient Africa was, and is, Africa south of the Sahara. To the north there is the coastal strip, which is part of the Mediterranean world, the world of Egypt and Carthage, of Greece and Rome, and the later Arab Empires of the west. This northern strip was called Libya by the Greeks and Africa by the Romans; both names were from local dialects and both were gradually transferred from a local district to the whole unknown continent. In both cases the names are so old that both their origins and meanings have been forgotten.

But south of the Sahara there is another Africa altogether, the real continental Africa stretching 3,500 miles to its southern tip against the Southern Ocean. This Africa is made up, broadly, of three portions each very different in their size, character, and history.

The first portion is a broad east-west belt immediately south of the Sahara between the Atlantic and Indian oceans. This is itself a belt of great diversity, from the semi-arid savanna next the Sahara in the north, from the green highland valleys of Abyssinia in the east, to the fever-thick coastal swamps in the south and west. This Africa is the scene of the great medieval African Empires, Mali and Songhai, Fulani and Bornu and the famous gold of Wangara. This was later the coast par excellence of the European slave traders, stocking up as fast as they could, both the Americas with black Africans and their future racial problems, for the best part of two centuries. This is still the same setting of the new modern African states, of Liberia and Ghana, Nigeria, Togo, Sierra Leone, and many others. This is the seedbed of Negro Africa, the source from which so much of Africa has been peopled, in spite of the centuries-old human denudation caused by the slave trade.

The second portion is the smallest in area but by no means the least important—the great belt of the equatorial rain forests covering the basin of the Congo, the second largest river in the world. These stretch from the Atlantic on the west to the

Mountains of the Moon and the great lakes on the east. This is the home of the largest apes, the gorillas, and equally of the smallest men, the Pygmies of the equatorial forest, a vestigial relic of the earliest human days. Although the very opposite of the desert, yet this belt of the rain forest is just as effective a barrier, its central position barring access both ways—east-west and north-south.

The third portion is the remainder of the continent—a great L-shaped slab covering the whole east coast fronting the Indian Ocean and all that is left, south of the equatorial forests. This is—beyond a low coastal fringe—a vast interior plateau 3,000 to 5,000 feet above sea level stretching from the tropics to the Mediterranean climate of the Cape of Good Hope, and from the Atlantic to the Indian Ocean.

This central plateau is generally tilted from a long line of mountains behind the coastal plain on the east to a difficult and semi-arid country on the west against the Atlantic. One great river, the Zambezi, starting only 300 miles from the Atlantic and flowing 2,000 miles to the Indian Ocean, dominates the northern portion of the plateau; south of its basin lies the Kalahari desert, the southern equivalent of the Sahara and like the Sahara effectively cutting off north from south, east from west. South of the Kalahari again, the semi-arid Karoo of South Africa continues the same story.

Everywhere in this eastern and southern third portion of Africa it was only on the east, along the line of the great lakes or on the high edge of the plateau above the coastal plain, that north-south movement was possible.

Along the coast there was, to reinforce this movement, the uncanny god-given constancy of the monsoon winds, blowing half the year south and the other half north, asking for exploitation by man with his very ancient invention of the sail. It was along this eastern edge, linked to the coast and its sea lanes, that all life and movement was concentrated; here is the source of most of its history. It is essentially an eastward-looking land, with its back to the Atlantic and its face across the ocean, towards the Indies, Indonesia, and faraway China. It is this third portion of Africa that is the home of the oldest living things left in the world today: relics of a remote past far older than the emergence of humanity.

There are the cycads, giant ferns, still living and growing as they did in the Mesozoic forests, contemporary with the great reptiles, 100 million years ago. There is the huge baobab tree, the tree that looks all wrong with a trunk one hundred feet in girth and branches at the top suddenly ending in nothing: a relic of primeval forests dead many millions of years ago, a tree that can last 1,000 years and never seems to grow, only shrinking and swelling with the longer rhythms of the years. In its eastern waters still living was the coelacanth, and in its western deserts, a spider, both belonging to species thought extinct 250 million years ago.

Here too, more recent, only two to three million years ago, are the earliest relics of what was to be the greatest predator of all time—man himself, at first so scattered, small, and weak. Here were found the tiny skulls of *Australopithecus africanus* linking the apes and men, found in Southern Africa halfway between Great Zimbabwe and the southern tip of the continent. Here too are the later but still unique relics of another animal past: the hippopotamus wallowing in mud and water; the rhinoceros with the surprising single or double horn in the centre of his skull; the unicorn of medieval legend.

Africa is an old land, with queer and strange survivals. It is the dark of the world's past, closed to the casual, compelling to the curious or determined. It is another world, old beyond memory and strange beyond experience, sending unhappy vibrations down the spine of the

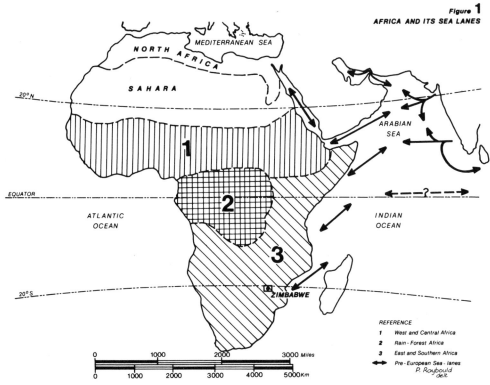

Figure **1**
AFRICA AND ITS SEA LANES

REFERENCE
1   West and Central Africa
2   Rain-Forest Africa
3   East and Southern Africa
◄► Pre-European Sea-lanes
P. Raybould
delt

Africa, south of the Sahara, looks east, not west, and
Zimbabwe lies at the southern end of these sea lanes.

mind, questioning all accepted truths, all accepted interpretations of one's own experience. It opens a void that only study and time can fill.

It is in this old and strange central-southern portion of Africa that the Great Zimbabwe lies, and so it is this part of the sub-continent, south of the Zambezi River, that gives the African setting for the long Zimbabwean story.

CHAPTER 1

The Setting

For there is no going so sweet as upon the old dreams of men.
—*Edward Thomas*

SOUTHERN AFRICA— "ONE VAST RUIN FIELD"

THE ruins of the Great Zimbabwe, lying about 300 miles south of the Zambezi and 250 miles from the Indian Ocean, form one of the most extensive, impressive, and extraordinary group of ruins anywhere in Africa, and indeed, of their kind, in the world. They have been called the greatest stone monument on the African continent, apart from Egypt, and they remain still today largely unexplained, with queer anomalies that make them virtually unique, without parallels elsewhere that might give some lead to their identity.

These ruins are, however, only the most outstanding and astonishing of a vast extent of stone ruins, scattered very unevenly over Southern Africa between the Zambezi and the Orange rivers—a distance of 900 miles north-south and 300 miles east-west, making a total of 270,000 square miles. This covers present-day Zimbabwe, Botswana, Maputo, and the northern half of South Africa.

Within this area there are wide divergencies in type, size, age, and interest. Some, like the Great Zimbabwe, are grand, exciting monuments to see at any time; others are intriguing because they are imposing to see at first and then frustrating because their plan and meaning is any-thing but obvious; others—and these are many—are so ruinous and disjointed with low, stunted walls that although they are clearly the work of people with definite skills and some sense of purpose, they seem to defy forever any complete solution to the puzzle they present.

Their number is as surprising as their distribution. There are over 600 listed stone ruins in Zimbabwe alone, between the Zambezi and Limpopo rivers, and nearly 7,500 further ruins have now been identi-fied in the northern areas of South Africa—that is, in the Transvaal and Orange Free State. Reports of ruins from other areas, in Botswana and the northern part of the Cape Province, suggest these figures, if all the ruins were known, could be much fur-ther increased, since much of our knowl-edge comes from air photos, where often thick vegetation makes identification of ruins impossible and ground surveys do not exist. For this reason, it is thought this number could be more than doubled, making the total number of ruins in South-ern Africa run to 18,000 or even 20,000. A production of this magnitude, spread over many centuries, peoples, and countries, represents a major part of Southern Afri-can history both before and after the white man came. Some ruins may be as many as 1,500 or even 2,000 years old, while some were built only yesterday. This compares

5

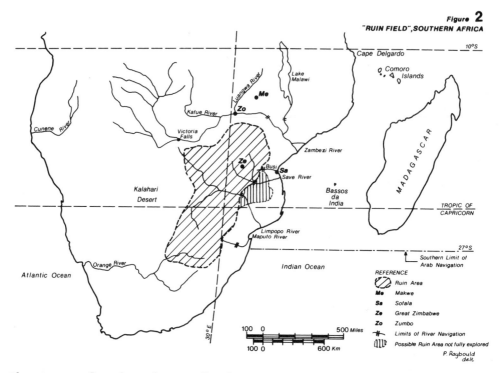

The ruin area reflects the modern as well as the ancient extent of human settlement, due to the same causes—climate, food supply, and access to Indian Ocean ports.

both in space and time with the 4,000 or so megalithic monuments of Western Europe built over an even longer time— up to 2,500 years; and the seemingly endless expenditure of time and energy that these European monuments represent is equally though very differently reflected by the Southern African ruins. Both groups show the same determination to make some statement beyond immediate necessity, beyond the next rainstorm or next planting season; both must have believed in some overriding purpose that appeared to them, at the time at least, permanent, stable, and beyond doubt worth working for, perhaps fighting for. The measurement of the seasons for a settled agricultural society such as seems the almost certain purpose of Stonehenge and other stone circles of Europe is intelligible enough. But what purpose did these Southern African stone ruins serve, in a society where the price of

survival was continual movement, agriculture was a small garden near one's hut, and staying too long in one place spelt famine and disaster? Such a fundamental anomaly deserves some attempt at an answer.

What is most surprising about this mass of ruins is how little is known accurately about them. There are, to begin with, no proper surveys. The Great Zimbabwe itself has never been accurately surveyed and the actual plans published often disagree, so that it is impossible to decide what was the original plan even after a detailed inspection on the site. Then again, immense damage was done in the first decade or so of European settlement before the ruins became legally protected. The Ancient Ruins Company was specifically formed by enterprising pioneers to "rape the ruins" by ransacking the ruins for gold and then melting the gold down to sell it. These pioneers not only removed the vital objects that could have given the key to the meaning of the whole culture for later archaeologists but also actually pulled down walls in their lust for treasure so that the actual plan became dismembered and less intelligible. From the early plan drawn up by the surveyor Robert Swan of the Great Enclosure, it would seem some vital portions of the central portion of the plan either disappeared completely or became meaningless heaps of stone.

For the wider problem of the distribution of ruins in Southern Africa as a whole, while air photos in the last twenty years or so have helped to some extent, their utility is not the utility given in Europe, where the cultivated landscape, by its reduced soil depths and vegetations over old foundations, can reflect a skeleton picture of the past. Not so in Africa: here there are no foundations, no roads or streets, and no long-standing cultivation. Thick vegetation cover often completely obscures the ruins and eliminates shadow, the great identifier. The air photos, however, have helped to establish the extent of ruins, stimulated the study of their shape and nature, and are making possible some overall perspective of distribution patterns. In this way a comparative analysis of the various forms and differing purposes of the ruins can be attempted, to give a setting in time and place to the Great Zimbabwe.

From the point of view of planning and design, three major groups can be identified, with sub-groups in the first two groups.

THE FIRST GROUP: ZIMBABWE STONEWORK

The first is the group associated with the Great Zimbabwe, the chief characteristic being its walling: regular courses of stones, generally granite, of fairly standard shape and size and very similar to large bricks, and built up into walls like brickwork but without any mortar. This is one of the first and most obvious anomalies of the Great Zimbabwe. Within this general group of Zimbabwe Stonework are the three major sub-groups, all very different in design and so in function.

The first sub-group: the Hill-Fortress

The first sub-group is the hill-top fortress, of which the so-called Acropolis at the Great Zimbabwe is the outstanding and most famous example. This type would appear to be, from its design, by far the oldest type, for the planning of these hill-top hide-outs or forts goes far back into the Neolithic Age, when caves surrounded by boulders, with very limited means of access, provided a naturally defensive post for protection from other raiding parties and a look-out for game which had to be tracked and killed for food. The great rock shelter at Makwe in Zambia, which was occupied as early as 3000 B.C., shows the human exploitation of a natural facility; and this is mirrored by the great rocks of Zimbabwe and their much greater and later exploitation into an artificial fortress. Such an example shows the long historical tradition of unconscious planning and invention that lies behind the Great Zimbabwe fortress. It was no sudden improvisation of alien people working from scratch: rocky hide-outs had long been a natural habitat of African man. Scattered over Southern Africa they were a natural invitation for men to use and exploit.

The second sub-group: the undefended ruin

The second sub-group, although still made of brick-like stones in regular courses, is otherwise exactly the opposite of the first. It consists of a series of enclosed spaces in more or less open ground often on top of a low granite dome, with good views but with no other apparent reason for its particular location, and with little natural defensive characteristics. The ruins are smaller in area, more simple in layout (often with no internal divisions), and much less interesting.

The Valley Ruins at Great Zimbabwe are all examples of this second sub-group, being simple enclosures on open ground, with no defensive characteristics in their siting. The Majiri ruins, about twenty-five miles southeast of Great Zimbabwe, and apparently the first night stop in the journey to the coast, are another example of this type, a series of sixteen enclosed areas grouped together on ground gently sloping to a little stream two hundred yards away. Another whole group of nine ruins in the Chiredzi area to the southeast in the Lundi Valley, only fifty miles or so from the Maputo border, are also similar low-walled enclosures, sometimes on a slight rise, lost in heavily bushed country. There could not be a greater contrast than the contrast between this type and the great hill-fortresses.

The third sub-group: the "status" platform

The third sub-group is in planning somewhat of a mixture of the first two. It is situated mainly to the west in old Matabeleland round Bulawayo and is considered to be later in date, but before the coming of the Portuguese to the east coast. The ruins consist basically of stone walls, often with patterned brickwork, and used as retaining walls for flat terraces on which living huts had been erected. These terraces at different levels, sometimes dispersed (such as Khami), or grouped tightly together (as at Dhlo-Dhlo or Naletale), formed the setting presumably for a chief's residence, with the huts of the rest of the population grouped round it but outside its perimeter. All that is now left are the terraces and their retaining walls and the indications of hut foundations and sometimes the chief's seat where he must have held audience. In this sub-group the high stone walling that dominates the Great

Zimbabwe and gives its character has shrunk to a secondary role of merely a retaining wall or an additional foundation to a complex of huts, even if the huts are those of the chiefs, their senior retainers, and their wives. Such places could in fact be described as "status" (or even more rudely "fun") palaces—they had no defensive characteristics whatever and their main purpose was apparently to give "image" to the place of the Great Chief. In one case, Naletale, it was to provide a decorated backdrop from the top—or the front—of which the chief could address the assembled multitude of his subjects in the open space; exactly as from any palace to any plaza at any time in any part of the world. Certainly at Naletale the relationship between the wide-open surface of rock immediately in front of the most spectacular (and most photographed) piece of walling seems very obvious, as the link place between palace and people. The siting of the ruin as a whole, moreover, is magnificently chosen: a clear view of ten to fifteen miles in practically all directions.

Naletale has another interesting aspect, perhaps typical, arising from its siting. It is the centre of a cluster and from its appearance the most important. The other members are so situated that they could have formed warning outposts—at such heights that there is a clear view between them for signalling (such as smoke signals, or drums), in case of danger. Figure 3 shows their relationship—one outpost to the west, three to the east and northeast. It is unlikely that this relationship is accidental.

These three sub-groups have always been grouped together as forming the products of one historically evolving culture, with its origins in Great Zimbabwe. The general belief is that the Zimbabwe culture, starting in the centre and east of the country, moved northwards and westwards; and the third sub-group was later in date and reflected the westward movement with different forms of political power, with a different economic base. The need for

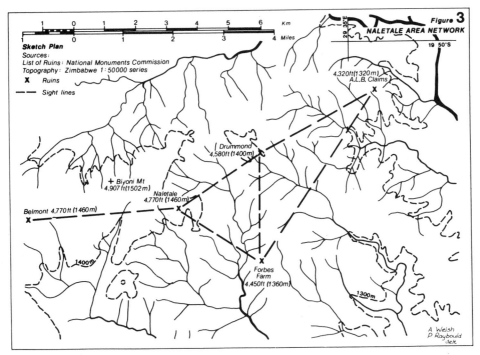

The relative heights show the possibility of inter-communication between strong points by sound, smoke, or other signals—but this needs further investigation.

extreme defensive measures caused by an acute dependence on overseas traders for economic and political strength, or by equally acute fear of jealous neighbours, may have disappeared, and with that disappearance, the simple functional fortress gave way to a decorated and image-conscious palace.

THE SECOND GROUP: TERRACED LANDSCAPE

This group has no visible connection with the Zimbabwe culture except that it is almost certainly pre-European, and used stone as a building material. The ruins here are connected with the vast terraced hillsides in the Inyanga district, north of present-day Mutare, close to the eastern border with Maputo in the high mountains, which form the inland border to the coastal low lands.

Here the stonework, the type of ruin, its layout, and above all the extent of the terracing are entirely different from the Great Zimbabwe complexes. The stonework is undressed, of random size as found in nature, and the consequent irregular gaps between the stones filled with small stone chips and wedges. This is usual the world over for random undressed masonry, but it is far away from the regular, coursed, dressed, and brick-like masonry of the Great Zimbabwe ruins. The plan and design of the ruins within or at the margin of the terraced area are also very different. There are two kinds.

The first kind: the simple fort

This is a simple fort, at the top of a hill or rise, built of the random masonry described but without the assistance of natural rock outcrops, which were not available here. These forts are sometimes just one enclosure, or a series of enclosures clustered round a central enclosure. Some have small holes in the walls, which have been called loopholes, but they are at unusual heights—2' or 4' above the ground—and their use is doubtful: one African story is that they were used to drag the enemy to the wall by a kind of harpoon and then to kill him there. It would seem most of them were places of refuge, used in emergencies only, and not permanent garrison stations.

The second kind: the sunken pit

This second kind in the Inyanga terraced area are what Cecil Rhodes first called "slave pits" but which are now thought most certainly to have been small stock shelters, for sheep or goats or quite possibly very small cattle. The ruins consist of a built-up circular stone platform round a sunken pit 20' to 25' in diameter and up to 8' deep, generally on a hillside so that the central pit can be approached by a covered passage under the surrounding platform on the uphill side with a drain as the only outlet on the downhill side. The pit sides are lined with stone and the floor is carefully paved—for what? To thresh and store grain? To collect manure every morning and take it to the fields?

Whatever was put in the pit was limited in size: passages were only 1' to 3' high and halfway through had a small light-well in which a vertical bar could be placed effectually blocking the passage. This vertical bar ended above in a hut so that immediate notice could be taken by the guard in the hut of any movement in the passage. A more sophisticated lock could be provided by a horizontal bar in a slot, with a vertical plug at one end locking it in position across the passage, and the plug controlled similarly by a guard in a hut on the platform above.

The terraced hillsides

But the most astonishing element of this second group is what must have been their economic base—the endless terracing of the hillsides themselves. The sheer quantity is

what makes this second group of stone users a group apart and of a special, unexplained importance both economically and historically. Whatever caused such effort? The only similarity with the Zimbabwe area was a possible gold trade, but in this case it was alluvial gold; but that must have been a peripheral seasonal activity, quite independent of the terracing. No full plans of the whole terraced area are available, but the importance of this area was realised in the very early days of European occupation by a mining engineer, one Telford Edwards, who knew very well what earth moving and stone construction meant in real life. Here is his account, from his journey through the area, the first ever made by a trained man, in November 1898:

For fifty miles I saw these ruins. I saw at least one and a half miles each side of the road, equalling fifty by three, that is one hundred and fifty square miles.

If the whole of the stones, mullock, earth, etc., which we saw on the slopes of the hills and valleys in terraces and ruined buildings could be distributed evenly over a flat surface it would run to about one and a half feet thick. This means 27,878,400 square feet (1 square mile) multiplied by one and a half feet, or 41,817,600 cubic feet. Taking this at twenty-four cubic feet to the ton we have, about 1,739,190 tons of ground per mile square and as we have a hundred and fifty square miles to deal with, we get a total tonnage of manipulated "ground" of something like 261,773,750 tons!

. . . The ruins are principally terraces, which rise up continually from the base to the apex of all the hills in the district in vertical lifts about two or three feet, and extended backwards over a distance of mostly about seven to twelve feet. The terraces are all made very flat and of dry masonry. . . . the way that the ancients seem to have levelled off the contours of the various hills around which the water courses are laid is very astonishing, as they seem to have been levelled with as much exactitude as we can accomplish with our best mathematical instruments.

So much for a first intelligent impression: but Edwards' estimate was wildly out. A later researcher, Roger Summers, estimated that the terraces and ruins cover not 150 but up to 3,000 square miles to form, as Summers states, "one vast ruin field", although the distribution of ruins over such an area is of course uneven. But even so, by how much more must Edwards' estimate of human effort be multiplied? Twenty times more—the difference between 150 and 3,000? 5,200 *million* tons of earth and stones moved—all by hand without any wheeled equipment whatever? The calculation becomes absurd and cries out for accurate detailed surveys of the whole area before any sensible answer can be found; but whatever the final answer, the total figure is bound to be so large that it will need a lot of explaining to make any economic or historic sense, in that wider perspective of human affairs that is world history.

As one of the excavators of the ruins remarked, the inhabitants, whoever they were, were unusually tidy in everything they did—including their final abandonment of the ruins and terraces at the end. The impression gained is that they must have left as they had lived—"in perfect marching order", without haste and without the slightest confusion. A queer people with another flavour altogether, almost naval in its trimness: why did they come here in the first place and not elsewhere, and then do such gigantic work on those hillsides? Still more inexplicably, why did they leave everything when in such good order, and, having left, where did they go?

THE THIRD GROUP: FARMING SHELTERS

The third group of stone ruins in Southern Africa south of the Zambezi is by far the largest, most widely distributed, and most widely ignored by all except the professional archaeologist and to some extent the professional historian. Yet from the human point of view they are vital and illuminating since they have a continuous history, probably from Zimbabwe times right down to the present day, when blacks can be found still building stone walls, in modern towns, impelled by the sheer folk-momentum of a thousand years or more.

The ruins are spread over the whole area south of the Limpopo River—say south of 22° South—and were made by simple, straightforward farming people, agriculturalists and pastoralists, looking after their flocks and herds and cultivating their small gardens very much as pictured in the Jewish and Muslim scriptures. The stonework formed the base of their circular mud huts and their smaller, sometimes semi-conical granaries. Low stone walls surrounded a group of huts or inversely a walled enclosure itself was surrounded by huts, to ensure their basic wealth, cattle, were safely under control in their midst. The safety these stone walls represented in fact was the safety of keeping cattle in, not intruders out: none of the walls could do more than hinder very temporarily any determined invader. The tradition of the great fortified hill-top hide-outs of the Zimbabwe people, whoever they may have been, had been largely forgotten—except for one very interesting and significant example. The BaVenda tribe, just south of the Limpopo, having according to their own traditions migrated from the Zimbabwe country north of the Limpopo and finding themselves in hill country, continued the tradition of the hill-top fortress and built villages "perched on inaccessible sites or precipitous slopes". When the testing time came in the murderous Mfecane, or Time of Troubles, in the early nineteenth century, only the BaVenda were saved from destruction. Elsewhere the lack of this tradition and the virtually defenceless state of all stone settlements brought to a bloody and appalling end thousands of peaceful and prosperous people. All that was left, as the early missionaries saw, were their bones picked white and clean by vultures and the blackened and shattered remnants of their stone walls.

It was the end of a thousand years or more. The great tradition of stone building had been given a death blow: for when recovery came after several decades, it was in another world altogether, dominated by strange and foreign ways, of houses that moved on wheels, and men on horses. In this world the slow building of stone walls, wooden huts, and grass roofs was no competitor to corrugated iron and mud bricks.

Building in stone lingered on only in forgotten corners as a fossilised habit, a silent testimony to inherited skills of many centuries, and perhaps a warning that all change is not necessarily progress and that every gain carries, within itself, its own loss.

CHAPTER 2

The Great Zimbabwe Complex

The Pyramids themselves, doting with age, have forgotten the names
of their founders . . .   *—Sir Thomas Browne*

THE GREAT ZIMBABWE AS A WHOLE

OF all this mass of stonework and stone building in Southern Africa, Great Zimbabwe dominates beyond any possible competition by its size, its quality, and its unexplained, absorbing, even infuriating, interest. These astonishing ruins lie in two quite discrete and opposing groups.

There is first the group on the hill-top up till now called the Acropolis but more accurately Hill-Fortress; and down below, half a mile away from the hill and the opposite side from the Fortress' entrance as if deliberately avoiding any connections, a group of queer, nondescript assemblages of walls called the Valley Ruins. These are dominated on the higher ground to one side by the vaguely elliptical-shaped enclosure originally called the Temple but now more accurately and modestly called the Great Enclosure, encircled by its own Great Wall.

Beyond the physical proximity of these two groups and a similarity in the type of stonework there is nothing to connect the two groups, or to say that they were built at the same time, by the same people, or for the same ends. The one connection that is very evident, certainly in the Great Enclosure, is a visual one. To anyone standing almost anywhere in that Enclosure, the visual dominance of the Hill-

Fortress is always present, as if Big Brother (or Big Sister) could be—if he or she so wished—watching one all the time. Conversely, when one is standing on the south side of the Fortress, in one of the several look-out points that have been provided on that side, the Valley Ruins and particularly the Great Enclosure seem to lie at one's feet, very much under one's control—or at least visual control. Certainly nothing could happen in the Great Enclosure without anyone on the look-out on the south side of the Hill-Fortress becoming immediately aware of it.

There is another connection between these two groups that is less obvious but as, if not more, important—and that is a sound, as distinct from a sight, connection. This may go back to remote times and have many cultural and historical undertones. For on the south side of the hill-top there is, under one of the larger rocks which form the southern boundary of the main living space of the fortress, a cave that has remarkable acoustic properties. Anyone speaking there can be heard with distinct clarity in the Valley below and more particularly better than anywhere else, in the Great Enclosure.* This excellent reception may be partly due to the curved east-

*There is also an echo from a focal point in the eastern enclosure above this cave which gives better reception down below than the cave itself, but the reception area is more limited.

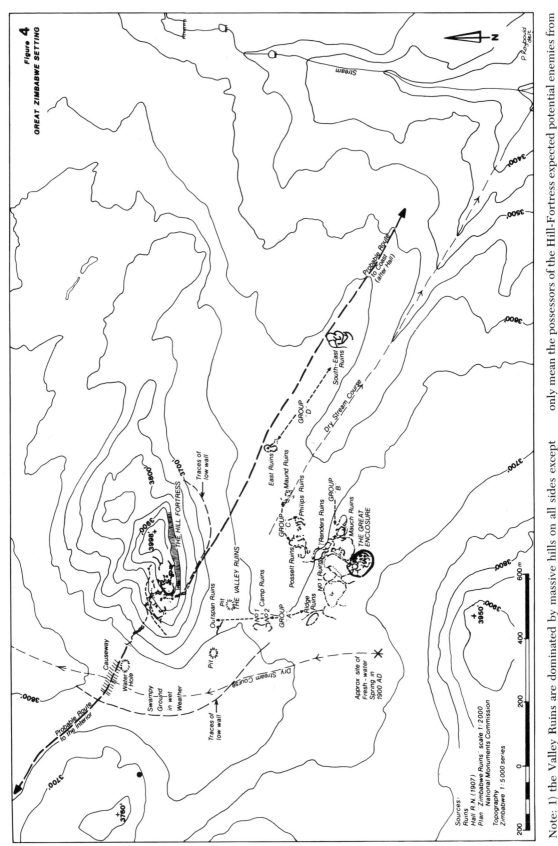

Figure 4

GREAT ZIMBABWE SETTING

Note: 1) the Valley Ruins are dominated by massive hills on all sides except the southeast, the approach route from that side being also the only escape route; 2) two ruins, the East, and South-East, guard the approach from the only mean the possessors of the Hill-Fortress expected potential enemies from the coast, potential friends from inland; and 3) the Valley Ruins stand apart from both main routes to the Hill-Fortress.

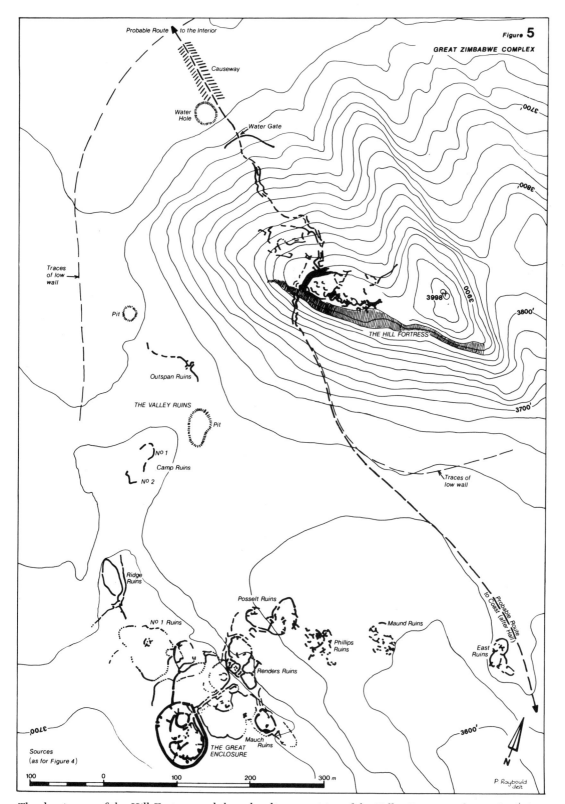

The dominance of the Hill-Fortress and the subordinate position of the Valley Ruins are shown clearly here.

PLATE 1. View from the Balcony above Eastern Enclosure, Hill-Fortress (*Photo by courtesy of the Zimbabwe Tourist Board*)

ern end of the Enclosure, which would concentrate toward the centre any sound received from the hill-top. Such an effect would reverberate everywhere inside from the outside wall as a whole.

Apart from this sight and sound connection however, the linkage on the ground appears very tenuous: at the best casual, at the worst deliberately divisive. There is no straightforward path or route linking the two groups. The natural one would be the high ground to the northwest of the Great Enclosure, a ridge between the heads of two small valleys, on the west and east, along which lie disjointed remains of four minor ruins, the last a queer kind of doorway ruin called the Outspan Ruin, though what it was the doorway to (or from) is very unclear.

But there is no indication in the planning of the Valley Ruins that this high ground was used as a route to the Hill-Fortress. The internal passages of the Valley Ruins connect the ruins together but do not lead towards this ridge, as would be expected of any plan that had grown up spontaneously. Nor do they lead anywhere else, except to the North Entrance of the Great Enclosure. In short, the Hill-Fortress and the Valley Ruins remain obstinately two separate systems with the appearance of each turning its back upon the other, except for the double connection of sight and sound. This divorce is one of the first great anomalies, one of the inexplicable surprises to any planner of the Great Zimbabwe, for all hill-fortresses, all over the world, have given rise to a town of the poorer classes very close at their foot, hard against the main Fortress Entrance as the old hymn says:

The Rich man in his castle
The Poor man at his gate.

The operative word as regards the poor man is "gate." For he was near the gate for two good reasons: firstly to pick up the economic crumbs—employment, charity—from the rich man's table and secondly to be able to get inside the Fortress fast when danger came. A well-known European example is Corfe Castle in Britain: the close sequence of Castle, Gate, and Village is obvious. A close examination of the ground immediately below the west wall of the Fortress to some extent resolves this anomaly, for here on the hillsides are the scattered remains of low boundary walls, hut foundations, and the usual detritus of human settlement. This means there was a normal village in the normal position attached to the Fortress at some time, probably early. But this makes the walled areas of the Valley Ruins being divorced from both village and Fortress all the more extraordinary. The siting of the Valley Ruins effectively prevented its inhabitants (whoever they were) from enjoying either the charity or the protection given by closeness to the Fortress. In fact the reverse: the planning suggests it was purposely done to prevent these benefits becoming available under any circumstances. What could have been the game in this inversion of all normal planning?

There is one other major fact that also makes the whole pattern queer. No cemetery, no necropolis of any kind has ever been found: only occasional burials in the Hill-Fortress, in common with the established practice of burying chiefs in caves and remote hill-tops. But what of the population as a whole? If there was a permanent settlement, people must have died regularly and needed formal burial of some sort. Yet the burials in the Fortress are far too few for a settled population . . . and there is no other place for the dead yet discovered. . . . Another unanswered question . . .

THE RUINS SEPARATELY

Great Zimbabwe, when studied in more detail, is best divided into three groups: the Hill-Fortress, the Valley Ruins (excluding the Great Enclosure), and the Great Enclosure itself. Each of these has its own common characteristics and deserves separate discussion.

THE HILL-FORTRESS

The Neolithic ancestry

To get this plan into historical—and functional—perspective, it is useful to look at its Neolithic ancestry, and the centuries that lie behind such a living space. The later Stone Age hunters had to survive defensively against predators—both animal and human—and offensively by watching accurately the movement of their food

supply, the great herds of buck and other game. Elevated rock shelters, with limited means of access, gave both requirements: intruders could be seen in good time to be stopped, and the movement of game could be monitored as from an eagle's nest.

The rock shelter at Makwe is a good example of this very ancient type-plan. It is situated in northeastern Zambia, about 130 miles northeast of Zumbo (in Maputo, at the junction of the Zambezi and Luangwa rivers), and lies on the side of a small hill 80' above an open swampy plain (or *dambo*). This is the headwaters of a river flowing southwards, the water and pasture of which would be a natural attraction for game. The known occupation dates are the fourth and third millenia B.C., then a gap of 2,000 years and renewed occupation in the first millenium A.D.

The component spaces of the plan are four (marked A through D on the plan):

(A) The only approach to the shelter (decorated with some rock paintings to greet, or distract, the visitors) is a sloping ledge 5' to 13' wide with a vertical precipice on the right. This could be guarded from a boulder directly over the entrance passage.

(B) A very narrow entrance passage, the only practicable way in, 3'0" high, 3'7" wide, and 12'9" long. Like many later passages and doorways a visitor had to bend down to come in head first, a useful position for the defenders to deal with an unwanted intruder. The combination of A and B meant access was, in military terms, "fully under control".

(C) The large entrance hall leading to the main living area. Here there was a smaller but still noticeable series of rock paintings.

(D) The main living area furthest from the entrance, inaccessible from any other direction and divided by rocks into two look-out vantage points, D1 and D2, from which all animal movement in the valley below could be monitored. It was here

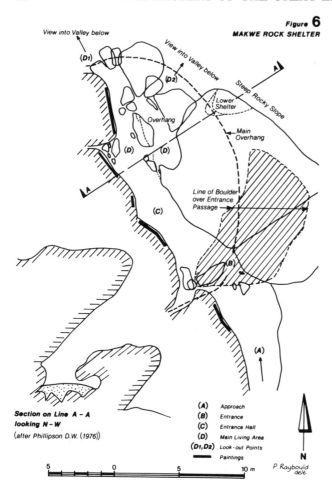

Figure **6**
MAKWE ROCK SHELTER

View into Valley below
(D1)
View into Valley below
(D2)
Steep Rocky Slope
Lower Shelter
Overhang
Main Overhang
(D)   (D)
Line of Boulder over Entrance Passage
(C)
(B)
(A)

Section on Line A - A
looking N - W
(after Phillipson D.W. (1976))

(A)   Approach
(B)   Entrance
(C)   Entrance Hall
(D)   Main Living Area
(D1,D2) Look-out Points
━━   Paintings

5   0   5   10 m

P. Raybould
delt

N

The inaccessibility of this shelter except through the narrow, easily guarded entrance gives the long historical background to the Great Zimbabwe planning.

where the action was, where the heart of the community rested, and which was honoured with the bulk of the paintings, whether that decoration should be labelled religious symbolism, ritual target practice, or simply leisure-time doodling: for after all, evidence suggests early societies had a lot of leisure time.

Once inside, the living environment was not bad: protection from wind, rain, or the hot sun of the summer afternoon was given by two vast overhanging boulders, one over the entrance passage and another (the larger one) over both the large entrance hall and the main living area. The beginning of

human living space had been created, by the ingenuity of Stone Age man.

The four components of the Hill-Fortress

If we turn now to the Great Zimbabwe Hill-Fortress, we see that it also has the same four major components, but in a much more developed and sophisticated form. In spite of this, it still clearly displays its environmental pedigree from prehistoric Makwe:

(A) *The long approach passageways,* the awesome Ancient approach from the south and the Watergate approach from the north (A1 and A2 on Figure 7).

PLATE 2. Air view, Hill-Fortress from the west (*Photo by courtesy of the Zimbabwe Tourist Board*)

(B) *The great western enclosure*, controlling all important entrances (B on Figure 7).

(C) *A series of intermediate smaller enclosures linked by narrow passages*, some natural, some artificial (C on Figure 7).

(D) *Lastly, the culmination of the plan, the two great Eastern Enclosures and the east Cave* (D on Figure 7).

This fourfold division is a natural and permanent feature of all fortress planning, since it reflects directly the social structure of a warrior society—firstly, control of access; then the garrison troops for defence; then the immediate and more personal supporters of the rulers; and lastly, the ruling clique. The same division can be seen in any fortress, independent of time and place: Tiryns in 1500 B.C. Greece, the medieval fortresses in Western Europe, Margat and Saone Crusader castles in the Levant, or fortresses in India. They have the same plan for the same reason: protection and power. The detail, however, varies, and these four components in the case of the Great Zimbabwe Fortress need more explanation.

There are only two ways of approaching the Fortress—one from the coast coming up from the southeast, called the Ancient approach, and one from inland coming in from the northwest, called the Watergate approach. No two approaches could be more different and distinct from one another. The first comes across from a range of hills to the southeast and, slowly climbing the lower slopes of the "dark side of the mountain", finds itself becoming a walled-in path, with unexpected turns and a guard post enclosure; and then suddenly, without warning, entering a deep, overwhelming cleft between two towering rocks through which only a single person can move, with the width down at one part to 1'10". After this cleft the high southern wall of the western enclosure looms over one on the right side till a sudden turn and another guard post lead past the end of the great West Wall into the narrow southern passage within the Fortress. The overwhelming impression of this approach is that whoever planned it and engineered it must have been very frightened people: there must have been some very compelling reason in their minds to put visitors under such strict, awe-inspiring control when coming from the coast. What was their motive? It is all the more inexplicable against the totally different character of the northwest approach—across the gently sloping open hillside through what

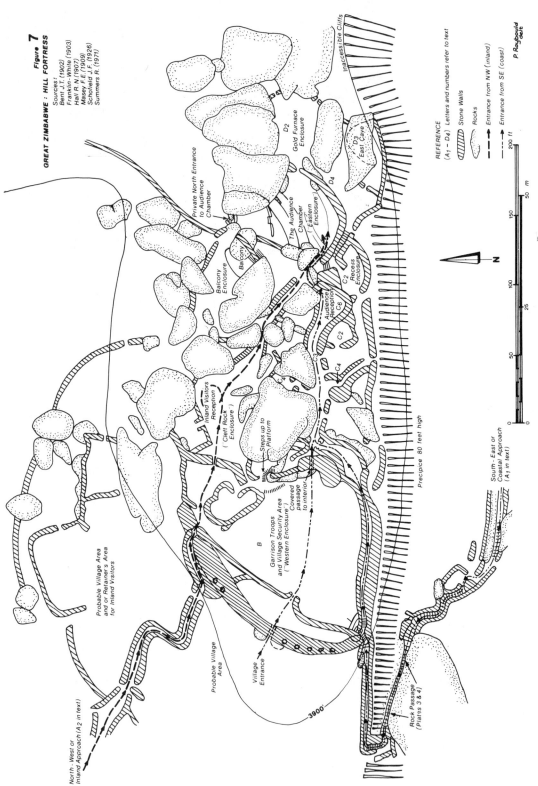

Figure 7

GREAT ZIMBABWE : HILL FORTRESS

Sources:
Bent J.T. (1902)
Franklin-White (1903)
Hall R. N. (1907)
Masey F.E. (1909)
Schofield J.F. (1926)
Summers R. (1971)

Private North Entrance
to Audience
Chamber

Balcony Enclosure

Balcony

The Audience
Chamber
('Eastern
Enclosure')

D2
Gold Furnace
Enclosure

D3
East Cave

D4

C2 Recess
Enclosures

C6

Audience
Reception

C4

Inland Visitors
Reception
('Cleft Rock
Enclosure')

Steps up to
Platform

Garrison Troops
and Village Security Area
('Western Enclosure')

Covered passage
to interior

B

Probable Village Area
and/or Retainer's Area
for Inland Visitors

Probable Village Area

Village Entrance

North - West or
Inland Approach (A2 in text)

3900'

Precipice 80 feet high

Inaccessible Cliffs

Rock Passage
(Plates 3 & 4)

South - East or
Coastal Approach
(A1 in text)

REFERENCE

(A1 – D4) Letters and numbers refer to text

Stone Walls

Rocks

Entrance from NW (inland)

Entrance from SE (coast)

0   25   50 m

0   50   100   150   200 ft

N

P Roybould delt

This plan, a compilation from all available earlier plans, gives some idea of the stringent control of movement before reaching "the heart of the matter", the king's Audience Chamber, whether visitors were from inland or the coast.

must have been the village resting at the foot of the Fortress.

This inland approach starts with an entrance, and possibly a Guard House, on the side of the Valley away from the Fortress, through the low wall called the Outer Defence Wall, which, in spite of its name, in size suggests merely some control for cattle. The path then crosses the Valley bottom on a raised causeway, apparently the dam wall for the main water reservoir, for in the rainy period the Valley above the dam for five hundred yards or so is still today a water-logged marsh. Where the hill starts on the Fortress side of the Valley there was another wall, the Watergate. It is next to a large depression now full of

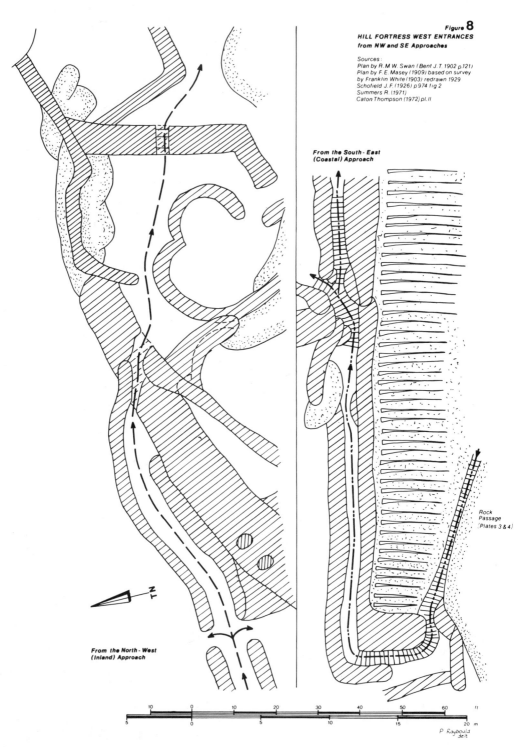

Figure 8
HILL FORTRESS WEST ENTRANCES
from NW and SE Approaches

Sources :
Plan by R.M.W. Swan (Bent J.T. 1902 p.121)
Plan by F.E. Masey (1909) based on survey
by Franklin White (1903) redrawn 1929
Schofield J.F. (1926) p.974 fig 2
Summers R. (1971)
Caton Thompson (1972) pl. II

From the South-East
(Coastal) Approach

Rock
Passage
(Plates 3 & 4)

From the North-West
(Inland) Approach

10   0   10   20   30   40   50   60   ft
5   0   5   10   15   20   m

P. Raybould
delt

These, the main, entrances to the Hill-Fortress show the extraordinary lengths the designers of the Fortress went to to control all visitors. The design is entirely pragmatic without the slight-est pretence of display or grand architectural statement as has been given elsewhere in the world to the main entrance to a major strong-hold.

PLATE 6. V.I.P. Entrance, Cleft Rock Enclosure, Hill-
Fortress *(Photo by courtesy of National Archives)*

water, surrounded by trees and the home of very varied bird life.

After this second "gate" the path crosses some bare rock and starts ascending the hill through low stone walls, which become higher as the path ascends the hill and traverses the area of the village next the Fortress. On this section there are some twists and turns and small side enclosures that could have been used by guards, but there is nothing to compare with the precautions taken in the coastal approach. The path then runs along under the West Wall and originally entered the Fortress through a tunnel under the West Wall. This section collapsed and has been rebuilt incorrectly so this approach now enters the first reception area of the Fortress, the Cleft Rock Enclosure, by a winding open path.

Nevertheless, it is clear even now that any guard on the summit of the West Wall would have had full control of people using this approach both along the base of the wall and as they emerged from the tunnel, before they reached the V.I.P. entrance to the Cleft Rock Enclosure itself. It is clear from this planning that though the inland approach route was very open compared to the coastal route, the actual point of entry was strictly controlled.

It has been generally assumed this was the V.I.P. entrance: but why V.I.P. from inland only? Were there no V.I.P.s from the coast too—the traders and the foreigners who wanted to do business? And why such protection on the side of the Valley Ruins and the Great Enclosure, when such a clear view of what was happening in the

Valley could be obtained in any case from the Hill-Fortress?

There was one other minor entrance into the Fortress, through a tunnel in the Centre of the West Wall. This appears from its position to have been planned to be a direct connection only to the village outside the West Wall, giving quick access to the Fortress in times of trouble. It is not directly connected to either of the main east or west approaches.

The Great Western Enclosure, the first to be encountered on entering the Fortress, is by far the largest of any single space, being about 11,000 square feet or slightly over one-quarter of an acre. It is an irregular, five-sided figure, with high walls on the inside on the top of high boulders. The main wall is the West Wall that greets one first on approaching the Fortress and gives almost a celebration of arrival by having originally along its very broad top a series of 6 conical stone turrets at 12-foot intervals with large 5'9" stone uprights placed between them: an unusual and striking form of wall decoration. The same idea, in a slightly different form, was used at Naletale, also on the West Wall, fronting the assembly area outside. This decorative effort is increased by the wall itself having the widest summit of any wall known in Africa—from 12' to 14½'. Its summit could therefore—as with in fact most important walls in all Southern Africa—be easily patrolled on foot. It seems made for sentry-go—even for bare-footed soldiers, since there is some evidence the original summits were finished with relative flat slabs. Its original height was between 20' and 25', similar to the lower sections of the Great Wall of the Great Enclosure.

The possibility of sentry-go is the more likely, since the summit controlled directly all three entrances. The southern coastal one creeps around the southwest edge of this West Wall and the northwest Water-

gate entrance creeps round the opposite end, as already described, while the village entrance is directly in the centre. In this way all three entrances could be easily controlled by a few well-directed stones aimed at unwanted intruders, since all entrance passages were between walls that only permitted single-file movement and were directly at the base of the West Wall.

Similarly, the exits from this Western Enclosure onwards to the eastern quarters were well controlled. There were only three of these: (1) *on the south*, to the internal passage continuing the southern coastal approach leading to the central and eastern areas; (2) *on the north*, by a staircase (now ruinous) to a Platform Enclosure and so to the Cleft Rock Enclosure (and probably the main access to the top of the West Wall); and (3) *on the east*, another wall tunnel leading to the passageway network of the central area and so to the Eastern Enclosure—"the heart of the matter".

All these three exits were again single-file exits, so they could all be easily controlled by a few guards, say two to each. It meant that even if an enemy penetrated into the Western Enclosure, there were still strong defences guarding the rest of the Fortress.

The whole planning of this Western Enclosure makes absolutely clear its function: it was the guard house controlling all primary entrances from the outside and all secondary entrances to the heart of the Fortress. It is here where the garrison troops would live, where parades would be held, where even war dances might have been performed. Throughout its long history, long after probably the original purpose of the Fortress had been forgotten, this was the space everybody made for and lived in—so much so that when first discovered by the white pioneers of 1890, its surface level had risen to within 6' of the summit of the West Wall: a fill of rubbish, earth, and all the usual detritus of human settlement 20' deep. Even if filled at a yard or so a century, this means an accumulation of nearly seven centuries—and probably much longer. The castles already referred to (p. 19) all have the same garrison areas as a lower or inferior court through which one has to go to reach the heart of the plan. In this way the Hill-Fortress follows the rules of fortified planning anywhere else in the world. The same imperatives always produce the same results.

It is the intermediate portion between the main Western Entrance Enclosure on the west and the main Audience Chamber Enclosure on the east that appeared to the early explorers as a hopeless confused labyrinth of passages out of which no sense could be made. Full of fallen stones from ruinous walls, vicious stinging nettles, and all kinds of undergrowth, there was every reason for this impression. Cleared of stones and growth, with the passages clear, the plan becomes extremely logical. With the greatest bulk of piled-up natural boulders on the northern edge of the hill, most of the small enclosures in this middle section were placed on the southern edge, with ample shade from the hot afternoon sun, and an 80' precipice which, besides protection, gave an uninterrupted view of everything going on in the Valley Ruins below.

Four of these small enclosures cluster together. The easternmost is the most interesting (C1 on Figure 7), for it has five vertical recesses built into the south wall. These are about 5" wide and about 2'0" apart and at the present roughly 5'0" high—though Richard N. Hall thought they may have been higher. It seems fairly obvious these recesses must have been built to house the "cult" objects, namely the famous birds carved on their soapstone posts, for the sizes fit and this room is immediately next to the Audience Chamber enclosure, where most of the soapstone birds were

found. If this was so, then this recess becomes the priests', or rather the priest-king's, vestry, where the cult objects were held when not in use. On this assumption the next enclosure (C2 on Figure 7) becomes either the priest-king's private apartment, if the priest-king lived and slept—as well he might—near the vestry housing the national treasures, or a V.I.P. accommodation for strangers.

On the north side in this central section two other spaces were created by the ancient planners by capitalising on the peculiarities of the rock formation. In the first place, to the east a small cleft behind a large 26' boulder, at the rear of the terraces on which the king kept court, was used as a stair to climb to the top of the same boulder and make the top a "balcony" that overlooked the whole Audience Chamber, and the space behind has become known as Balcony Enclosure. From this vantage point anyone could rain death and destruction upon the court below, so it must have been always manned by the garrison troop defending both the person of the king and the whole fortress. It is obvious that the king and his court when in session would have needed protection like this, and the Balcony was ideal for the purpose.

In the second place, another space—not so dramatic, but very appropriate—was formed on the north side of the mass of central boulders and was developed as a Reception Area, the Cleft Rock Enclosure already mentioned at the head of the northwest access from the Watergate. From here, passages led directly to the Audience Chamber and to the smaller private enclosures on the south side overlooking the precipice and the Valley Ruins. The Reception Area has become known as the Cleft Rock Enclosure because of a tilted cleft in the rocks on the north side. This cleft is about 4' wide throughout and may have once been a subsidiary entrance from

PLATE 7. Great West Wall, Hill-Fortress (1914) *(Photo by H. H. McNeil)*

PLATE 8. East Wall, Western Enclosure, Hill-Fortress (1929), showing the elevated Platform and the tunnel opening to the eastern portions of the Fortress *(Photo by Milton John Bell)*

PLATE 9. Northeast Wall, Western Enclosure, Hill-Fortress (*Photo by G. le Roux*)

PLATE 10. Entrance to Covered Passage, Western Enclosure, Hill-Fortress (*Photo by G. le Roux*)

the north—though later it appeared to have been blocked by a stone wall, since a heap of wall stones at its base outside was found by Hall.

The passage system of this central component (C on Figure 7) controlled all movement within the fortress. It consisted of:

(1) A central west-east passage leading directly from the Western Enclosure to the Audience Chamber (C3 on Figure 7).

(2) A passage crossing the west-east passage at right angles leading directly from the Cleft Rock Enclosure to the small southern enclosures and extending to the very edge of the precipice, which apparently was also used at some time as a subsidiary, if very dangerous, west-east path (C4 on Figure 7).

(3) A direct passage from the Reception Area Enclosure to the Audience Chamber.

This arrangement of passages makes clear the central area of the fortress was an extremely well-planned system of movement—the very opposite of a mad labyrinth. In fact, the way the natural gaps in the great rocks were used and systematised could not have been more skilful. A few men posted as sentries at the critical crossing points of the passages could easily have controlled all movement throughout the system. Again, in military terms, the position was "fully under control".

The Eastern Enclosure (see Figure 7) is the culmination of one's progress through the Fortress and seems without doubt to be the seat of authority. It is the most impressive space in the whole hill-top, being overshadowed by colossal rocks forty to seventy feet high, its south side above the precipice formed by a large wall with a raised seat or banquette facing the towering rocks. It was here that eight of the soapstone birds were found, several of them still standing upright with their posts firmly embedded in the stonework: presumably as cult objects, the symbols at once of the king's power and the nation's identity.

Opposite to this banquette at the back of the space under the overhanging rocks there was originally a series of rising terraces, each with its stone retaining wall, as if each level had been allocated to particular levels of the political and social hierarchy, with their accompanying claims to power and status. Much of this has now disappeared, but Hall's sketches show three such terraces, which could reflect the triple planning of the Hill-Fortress itself— the garrison troops, the personal supporters of the rulers, and the rulers themselves.

In the centre of the Audience Chamber is one of the unsolved details of Zimbabwe: a queer sunken passage or trench, starting where one enters from the west and ending against a buttress near the centre of the enclosure. Its length is 25'0" to the buttress; its depth, 6'10"; and its width varies from 4'0" on the west to 6'3" where it finishes near the centre of this chamber. Large flat stones found nearby suggest it might have been roofed: but for what purpose? The absence of steps at either end suggests a store filled from above with fairly large objects or bundles that could be handed up from the floor of the enclosure. The size of the passage does not suggest the storage of minute and very valuable material such as gold, which we know tended to be carried often as dust in porcupine quills. Perhaps, of course, the pioneers of the Ancient Ruins Company tore open the roof stones, and ransacked the trench in the hope of finding treasure, and having found treasure or not, abandoned the place, so that whatever knowledge might have been obtained from the contents (if any) has gone forever. But it must have had some specific purpose. More of this later.

The Gold Furnace Enclosure (D2 on Figure 7) earned its name through Theodore Bent, the first writer and investigator of the ruins, who said he found relics of a gold furnace here, "a gold-smelting furnace made from very hard cement of powdered granite, with a chimney of the same material and with neatly bevelled edges. Hardby, in a chasm between two boulders [probably D4 on Figure 7] lay all the rejected casings from which the gold-bearing quartz had been extracted by exposure to heat prior to the crushing. . . . Near the furnace, we found many little crucibles, of . . . clay, which had been used for smelting the gold and in nearly all of them exist small specks of gold adhering to the glaze formed by the heat of the process. . . ."

This description by Bent of his finds in this easternmost and innermost enclosure of the whole Fortress is significant, since it is one prime piece of evidence, which has now disappeared, that Zimbabwe was directly connected with the gold industry. Whether it was the main or only one of many smelting centres it is in the present state of research impossible to tell. But the fact that it was one such centre is highly probable, apart from Bent's evidence, because its topographical position on the eastern edge of the gold-mining area was a natural collecting point for storing trade goods prior to their annual transshipment to the coast.

The East Cave (D3 in Figure 7) is famous for having such acoustic property for the Valley Ruins and the Great Enclosure below: a gigantic megaphone in fact, as was discovered by experiment shortly after 1950. Though the connection of those acoustic effects with the worship of the great god Mwali, or Mwari, has been doubted, there seems good reason to connect them, as there remained into the twentieth century the folk-memory of such effects, probably referring to Zimbabwe, among the BaVenda nation now on both sides of the Limpopo River.

As regards gold, Bent continues his account by saying, "in the adjoining cave we dug up an ingot mould of soapstone of curious shape, corresponding almost exactly to an ingot of tin found in Falmouth Harbour". Falmouth, England, is far away, and there may be simpler explanations nearer home. But the connection with gold working and the possible worship of a god still needs explaining.

Figure 9
THE "EASTERN ENCLOSURE" OR AUDIENCE CHAMBER
HILL FORTRESS
Reconstructed Plan

North Entrance
✦ Possible position Soapstone Birds
For Section A – A see Figure 10
Way up to Balcony
Possible Chief's Throne
From NW approach
Steps up
Terrace 3
Terrace 2
Bent's "Altar"
Terrace 1
Gold Furnace Enclosure
Sunken Passage (Fig 28)
Pattern Passage
"Banquette"
From SE approach
Recess Enclosure
Way down to Cave
Acoustic Cave Under
TN
80 feet Precipise
0 10 20 30 40 50 ft
0 5 10 15 20 m
P. Raybould delt

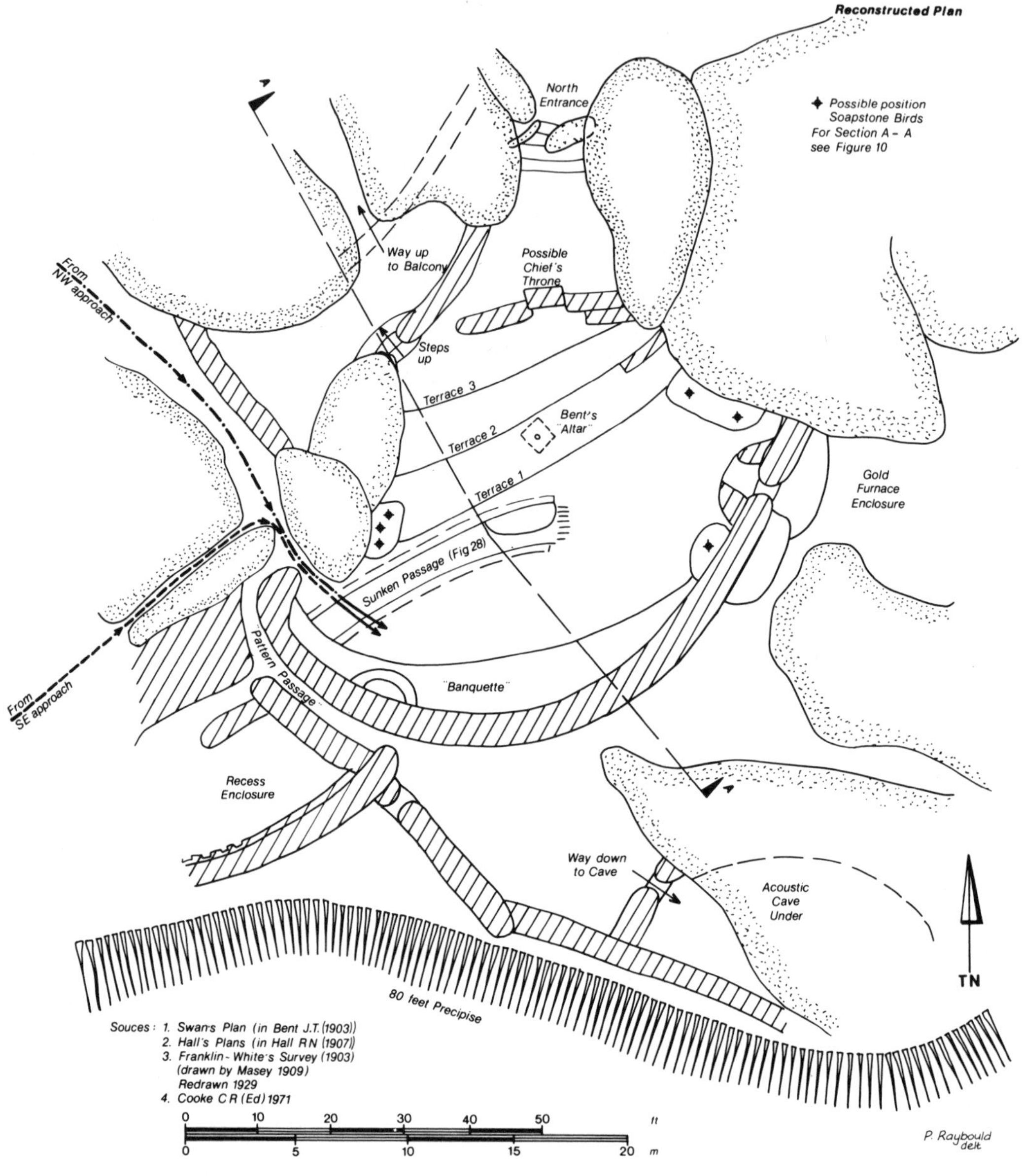

Souces: 1. Swan's Plan (in Bent J.T. (1903))
2. Hall's Plans (in Hall R N (1907))
3. Franklin-White's Survey (1903) (drawn by Masey 1909) Redrawn 1929
4. Cooke C R (Ed) 1971

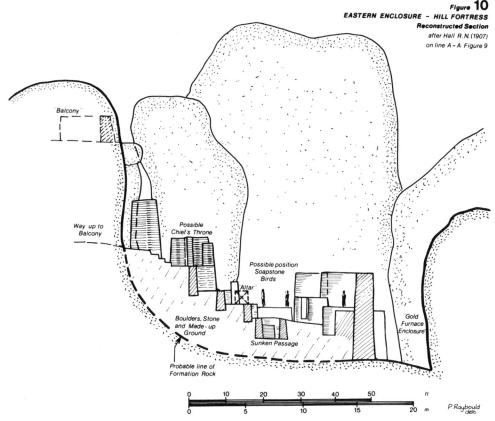

Figures 9 and 10 are an attempt to reconstruct from the earliest plans and from the logic of the entrances what might have been the origi- nal way in which the space was used: the chief, or king, high up above the three ter- races, the visitors below on the banquette.

THE VALLEY RUINS

The Valley Ruins, dominated by the mass of the Great Enclosure, present another kind of riddle altogether from that of the Hill-Fortress. Compared to the Valley Ruins, the Fortress is simplicity itself, a straightforward piece of military planning. But the ruins down below at first sight present an inextricable series of spaces and passages without coherence, sequence, or sense. They can be divided into four main groups, and are marked A, B, C, and D on Figure 4.

Group A

These are on the small watershed between the northwest and southeast val- leys and are known as the Outspan, Camp No. 1, Camp No. 2, and the Ridge ruins. Collectively they can be called the watershed ruins. They are as a group the least interesting, but they are significant as lying on the natural route (being on the high ground of a watershed) that leads from the bulk of the other Valley Ruins, partic- ularly the Great Enclosures, to the Ancient Ascent up to the Hill-Fortress. The Out- span Ruins are the most interesting because they are the most inexplicable, both in their siting and their design. They apparently formed part of a low wall that ran around the lower slopes of the Hill-Fortress, but judging from the remains, the wall was so low that a man could jump or certainly climb over it, and it could never do more than keep cattle out. Why therefore the extremely complex control of the entrance? Why that extraordinary conical tower as part of the wall line, with a stone shelf built in to link it with the wall on either side? Finally, why the entrance path divided immediately on the inside, so that one has either to go through what might have been a guard room or double back behind the tower with its two stone shelves going off in another direction, thus avoiding the guard room altogether? Nothing seems to make sense.

Group B

This group consists of four ruins known individually as No. 1 Ruin, Renders Ruin, Mauch Ruin, and the Great Enclosure, together with all intervening enclosures. The first three ruins are on the edge of a small rocky plateau that is an extension southeastwards of the watershed, so they have good drainage characteristics. Their siting is carefully adjusted, like the Hill-Fortress itself, to the contours of the granite, the Renders and Mauch ruins being carefully placed on small promontories of granite that project into the valley. As the stonework of Group B links it to the Hill-Fortress, it appears the designers of one had a hand in the other and had time to consider both sitings carefully.

This group as a whole is by far the largest, occupies the bulk of the space, and is interconnected throughout with passages and continuous walling. It also has a very clearly defined passageway between stone walls to the Great Enclosure and this passageway leads directly to the internal passages of that Enclosure. Yet the Great Enclosure as a whole appears, as a plan, to be tacked on to the southern side of this main group, and there is no trace of anything beyond it. Moreover, as will be seen, the Great Wall itself is different from the internal walls of the Great Enclosure and is linked by the character of its stonework not to this group but to Group C.

Group C

This group, comprising the Posselt, Philips, and Maund ruins, is sited unexpectedly on the valley bottom with the Maund Ruins in the lowest and dampest part—so damp, in fact, that underneath the cement floor, which appears to relate to the walls and the first occupation period, there was a series of paved stone paths linking the enclosures as if the site had been wet enough to need pedestrian causeways, possibly to a group of huts that later were reformed at a higher level to make a set of walled enclosures. For some reason the Maund Ruins stand apart, more dissociated than any other ruin from the main group.

Why was this siting so un-African? The true African settlement always shows the greatest sensitiveness to micro-climate, avoiding the cold inversions of the valley bottoms and facing east or north to catch the maximum sun on winter mornings. Moreover, the valley bottom would have been best for cultivation and the African naturally avoided good agricultural land for settlement.

The group as a whole is also much looser in plan and has not the tight coherence of Group B; it has neither interconnecting passages to link the ruins together, nor any direct means of access to the Great Enclosure. Yet, as will be seen, it is technically linked by its stonework more to the Great Wall of the Great Enclosure than to anything else in the Valley or on the Hill.

It was as if the siting of this group and, in particular, the Maund Ruins, was done by foreigners in a hurry, very carelessly, as if it didn't matter where it was done as

Figure **11**
VALLEY RUINS - GROUP B
Sources as for Figure 4

Posselt
Ruins

Philips
Ruins

Renders
Ruins

B
+
3662'

A

No. 1 Ruins
+
3681'

+
3681'

+
3681'

Mauch
Ruins

T (foundation only)

The Great
Enclosure

MN TN

Plan

● T Stone Towers

3690'

T

T

10   0   50   100 m

10 0   50   100   200   300   ft
                                                    P. Raybould
                                                    delt.

Note: 1) trade goods—"Ancient gold, Arabian pottery and glass"—found in Enclosure "A" of Renders Ruin (Hall's Enclosure 1); and 2) 30,000 beads and other trade goods found by Mrs. Goodall in Enclosure "B" of Renders Ruin (Hall's Enclosure 8). There is good reason to suppose that these Valley Ruins at least for some time in their history were traders' camping sites.

long as it was done quickly. Its siting contrasts sharply with the careful siting of Group B; worse siting, yet better stonework—a very queer anomaly.

This is but another example of the anomalies, the non sequiturs, that continually occur at the Great Zimbabwe.

Group D

This group consists of two isolated ruins known as the East Ruins and South East Ruins. They are remarkable for their very careful siting on the relatively narrow ridge that forms the northern border to the southeast valley of the Ruin Area. It was on this ridge that the coastal route up to the Hill-Fortress must have gone, and these ruins, situated close to or even astride this route, must have been normal military guard posts to the route as it approached the Fortress. The East Ruins thus become the last point of control before that route begins the long climb up the Ancient Ascent already described.

It is to be noted the bulk of the Valley Ruins—that is, groups A, B, and C—all lay well clear of this route to the Fortress, and may have used, when needed, the other route, the watershed or Group A via the Outspan Ruins, to join the Ancient Ascent halfway up the hill.

THE GREAT ENCLOSURE

Finally we come to the Great Enclosure itself, in many ways the real heart of the Great Zimbabwe riddle. Fundamentally it is simply a Great Wall in the shape of a rough ellipse flattened on the north end facing the Hill-Fortress, with only three narrow entrances and with a very queer arrangement of spaces inside. Yet this building is by far the most impressive and interesting ruin in Southern Africa—if not the whole of Africa—because of:

(1) The Great Wall—unique for its unusual height, width, construction, and

extent—830′ in circumference and varying from 16′ to 35′ high.

(2) The Conical Tower inside and close to the Great Wall.

(3) The long internal "parallel passage" following the inside of the Great Wall and connecting the main entrance with the space round the Conical Tower.

(4) Three "platforms" with their back to an inner parallel wall.

(5) A ruinous and seemingly inexplicable arrangement of lower walls and spaces inside the Great Wall, with other narrow passages leading to nothing and walls that start and stop without meaning and half-enclosed spaces unconnected to anything else. Of course a great deal is ruinous and incomplete, but even so, what remains seems to make little sense.

All these aspects contain riddles whose solution must wait till a later chapter. Some things, however, are clear from established facts. These are:

(1) The Great Wall, the Conical Tower, and some (minor) portions of the internal walls are all the best workmanship and appear to have been built as one operation, while the other internal walls are less well built.

(2) The long internal passage must have been deliberatively planned as such, otherwise the inner wall of that passage need never have been built, or if built previously could have been made itself the main outer wall. There was therefore some overriding reason to get from the North Entrance to the Conical Tower, and so to the back entrance to the large Platform C, without being seen from the rest of the interior.

(3) The control of movement as shown by the distribution of buttresses and grooves was concentrated in the eastern and southern portions and did not affect the northern or western portions, save for the exceptionally heavy buttresses on the inside of the western entrance.

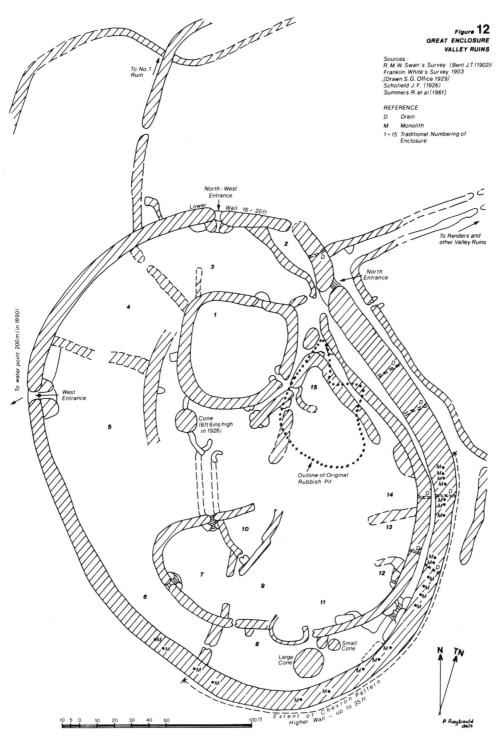

Figure **12**
GREAT ENCLOSURE
VALLEY RUINS

Sources :
R. M. W. Swan's Survey (Bent J.T. (1902))
Franklin White's Survey 1903
_(Drawn S. G. Office 1929)
Schofield J. F. (1926)
Summers R. et al (1961)

REFERENCE

D   Drain

M   Monolith

1 – 15   Traditional Numbering of
          Enclosure

To No.1
Ruin

North - West
Entrance

Lower   Wall 16 - 20 ft

2

To Renders and
other Valley Ruins

North
Entrance

3

4

1

To water point 200 m (in 1890)

West
Entrance

15

5

Cone
(6 ft 6 ins high
in 1926)

Outline of Original
Rubbish Pit

14

Me
Me
Me

D   D

Me
Me
Me

13

10

12

7

9

6

11

8

Small
Cone

N   TN

Large
Cone

M

M

M

M

M

M

Extent of Chevron Pattern
Higher Wall - up to 35 ft

P. Raybould
delt

10 5 0   10   20   30   40   50   100 ft

The outline of a rubbish pit as outlined by R.
Summers et al. (1961, p. 308) suggests that
this area was on the periphery of the original
settlement and may also have been on the
footpath from the settlement to the water
point 200 metres to the southwest. The need
for access to this water point after the Great
Wall had been built also explains the position
of the West Entrance, which otherwise
appears unnecessary, as it leads to no other
ruins.

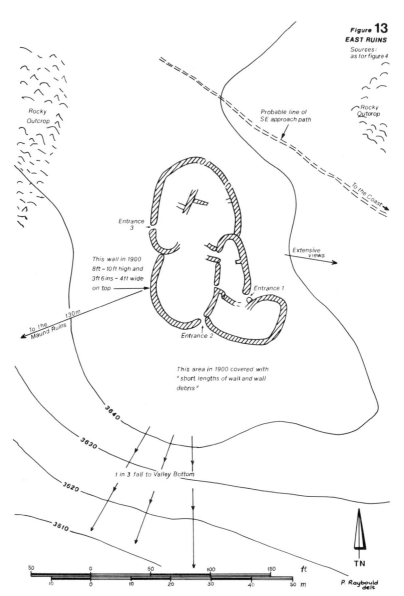

Figure **13**
EAST RUINS
Sources:
as for figure 4

Rocky
Outcrop

Rocky
Outcrop

Probable line of
SE approach path

To the Coast

Entrance
3

Extensive
views

This wall in 1900
8ft – 10ft high and
3ft 6ins – 4ft wide
on top

Entrance 1

To the
Maund Ruins

130m

Entrance 2

This area in 1900 covered with
" short lengths of wall and wall
debris "

3640

3630

1 in 3 fall to Valley Bottom

3620

3610

TN

50   0   50   100   150   ft

10   0   10   20   30   40   50   m

P. Raybould
delt

Whoever chose this site knew his business. Sited on a smooth granite outcrop overlooking the Valley Ruins to the southwest and with extensive views to the southeast, it both supervised the Valley Ruins and guarded the southeast approach to the Hill-Fortress. The entrances reflect this function. Entrance 1 controlled the approach to the Hill Fortress; Entrance 3 gave direct access to the Valley Ruins, with the nearest Maund Ruins only 130 metres away; while Entrance 2 was the back door from which domestic rubbish, according to Hall, had been thrown down the steep southern slope to the valley bottom.

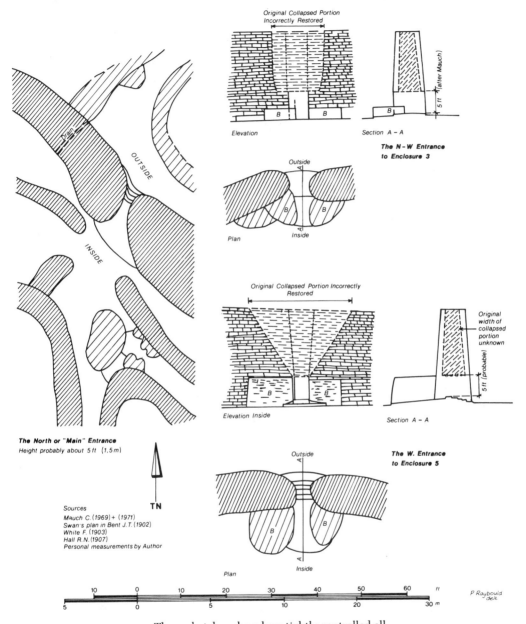

Figure **14**

ENTRANCES AND EXITS – GREAT ENCLOSURE

Original Collapsed Portion Incorrectly Restored

Elevation

Section A – A

5 ft (after Mauch)

The N–W Entrance to Enclosure 3

Outside

B   B

Plan   *Inside*

Original Collapsed Portion Incorrectly Restored

Elevation Inside   *Section A – A*

Original width of collapsed portion unknown

5 ft (probable)

The W. Entrance to Enclosure 5

OUTSIDE

Drain

INSIDE

The North or "Main" Entrance
Height probably about 5 ft (1,5 m)

TN

Sources
Mauch C. (1969) + (1971)
Swan's plan in Bent J. T. (1902)
White F. (1903)
Hall R.N. (1907)
Personal measurements by Author

Outside

B   B

Plan   *Inside*

10   0   10   20   30   40   50   60   ft
5   0   5   10   20   30 m

P. Raybould
delt.

These sketches show how tightly controlled all
access and egress was to this main enclosure.

Figure **15**
INTERNAL PASSAGES - GREAT ENCLOSURE

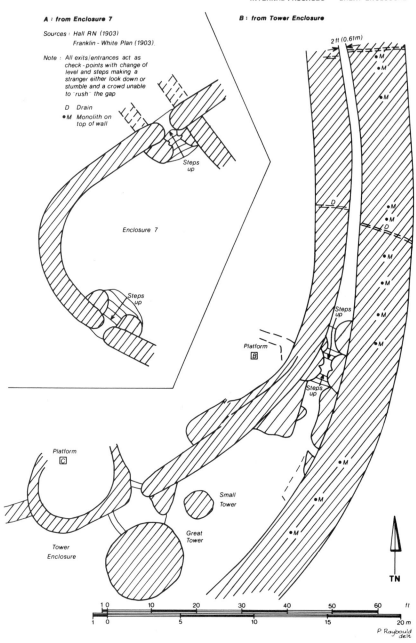

A : from Enclosure 7

B : from Tower Enclosure

Sources : Hall RN (1903)
Franklin - White Plan (1903).

Note : All exits/entrances act as
check-points with change of
level and steps making a
stranger either look down or
stumble and a crowd unable
to "rush" the gap

D Drain
•M Monolith on
top of wall

2 ft (0.61m)

Steps up

Enclosure 7

D

Steps up

D

Steps up

Platform
B

Steps up

Platform
C

Small Tower

Great Tower

Tower Enclosure

TN

1 0   10   20   30   40   50   60   *ft*
1 0   5   10   15   *20 m*

P. Raybould
delt

These passageways indicate the method of controlling movement: a wooden beam bridging between the portcullis grooves could be used to count the number of persons moving through.

(4) The western entrance was the only entrance to lead to the open and not to another series of walled enclosures, and this had the largest buttresses.

(5) There seem to have been two foci of interest—a minor one in the recess in Enclosure 15, and a major one in the rather grand semicircle behind Platform C.

(6) There is a considerable difference between the northern and southern portions of the Great Wall. The south has all the best work, it is wider, higher, and better finished, and it has a famous chevron pattern along its crest outside. The north, on the contrary, is narrower, lower, and less well finished, though still classed as better walling. Many theories have been put forward to explain this: a different group of builders, a different intention, a different time. But one obvious and perhaps critical fact has never been mentioned: namely, that the lower wall on the north permitted any onlooker in the Hill-Fortress above to have a clear line of sight into the interior, whereas if the north portion had been the same height as the south portion this would have been impossible. With the lower wall, Big Brother or Big Sister, watching from the Hill-Fortress, could keep strict control.

One further fact about the Great Wall is interesting and not immediately obvious. It has been calculated that 18,000 man-days would have been required to quarry, transport, and erect the 182,000 cubic feet of stonework in the Great Wall alone. This means that with a work force of fifty men all told in all three operations, the whole of the Great Wall could have been built within one year: in short, remarkably quickly. As this represents the best quality work, it follows all the other ruins could have been built equally fast, if not faster, as an emergency operation if that had been necessary.

There is one big doubt about the plan of the internal walls. In the plans drawn in 1892 for Bent, a walled passage is shown connecting the north entrance of Enclosure 7 to an area south of Enclosure 1 (see Figure 12). These walls have completely disappeared in the plan of Franklin White of 1903 and presumably if they ever existed were destroyed by treasure seekers, the ruin robbers, in the interval. But if they did exist they are important as providing a connection between the southern and northern portions of the interior.

The riddle of the Great Enclosure still remains. Why was the Great Wall built so differently, so much better, than all the other walls? Why did it enclose spaces that apparently had already been built, and why was movement so carefully controlled and contrived in some of its parts and not in others? Why was the Great Enclosure so different from anything else here or anywhere else in Southern Africa and why was it here in the valley separated almost from everything else? Whatever the reasons, it remains, in both its siting and its design, a very queer phenomenon.

One further general comment can be made before some specific features are considered. It is that in the physical planning of the ruins, there is virtually no geometry, in the Euclidean sense, anywhere. There is not one straight wall, not one rectangular space, no true right angles or circles or true arcs of circles in any portion of the plan. There are some approximations to rectangularity in some minor details that will be mentioned later; but in general it can be said that the Great Zimbabwe is devoid of geometrical control. All the planning shapes are curving, sinuous, infinitely flexible to fit any topography or any function, as if the laws of geometry had not yet been invented or, if known, had by choice been avoided. It was a technique of direct adjustment to necessity, whether of nature or of man: functionalism unlimited, the very essence of grass-roots.

One aspect connected to this non-rectangularity is that the walls were never

PLATE 12. Great Enclo-
sure, air view from the east
*(Photo by courtesy of the
Zimbabwe Tourist Board)*

PLATE 13. Great Wall of
the Great Enclosure *(Photo
by G. le Roux)*

PLATE 14. Chevron pattern on the summit of the Great Wall, Great Enclosure (*Photos by R.H.G. Erasmus*)

A: Southern face with monoliths

B: Eastern face with sudden stop, with no apparent reason inside or outside

planned to carry roofs. Not only is there no preparation at the top of the wall to carry any roof timber, or other suggestions of a roof, but more important, the actual shapes enclosed by the walls, by their lack of geometric form, make roof construction impossible. It is clear the walls were originally designed as walls, as a means of enclosing space, and for no other purpose. The only protection they could have given against the force of nature, apart from wild animals, would have been protection against wind, and grass and forest fires, the latter a real danger.

This characteristic of non-rectangularity alone makes the Great Zimbabwe ruins unique in the world. No other prehistoric or historic stone ruins exist anywhere with this kind of non-formal, non-geometric, planning: all the other great ruins or monuments the world over have been laid out on the principles of Euclidean geometry, long before Euclid's lifetime, for practice always comes long before theory.

The Egyptian pyramids, the oldest stone monuments in the world, are exact squares or rectangles in plan; Stonehenge in England 2,000 years later, and still 4,000

PLATE 15. Conical Tower from Enclosure 12,
with Great Wall behind (*Photo by G. le Roux*)

PLATE 16. Conical Tower from north end
of Sacred Enclosure, with Great Wall on
the left (*Photo by G. le Roux*)

years old, is a true circle; Ur in Sumer, the Ziggurats at Babylon, the Palaces in Crete, the temples and shrines in Greece, Rome, India, Java, and Japan—all without exception were rectangular or circular.

The same applies to all the Americas, from south to north. Pre-Inca Chanchan on the Peruvian coast, the Inca streets in Cuzco and Ollantaytambo, the temple complex at Teotihuacan, even the sand designs of the Navaho Indians—all were geometric in concept, rectangular or circular in execution.

This geometric control of early religious buildings was not accidental. It repre-sented the determined belief of early man that the universe was either square or circular—generally the earth square and the heavens circular—controlled in either case by the four cardinal directions. Early man invented this concept in order to measure the changing movement of the sun and other heavenly bodies and by that calculate the change of seasons, and so construct a regular calendar for the great river systems where survival depended on correctly estimating the arrival of the annual floods.

Africa, and so the Great Zimbabwe, had none of these things. Africa never had the

43

PLATE 18. Detail of Great Wall, Great Enclosure; typical Q-type walling *(Photo by G. le Roux)*

need to measure the movement of the heavenly bodies, nor calculate the seasons in advance, or invent a calendar; her soils were never given an annual renewal of silt and flood water; she had been given by nature no opportunity to measure time accurately for intensive agriculture.

So Africa never had a formal institutionalised set of beliefs about the universe as a whole, never thought of it as having to be circular or rectangular, never developed power-groups of priests to regulate work and time and build great rectangular temple complexes. Her settlement patterns remain the simple and direct patterns of a subsistence economy, dwelling units clustered round the chief as the social hierarchy dictated and nature permitted.

What is extraordinary about the planning of the Great Zimbabwe is not its nature but its size. It remains obstinately with its roots in Africa, but its scale and extent of building is found nowhere else in Africa. It is amazing and unique that all this manpower and energy were expended without any of the great religious compulsions that operated everywhere else. Some other compelling forces in this part of Africa must have been at work, and these must lie at the heart of the mystery.

To try and identify some of these forces, a more detailed look must be given to certain specific features which do not appear to be typically African, and which may therefore begin to give some leads to break the code and solve the mystery.

CHAPTER 3

Walls, Towers, and Relics

The ruins of forgotten times . . .
—*Sir Thomas Browne*

SEVERAL specific and recurring features of the Great Zimbabwe that call for attention are: the total absence of mortar; stones used like bricks; variations in masonry technique; no foundations; the width and height of walls; no arches; timber lintels; drains; entrances and steps; raised platforms against walls; stairways and some other slight traces of rectangularity; conical towers; and finally the various relics—a divining bowl, a zoomorphic hollow pot, the soapstone birds on poles, one of which is still the country's national emblem, and then the relic that never was found—a fabled inscription over a doorway that nobody could read. Lastly, there was a story about a stone door to a town—which appears much later, in Madagascar.

1. *The total absence of mortar.* All walling, not only at the Great Zimbabwe but throughout the whole 270,000 square miles of the "ruin field" of Southern Africa, is without any mortar. It is all, without exception, dry-stone walling—stones fitted together with varying degrees of exactness to make walls without any bonding material in either the horizontal or vertical joints.

Dry-stone walling is of course common in many parts of Europe for field boundary walls on farms; but unlike those walls, the Great Zimbabwe stones have been standardised in shape, size, and weight to per-

mit a smooth and regular finish to the wall face. This is one of the most obvious abnormalities of Great Zimbabwean stonework to strike any visitor at once.

The absence of mortar has led to another unusual feature—the absence of any bonding of the stones at wall intersections. Such bonding needs either mortar or much longer and larger stones to tie togehter two walls meeting at a T-junction; and the absence of any variation in the building technique to provide such bonding at intersections indicates clearly the severely limited nature of the stone technology.

2. *Stones used like bricks.* The first impression of the best stonework is that it must have been built by bricklayers: the stones are roughly standard sizes and have been laid in regular courses. The only basic difference is that the size of the average stone used is larger than an average brick. This is obviously due to the fact that there is no mortar in the joints, which allowed the mason to use both hands to fit a stone into place, whereas the bricklayer has to fit a brick with only one hand, the other being required to handle the trowel to lay the mortar.

This, however, is not a normal thing to do: to cut stone down to such a small size that one man can handle it. The great stone cultures of the world—the megalithic cultures—have done the precise opposite.

45

They have used enormous stones needing masses of serf, if not slave, labour. Some stones at Stonehenge weighed from twenty-five to forty-five tons each; one Irish dolmen capstone, two hundred. But for some reason the Zimbabwe builders did not want to do this. They wanted a brick technique, a single-man technique, not a massed labour technique.

Many if not most writers on Zimbabwe have assumed stones of this size were formed naturally by the spalling of the granite domes due solely to the action of sudden thunder storms on rock after long exposure to a hot sun. But the small variation of rock size in most of the walling contradicts this assumption. The stones in the best walling, such as the Great Wall to the Great Enclosure, are standardised in size, shape, and weight within quite a narrow range, and this degree of accuracy can only have been the result of human intention, effort, and skill. In short, both the quarry men and the masons building the wall knew precisely what they were doing: it was no accident of nature.

Moreover, it would seem most stone cutting was done at the quarry, not the site, for no piles of chippings at the base of or near the walls have been found, except for one case—the Great Wall of the Great Enclosure, where small chippings were found at its base, no doubt due to the extra degree of precision fitting needed in this best-class work.

3. *Variations in masonry technique.* One aspect of the riddle of the ruins that has been attacked in detail over the last twenty-five years by some determined archaeologists and architects is the actual way in which the stonework had been built.*

Two significant facts were found, the first fact being that there is some variation in the workmanship of the walls—that is, the degree of regularity in the size and shape

of the stone bricks and the consequent degree of regularity in the stone courses, the horizontal rows of stones laid one upon the other. Four main categories of walling were identified and labelled Q, PQ, P, and R, each with the following characteristics:

Class Q: Regular courses and regular height, but some variation in stone length. Built with a batter, each course level but slightly set back from the course below to give a total set-back varying from one in six to one in nineteen. The whole of the Great Wall of the Great Enclosure is the prime example of this class.

Class PQ: Fairly regular courses, but variations in stone depth and length leading to some irregularity in courses; mostly in the Great Enclosure.

Class P: Large variation in stone size, courses very irregular, with small stones used as infill. Some stones so large that two men would be required to lift them.

Class R: Variation in stone size and shape (some not rectangular); small stones as infill; no batter and no courses of any length.

It was noted that although class PQ is intermediate in character between P and Q, there is no instance anywhere of an intermediate between P and R or Q and R. For the sake of the record three other classes, S, W, and Z, were identified, representing respectively walls too small to classify, modern restoration, and completely ruinous walls. These can be forgotten for our present purpose.

The second fact was less obvious but possibly significant. The absence of bonding at a T-junction of walls led to the assumption that the through wall (the head of the T) was built first. This may well have been so, but there is no evidence of the time interval between the two operations. As no bonding has ever been found, anywhere, the absence of bonding may merely have been the normal way of making walls meet one another and therefore the build-

*This analysis of stonework is from R. Summers et al. (1961).

ing of the two walls may have been simultaneous, or at a negligible interval.

However, on the assumption the absence of bonding at intersections indicated an appreciable time interval, every wall in the Great Enclosure was so tested, and the resulting evidence, both positive and negative, led to one conclusion and one only—the sequence of building was P-PQ-Q-R. In short, the start was mediocre, changing to much better, and then the best and finally the worst—with no evidence for any intermediate step between the best and the worst.

This conclusion, derived solely from the Great Enclosure, was then applied to all the ruins, including the Hill-Fortress, and a further conclusion appears: the three main classes, P, Q, and R, each have their own distribution pattern. Class P predominates in the Fortress, including the great West Wall and the upper Valley Ruins built on a rock face—the Mauch, Renders, and No. 1 ruins. Class Q, the peak workmanship, predominates in the Great Encolosure (with the Great Walls its finest example) and in the lower Valley Ruins (Posselt, Philips, Maund group); while the intermediate PQ occurs in the internal walls of the Great Enclosure and in some limited cases in the Hill-Fortress, such as the Western Enclosure and the small southern enclosures, suggesting a process of partial rebuilding from an original Class P building. Class R occurs in the outlying ruins or minor additions in the other main ruins.

The whole of this hypothesis, derived purely from the internal evidence of the walls, if correct, means there were four main periods of building: firstly, the Hill-Fortress and the bulk of the upper Valley Ruins; secondly, some re-building of the Fortress and some of the internal walling of the Great Enclosure; thirdly, the Great Enclosure in its final form with its Great Wall and the Posselt, Philips, and Maund ruins in the lower Valley; and fourthly, the outlying and unimportant additions.

The quantities actually built show the first period was the longest and the second and third much shorter. The third period appears as a sudden and brilliant burst, then to peter out into insignificance. In fact, Summers actually thinks the third period—the Q style—represented such a clear new step forward in technique that it may have been due to some sudden external influence, which, having done its work, disappeared never to return. The fourth period may have continued, at intervals, as need demanded, over many years and even perhaps centuries. This makes overall sense, for in the nature of things, the Hill-Fortress would have been first and have taken the longest time; then some of its village immediately below the West Wall, and then gradually the Valley Ruins.

The Valley Ruins themselves in fact show the sequence in greater detail, for they have all four classes of walls and their staging also makes planning sense. The first group to be built would have been Group A—the Outspan, Camp No. 1, No. 2, and the Ridge ruins. These are the nearest to the ancient southeast ascent to the Fortress and to the water sources in the head of both valleys—particularly the good spring in the northwest valley (now dried up) just west of the Great Enclosure. *Why* the community decided to build anything on this side away and separated from the village on the northwestern slopes is the million-dollar question. But the decision was made and these appear to be the earliest ruins, since they are closest to the Fortress, the heart of the settlement. Hall considered the walls left in Camps No. 1 and No. 2 ruins as "old" but not "ancient"—that is, not contemporary with the other ruins, but probably built on an ancient site, owing to the site's strategic position on the ridge. Very little was found in these ruins, and it may be they were little used after the other and larger Valley Ruins had been built.

Later, Group A was extended to form Group B along the same ridge, above the valley bottom—No. 1 Ruin, Renders and Mauch ruins. Most of the internal walls of the Great Enclosure, as well as some of the intervening large enclosures between the Great Enclosure and the other ruins, appear very similar to one another and may be contemporary.

Then suddenly for some unusual reason a new look was imposed, involving a new team of masons with a totally new level of competence and quality. The Great Wall of the Great Enclosure was superimposed on the southwest edge of Group B and new enclosures down in the valley bottom built to go with this new burst of activity. This is Group C—the Posselt, Philips and Maund ruins.

This practically completes the total complex, and any new building that took place after this burst seems to have been very minor or peripheral. The East and South East ruins (Group D) contain elements of all classes of wall, suggesting they were constantly being built and rebuilt and so spanned all periods. This makes planning sense, for they were almost certainly garrison posts on the trade route to the coast and so would naturally have been judged necessary at the start, when the Hill-Fortress was first built, and had to be maintained during all subsequent periods.

4. *No foundations.* Class Q, the best class of wall, is the only one to have in one or two cases any foundations, and these are minimal: in the case of the Great Wall, a trenching for one course projecting four inches from the general wall face above. That is all; everywhere else, with all the classes except for one or two cases built on rock, the walls were built directly on the natural soil without any preparation whatever. A very queer way of building: a lack of knowledge? and lack of care? a lack of necessity? There seems no easy answer, but it puts at least the Great Wall and therefore Q-type walls into a different class.

5. *The width and height of the walls.* In all dry-stone walling, or any walling, even

of brick, built without mortar, there must be a batter to both faces of the wall—that is, the wall thickness must diminish with height, to increase stability by lowering the centre of gravity of the wall mass. In addition, at the Great Zimbabwe there seems to have been a definite ratio between the width at base, the total height, and the width at the top. It is clear it would have been impossible to build these walls at all unless there was some rule of thumb that related these three dimensions to one another, for without it the builders would not have known how wide to make the base when they started building or how much to set back each course as they proceeded upward.

In the absence of any detailed survey of the ruins, it is fortunate that one of the best examples of any walling—the Great Wall of the Great Enclosure—was measured in detail by Hall at the turn of the century. The variations in the ratio of widths (at top and base) to height are quite large—at one point 19′ at the base, 12′ at the top, and a height of 33′; at another, 10′ at the base, 4′6″ at the top, and a height of 21′. The batter has an even wider range—one in seven to one in nine on the outside face and one in thirteen to one in nineteen on the inside face of the western section (Enclosures 4, 5, and 6) of the Great Enclosure.

Any rule of thumb must have been a simple one, for the wall masons had to apply it on the spot from memory without any documentation. Averaging from the above dimensions, it would seem that the width at the base was assumed to be double the width at the top and half the height. This would make the width at the top a quarter of the height and give a batter of one in eight—the face of the wall setting back one foot for every eight feet of height.

The final testing of such an hypothesis can only be done when all walls have been accurately surveyed for both the width at the base and the width at the present top, and some estimate made of their original height. But random testing on walls in the Valley Ruins and the Hill-Fortress seems to confirm such a rule, for very few walls are less than four feet thick at a base or two feet at the top. This brings out a characteristic of the walls that has hardly, if ever, been commented on—the top of the walls were never thinner than the average width of wall openings—twenty inches or a cubit—a one-man width. In short, all walls at the top were wide enough to let a man walk along them—a very important conclusion.

5. *No arch, either true or corbelled.* No arch of any kind has ever been found in any of the ruins, either the true arch or the corbelled arch. The true arch is a relatively sophisticated technique needing normally a custom-made timber framework to support it while being constructed, and given the simple building techniques used at Great Zimbabwe this was hardly to be expected.* But the corbelled arch (formed by each course projecting slightly over the course below till both sides meet together at the top) is simpler and easier to build, since it requires no timber framework to support it while building, or, at the most, one or two straight timber struts. It could easily have been used wherever there were regular stone courses, such as the Q-type walling.

The collapse of all walls, save one, over openings suggests the corbelled arch was never used, since a collapse of corbelled arch is most improbable, the load of stonework above acting as a compressive force to keep the corbels in place. Only an earthquake is likely to have been able to dislodge some corbels, which might have led to a progressive collapse of the remaining corbels and a total collapse of the walling above. Even a great monument like

Angkor Vat in Cambodia still includes many corbelled arches still intact, and this is in an earthquake-prone zone. It is therefore practically certain the absence of corbelled arches today means they were never used. *Why* they were never used in walling that was suitable for their use is just another of these queer questions that the ruins are always posing. Their absence indicates the very limited range of thought and action available to the wall masons, almost as if they were automatic men, programmed only to do one thing, and do it well, and never to invent, or even consider, any possible alternatives.

7. *Timber lintels over openings.* The collapse of all walls over openings, except one with stone lintels, suggests all openings were bridged with timber lintels. It was, after all, a very simple structural problem, for all openings were one-man width, for single-file movement, mostly not more than two feet. Mauch saw a timber beam in place in the north entrance to the Great Enclosure, took a splinter from it, compared it to the wood of his pencil, and concluded it was cedar of Lebanon imported by the Phoenicians or Solomon's agents. Mauch may have been nearer the truth than later investigators, derisive of such wild theorizing, would like to admit; for the one timber lintel found in place, spanning a drain in one of the inner walls in the Great Enclosure, from which the first famous and controversial carbon 14 dating was obtained, was in fact one of the hardest and most enduring African hardwoods—tambuti (*Spirostachys africanus*). Such a wood, or other African hardwood, could easily have been mistaken by any immigrant stranger for the best timber of his home country, such as teak from India, or cedar from Lebanon, for these timbers were the main ship-building timber that any stranger from the Indian Ocean lands would have been familiar with. An Arab many centuries before Mauch could well have made the same mistake and come to

---

*The true arch was probably invented in Persia or Mesopotamia owing to the scarcity of timber. The Greeks never used it, and the Romans learned it from the Etruscans, a people of eastern origin.

PLATE 19. The Great Enclosure north entrance, (before restoration). The wall originally (and in Mauch's time) was carried across the opening, at the height of the collapsed courses in the photo. (*Photo by courtesy of National Archives*)

the same conclusion. In fact, a few years before Mauch came to Africa, David Livingstone had reported tambuti being used by Arab slavers for ship building of dhows on Lake Nyasa (now Lake Malawi), to take slaves across the lake on their journey to the coast.

It is possible all wood lintels used in the Great Zimbabwe were tambuti, owing to their long durability, but whatever the timber was, they had all disappeared, except for these two known cases, by the time the white man had found the Great Zimbabwe. The result was all walls over openings had collapsed, with one exception—that over the tunnel in the east wall

of the Western Enclosure in the Hill-Fortress. This had been spanned with stone lintels, still in place today.

Unfortunately, the two main entrances to the Great Enclosure, the north and the west, have been restored as openings up to the top of the walls, which is quite incorrect and gives a totally wrong impression on entering. The original height of the opening can be seen by the difference in surface appearance between the original and restored wall surfaces, and was no more than needed to give entrance to a human being.

8. *Drains.* It is clear the builders had some hydraulic knowledge: they knew how

50

water behaves and they had some means of taking true levels—almost certainly water, in a long, narrow, wooden trough, similar to one found in an old gold mine. Drains occur in Class P, PQ, and Q walls—such as both walls of the inner parallel passage in the Great Enclosure—but the most obvious and best built are in the Great Wall. The drains in this wall were clearly no afterthought and must have been planned in advance, both in their horizontal and vertical position, for they are in the correct place in plan, and at the correct height in the wall, to drain the whole of the Great Enclosure. After a heavy rain the run-off water still gravitates towards them today. This means the builders must have taken some levels, or watched very carefully how water behaved after a storm, before they started the bottom courses of the Great Wall. In any case, some method of levelling would have been essential to obtain the stone courses of the Great Wall itself.

The other instance of the builders' hydraulic knowledge was the damming of the valley to the west of the Hill-Fortress by building the causeway approach to the Watergate and the V.I.P. inland approach to the Hill-Fortress. As already stated, in heavy rains this valley area above the causeway becomes a marsh, a vestigial relic of the original lake that must have been the main water supply for the Hill-Fortress and may have been a supply tank for irrigated lands below the causeway.

9. *Entrances and steps.* If the drains were no afterthought, neither were the steps in the entrances. The bottom courses of the wall were carried across the openings, forming steps up and down to enter the building; and in one case (the north entrance to the Great Enclosure, always assumed to be the chief entrance) these steps were swept round into a smooth, concave curve, almost as a welcoming gesture, an enticement to enter.

It is now generally accepted that walls everywhere in the Great Zimbabwe were carried across entrances so that entrances were never more than man-high. The wall over may have followed the curve of the steps under: the distance to be spanned would have been so much less and there would still have been sufficient width for a passageway on the top. This may have been the reason for curving the steps, to prepare the pedestrian for the wall over the entrance: but there is no firm evidence for this.

Two other interesting details occur at entrances. The first, is the use of low stone projections either side of the opening, almost always on the inside of the enclosure concerned, and the second is the design of V-shaped recesses in the side of the opening itself or in one of the projections. The projections have been called buttresses or bastions, the V-shaped recesses portcullis grooves. Figure 15 shows two typical cases, the north and south entrances to Enclosure No. 7.

Both these devices have one obvious purpose: they help to control movement, reduced as always in Africa to single-file movement. But they are not always used together. Two of the entrances through the Great Wall, the northwestern and western, have bastions but no grooves, and the main north entrance has neither, being very well controlled by narrow passages converging on it from both sides. But why no grooves? And why grooves in certain enclosures, such as Nos. 7 and 10, and none in others, such as No. 1? And why such long, narrow bastions with grooves effectively barring movement through the parallel passage? How these grooves were used in practice is another minor mystery of Zimbabwe, but the real question is, what were they for? In short, who was controlling whom or what, and, still more important, why?

10. *Raised platforms against walls.* These are another minor riddle. There are three spaced equally along the inner wall of the

Parallel Passage in the Great Enclosure, with the third being by far the largest, next the opening to the Conical Tower. There are others in both the Upper and Lower Valley Ruins and some in the eastern enclosure in the Hill-Fortress. They consist of two or three "blind" steps leading to a raised area, generally in a corner of two walls, so there is considerable physical protection at the back and good visual protection in front, the floor of the platform being well above the general floor level. No one has the least idea of what these platforms were for.

11. *Stairways and traces of rectangularity.* The use of steps was not limited to two or three steps at entrances or to platforms. Whole stairways were built in the approaches to the Hill-Fortress, and similar stairways have been found at other ruins, such as Khami. The use of steps in regular, standardised sequence to form a stairway is the result of rational, systematic planning; the earliest known stairways, in the valley cultures of the Indus and Tigris–Euphrates rivers, form part of very extensive and comprehensive rectangular planning.

Stairways are not the only traces of rectangularity and purposeful planning, though they are the strongest. Other slight traces are the regular, coursed stonework of the Q-type walling—including the carefully formed drain outlets—and the occasional right-angled ends to walls at entrances such as the V.I.P. entrance to the Hill-Fortress from the inland Watergate approach.

The use of stairways, and these other signs of rectangularity at the Great Zimbabwe, where there is no general rectangular planning at all, is one further queer anomaly that calls for some special explanation.

12. *Towers.* The main Conical Tower, by its very size, now 30', perhaps once 35' high, and 57' in circumference at its base, has caught everyone's imagination because it seems entirely useless. It is solid throughout, with nothing underneath below its shallow foundations and nothing on top. It is not strictly circular in plan nor conical in section; the batter increases in the upper half to give a curved profile, so even that seems to have been design, not accident. The same stone workmanship and shallow foundation are seen at the Great Wall, and standing as it does only four feet from that wall, it must be considered part of the same building operation. There is nothing else like it for size and character in Africa, or for that matter in the world. It remains one of the primary enigmas of Great Zimbabwe.

There are four other much smaller conical towers. One is only five feet away from the big one just described. With a base circumference of 21' and probable original height of 13', it is now only 5' to 6' much damaged and re-constructed. Two other small towers exist in the Posselt and Philips ruins, and a fourth forms part of the wall in the Outspan Ruins.

The two in the Posselt and Philips ruins, with a base circumference of 16' and 18', respectively, and up to 11' to 12' high, might have been nearly as high as the original walls. There is the possibility of another one in a circular bed of stones just outside the southwest corner of Enclosure 1 in the Great Enclosure, but there is not other evidence for this. With a circumference at base of 35', it could have been 20' high, as high or higher than the original walls of Enclosure 1 nearby.

All these towers have definite similarities. They are all (with the exception in the Outspan Ruins) of Q-type walling; they are all near entrances or passageways and, although always very near walls, are free-standing. The only slight clue to their purpose is the fact that the soapstone Zimbabwe bird, which, as mentioned, became the Zimbabwe national emblem, was found upside-down next the tower in the Philips Ruin, and had apparently stood as a kind of symbol or flagpole on its summit. Were these circular towers therefore simply image builders, or did they have some other purpose or significance?

13. *Relics.* If ruins are the macro, relics are the micro, remnants of the past. They can give a concentrated miniature of a culture and can open doors that otherwise remain firmly shut. But Great Zimbabwe is remarkable for a relative absence of relics found, some of which only deepen the mystery.

To begin with, no doubt most of the significant relics have been lost—taken by the ruin robbers, gold hunters of the early days, like the pyramid robbers of Egypt. Despite this, enough was found by Hall, ten years or more after Bent, to give some character to some of the ruins. Both Bent and Hall found small, stone, finger-sized phalli in many places, particularly near the Conical Tower. Of course, it could be said those two early explorers found only what they were looking for, being convinced of the existence of phallic worship. The Gold Furnace Enclosure and the curious ingot mould in the Fortress Cave have already been mentioned. Hall found indications of gold workings in Enclosures 7 and 10 in the Great Enclosure in the valley, together with traces of iron working in the adjoining Enclosure 6, so both the Fortress and the Great Enclosure were used at some time for productive purposes and presumably were, at least for that period, under the direct control of whoever was in power in the Fortress.

Investigations of the other ruins have produced equally scarce results:

Group A, along the watershed, have produced virtually nothing, even as early as 1893, when Sir John Willoughby excavated in the Ridge Ruins.

Group B, apart from the Great Enclosure, produced more. The No. 1 Ruins produced nothing, but Hall stated in his day the whole place had been "completely ransacked," so the absence of relics means nothing. On the other hand, the other two ruins of this group, Renders and Mauch, produced a lot. In the easternmost enclosure of the Renders Ruin (A on Figure 11), three ounces of gold wire and beads, with beaten gold, were found at the lowest level, on the rock; and above them four feet from the surface, Arabian glass with "arabesque patterns most delicately engraved", and white clay glazed pottery with "sunken designs under the glazes, sea-green and a delicate shade of foreget-me-not blue". Much later, in 1943, no fewer than 30,000 beads of all colours and descriptions were unearthed in another enclosure nearby (B on Figure 11), clearly some trader's store— but what happened to the trader, to leave such a store in such a place?

Next door literally, in the Mauch Ruins, more gold objects—sheating and wire— were found, as well as two pairs of the typically African double three-sided iron gongs, and more glazed white clay pottery. It would seem this Group B of the ruins was traders' territory, and if No. 1 Ruins had not been ransacked they might have told the same story.

All three ruins in Group C—Posselt, Philips, and Maund—have had some interesting objects, but not so much as they deserve, for they are all Q-type workmanship and so linked directly with the Great Enclosure. Beaten gold and unworked soapstone beams used as stoppers in grooved entrances were found in the Posselt, and portions of carved soapstone bowls, as well as the Zimbabwe bird, in the Philips. In the last of these three, the Maund, very little was found—only iron tools and arrowheads and fragments of soapstone bowls and pottery—the result of a very professional dig in 1929 by Gertrude Caton Thompson.

In Group D, the East and South East ruins, nothing has ever been recorded, but the ruin robbers may have done it all first. If it was the garrison post, it is logical it would have had nothing, for troops would be unlikely to use "Arabian glass, most delicately engraved". What was found were two sets of holes, cut into a rock face just outside for the Insufuba game (a sort of draughts): just what soldiers on guard duty would need, with nothing particular on their mind and very little to do.

One legend about the East Ruin makes sense—that it was the camp for the young mens' puberty initiation ceremonies, where they were taught the law of the tribe and were made men. That this should happen in what had been a military guard post, where young men would congregate anyhow, and where discipline would be enforced, is very probable. Beyond all these normal kind of relics, five "specials", three found either in or near Zimbabwe, can be taken as part of the Zimbabwe legendary history. They are: the wooden zodiacal bowl; the headless, hollow, four-legged pot; the famous soapstone birds; the relic that was never found—the inscription; and lastly a legend of a stone door.

The wooden zodiacal bowl

This was found in caves about ten miles from Great Zimbabwe, sometime before 1900. It is carved from a piece of wood about 12″ in diameter, with part of its rim destroyed. It is obviously in the same tradition as the later and well-known BaVenda bowls, some of which are as wide as 18″, and 1½″ to 2″ thick overall. The Zimbabwe bowl would be of no greater interest except that there can be no doubt there are at least six of the zodiac signs on the rim—on the left, Taurus (the bull); at the top, Gemini (the twins); and on the right, Sagittarius (the archer), Cancer (the crab), Pisces (the fish as a fishnet), Aquarius (water carrier), and (maybe) Leo (the lion). The remaining signs remain queries except for the four roughly rectangular signs with rounded ends at the top of the bowl, which without doubt represent the four wooden Karanga divining dice—two for men (young and old) and two for women (young and old)—for throwing in the bowl when filled with water

for divination. The real question remains, Where on earth did the knowledge of the zodiac signs come from?

The headless, hollow pots

This is a more extraordinary story. For a long time the legend of a four-legged pot that walked about on its own haunted the hills and mountains round Zimbabwe. It was said to have inside it some yellow substance that glowed red; that anyone trying to seize this substance would have his hand cut off by the pot closing in on it; and that if anyone disclosed the hiding place of the pot his arm would become withered.* It was also said there were two other pots, one male and the other female. One was called the most curious name—*fuko-ya-nebandge*—"the king's favourite adviser". Mauch had heard of this pot in 1871 as being on a mountain no one dare climb. He immediately climbed it, got to the top, and found nothing. It was the hunter and explorer, Harry Posselt, at Fern Spruit, about ten miles south of Zimbabwe, who after having heard stories about it from 1890 onwards eventually found it near the village of a chief who used to live at Zimbabwe. The pot is about 16″ long and 11″ high. The head, which would have been a stopper, was never found. It is black with dull red stripes—and so supposed to be a zebra, but the shape with the short legs is much nearer that of a hippopotamus. The animal's sex is undetermined, and the pot is now in the museum at Bulawayo; nothing more is known about it. The legendary second pot was never found.

Two other zoomorphic hollow animals have been found in southern Africa—a wooden buffalo in Botswana and a stone wild hog, or *vatolambo*, at Skaleona, on the east coast of Madagascar. The buffalo may have been a bellows for iron making,

*There is a story that in 1904 a black did disclose to some farmer the hiding place of another hollow pot shaped like a rhino, and came back later with a withered arm.

since it had some traces of leather nailed to it; and folklore connects the wild hog with immigrants from the west coast of India in the thirteenth century A.D. No evidence connects either to Zimbabwe, but the similarity of the model animal used as a receptacle for something presumably valuable (owing to its very limited capacity) may indicate some common cultural trait.

The soapstone birds

Eight of these were found at various times, seven in the Eastern Enclosure in the Hill-Fortress. Most of the seven were standing upright, according to Bent and Hall, either on a narrow terrace against a rock face on the west, or inside against the main wall on the east (see Figures 9 and 10); but it is not known exactly where.

Most of these seven are similar in feeling, and though they fall into two main groups, they have different subsidiary designs. But it is the eighth, found by Hall in the Philips Ruin, which stands apart from all the rest, for it is a far more dynamic design, a far more lively piece of sculpture in every way: upright, active, with a great elongated neck giving the impression it is on full alert and about to take off. In addition, it is the only bird that has a very definite second symbol—a crocodile (or a lizard?) climbing up the pole just below its feet. Finally, it is the only bird found in what must have been a traders' store, and not in the heart of the Fortress, the Eastern Enclosure.

The fabled inscription

No inscription or writing has ever been found anywhere in any ruin throughout Southern Africa. Yet João de Barros, in his book *Da Asia,* published in 1552, in describing the kingdom of Sofala, the mines within it, its prince Monomatapa, and the "Fortress in the centre of the mining country", said: "Above the door of this building is an inscription which some

Moorish merchants, learned men who went there, did not know how to read, nor could they tell what lettering it was in. And almost all around this building on some hills were other buildings of the same fashion, all worked in stone and without lime, among them a tower of a dozen fathoms. The natives of the land call all these buildings Symbaoe, which is to say 'Court' ". This is a very circumstantial statement, and the dry-stone building, the two groups of buildings, the size of the Tower, as well as the name, almost certainly all refer to the Great Zimbabwe. There was no possible reason why either Barros or the Moorish merchants should tell lies to expose their own ignorance, and on this evidence such an inscription must have once existed. Moreover, a contemporary of Barros, one de Goes, a keeper of the archives at Lisbon, recorded a similar rumour of a fortress built with heavy stones without mortar, with an inscription in stone over the entrance that no one can understand. This confirmation of the rumour may come from the same source, although the details vary.

What is really interesting is that these "learned Moorish" (that is, Arab Moslem) merchants not only could not read the inscription but could not even recognise the script. Yet they must have been traders, sailing continuously round the Indian Ocean in their ordinary way of business and so conversant at least with the coastal languages of that ocean. So what was the script? This is queer, to say the least.

A stone door

Finally, there was one rather remote legend. Hall was told by Harry Posselt that he had heard at several different times from several different natives that "large ruins with a stone door" could be found on the left bank of the Sabi, near the Portuguese (the present Maputo) territory. The reports all agreed, not only about the stone door but also about the carving of a man on the stone inside the doorway. Some ruins have been found near this area, but no stone doors, still less the "carving of a man".

Another time dimension

Looking back on all these ruins, one has to remember, as with all ruins in the world, one is looking at a palimpsest—a document that has been made, rubbed out, and remade many times over, till the original writing, the original plan, becomes almost lost and indecipherable. The sharp focus of the first idea has gone and what remains is layer upon layer of later events, like the successive skins of an onion each obscuring the one before. The most one can do is to take off some of the outer skins, get a little closer to the original heart.

However, much as one must discount the discontinuities of time, there is still at Zimbabwe the feeling of something unreal, something that defies all normal rules of thought and sense. It is not that there is no obvious thought in what one sees: on the contrary, again and again there is much thought; rather it is the sudden inconsistencies, the sudden invasions of the inexplicable mixed with the logical and sensible that is so disturbing. This is to any purely rational mind so unreal as to seem from another world.

The Hill-Fortress, for instance, has all the basic elements of a well-planned military fortress—the protected heart, the garrison station area, the controlled entrances. Yet the highest point of the hill is outside the fortress altogether, overlooking it; and this highest point has no defensive arrangements whatever, while the route to it from the Balcony in the Eastern Enclosure is also quite undefended. The only virtue of this high point can have been the possibility of an early warning system of any approaching strangers—a few minutes, or maybe an hour at most. Again, there were tremendous defensive precautions in the southeast approach, but practically none on the northwestern, except some walls on either side of the path. Beyond the carefully controlled entrances on the west, there were at least three weak points by which the central and eastern parts could be infiltrated by anyone determined to do so quite clear of any control from the garrison area in the west. And finally, there is within the fortress no visible means of storing water and certainly no spring, so it could never have withstood a siege of more than a few days, or a few weeks at most.

The same inconsistencies run through all the ruins. It is as if there was something inconclusive about the whole situation, something temporary or incomplete: perhaps a splendid and determined idea, great and brave, but then some hesitation, indolence, incapacity—what was it, simply no need?—to see it through to any hard conclusion. It is as if the makers found before they had finished that they had too much strength, and with 50 or 100 garrison troops that strength would never be tested. Fear may have started the planning, but self-confidence—perhaps later, over-confidence—completed it. A queer story, the opposite of the obvious and expected.

On a wider view, the ruins remain very African. The Great Zimbabwe has throughout one common basic theme, a purely instinctive feeling for shape, played without any Euclidean geometry, rectangular coordinates, squares, circles, or straight lines. It is another world of form altogether, a world of direct response to direct demand, without rules and without dogma. Perhaps one is not only in Africa: one is in another age or time dimension altogether. To understand it, to get inside its heart and mind, one must discard the remnants of neat and tidy thinking and immerse oneself in a kind of warm treacle of hand-made, sculpted shapes, of contorted boulders piled one on top of another, of twisted and turning walls spewed out equally from the wild imagery of early man and the inner entrails of the earth. It is at once smooth and fierce, calm and overwhelming: it is, like all Africa, nothing if not extreme, even outrageous.

Yet some humans, sometime, crept into these extraordinary shapes with a definite purpose in mind and slowly, with persistent care, tried to make them their own. Today, long after, it may be possible with imagination to creep back and live and share again with them some of their hopes and fears and dreams. To attempt to probe these shapes, to share these dreams, that is the next step. But before doing that, a short look must be given to this rather special land and even more what can be found out about the equally special people who lived in it and built the ruins.

CHAPTER 4

The Land and the People

[Zimbabwe] . . . is a relatively small, compact country but it enjoys
a rich and varied natural heritage which is unequalled by that of any
region of similar size in tropical Africa. . . . however it has continually presented its occupants with a tantalising mixture of prospects
and problems . . .   —*George Kay, 1970*

THE LAND

THE land of Southern Africa south of the
Zambezi is in essence a flat tableland 3,000
to 4,000 feet above sea level, with a major
mountain barrier on its eastern edge, set
back 100 miles or so from the Indian Ocean
and falling slowly to the west, where it dies
out to almost nothing on the Atlantic. Only
five major river systems breach this tableland and its mountain barrier to reach the
Indian Ocean—Zambezi, Save, Limpopo,
Incomati, and Maputo and so provide some
natural access routes, however tenuous and
difficult, from the east coast to the interior. Only one river system, the Orange,
flows westwards towards the Atlantic coast,
but that coast was unknown to the world
before A.D. 1500 and so proved useless for
the development of the interior. It may be
or may not be an accident that all the stone
ruins of Southern Africa have been found
between the Zambezi and Orange rivers,
and could have been reached with not too
great difficulty from one or other of the five
great river systems flowing eastwards to the
Indian Ocean.

There was, however, both difficulty and
danger in such routes from the sea. The
difficulty was the perennial sand bar at the

mouths of most African rivers, making
navigating upstream hazardous except in
flood conditions. The danger lay in the land
between the mountain barrier and the
eastern sea—the long, low flatlands and
lowveld of Southern Africa, where the
tsetse fly and anopheles mosquito created
a barrier of disease for man and beast
greater than the mountains or wild beasts.
It is this that gave the mystery and ignorance to what lay beyond and created
without doubt that enduring isolation that
protected the continental heart from
external invasion—of ideas as well as
exploitation.

In sharp contrast with these flatlands lay
the tableland behind the mountain barrier. Here there were climate and altitude
that combined to give the exact opposite—
a freedom from disease and a range of
temperature and rainfall that encouraged
people to stay and made the eastern and
central portions comfortable and productive.

The seasonal changes in climate increased
the attraction by eliminating monotony. A
rainy summer from November to March;
an intermediate season with decreasing rain
and lower temperatures till May; a cool—
even sometimes cold—season with frosts

till late August; and then a warm spring, with rains starting again in October or November. A routine of weather that was rarely too hot or too cold, with the only difficulty being that it was unequally distributed both in time—in summer storms—and in place—the greater amount caught by the eastern mountains. This reduced to a minimum the moisture available for the far south and west on the Limpopo and upper Zambezi valleys. Seasonal rainfall means seasonal rivers, dry for much of the year, and seasonal rivers mean a seasonal rhythm to human activity. It was a twist of nature, however, that the seasonal flood times of the rivers and therefore their navigability coincided with the northeast and not the southwest monsoon winds of the Indian Ocean, a fact of importance for visiting strangers, all of whom came from the north.

Over the physical surface of this upland, however, nature had through geological time imposed another dimension, of hidden wealth and power. Down the central land between the Zambezi and Limpopo, and even beyond the Limpopo, nature had scattered a long array of minerals, many only to be won in bulk once today's techniques had come to hand. But one, iron ore, in the shape of hematite ore, was widely distributed and had been known to Stone Age man for millenia as a source of specularite, the tiny, mica-like flakes that glistened in the sunlight and were used to decorate a young girl's hair when greased at initiation. A hematite mine in Swaziland, in the mountains near the upper waters of the Maputo River system, and within reach of the sea coast, has been dated at least to 40,000 B.C., and perhaps beyond the carbon 14 range to possibly 80,000 B.C.; and similar mines far inland, in present Botswana, were being exploited up to the nineteenth century. The existing mining for specularite must have identified for newcomers, bringing with them their new iron-making techniques, the sources of the

ore they needed for their novel product, and must have speeded up greatly this new use of an old metal. It was this new use that revolutionised the way of life of Southern Africa and attracted new peoples, new ideas—and new problems. The Iron Age arrived in Southern Africa somewhere about the start of the Christian era.

Iron was not the only metal to be developed at an early date: copper ores were widespread in the central upland between the Zambezi and the Limpopo, and there were large concentrations to the north and south of these rivers—in the Katanga district of modern Zambia and at the Phalaborwa and Messina districts in South Africa. Tin, the most precious and rare metal for early man, was certainly mined at Rooiberg 250 miles south of the Limpopo, but although copper was known and mined, there was no bronze in South Africa. There was therefore little reason to mine tin, and the only other generator could have been long-distance trade to overseas northern markets. But who mined, who sold, and who bought—and transported whereto—this ancient tin from this southern Tartessus of the ancient world? Nobody seems to know . . .

It was, however, the emperor of all metals, gold, that had the largest effect upon the local scene. Something like 4,000 gold mines and 500 copper mines were opened up between A.D. 600 and A.D. 1500, when the Portuguese arrived to try to seize the trade; and the proximity of the gold mines to many of the stone ruins proves the cultural connection of the two. The mines were both open and underground; stopes went down 20 to 80 feet, and in one instance (Gwanda) 120 feet vertically—280 feet on the incline. It would seem that water, which they had no means of controlling, was the ultimate determinant of the depth and extent of what they could mine. The shafts and slopes could be narrow—3 feet or less (one was reported only 10 inches wide)—and the work conditions

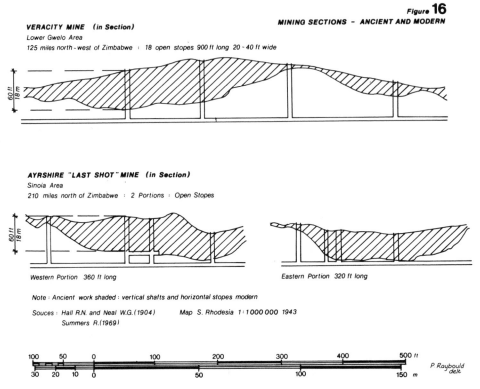

Figure **16**
MINING SECTIONS - ANCIENT AND MODERN

VERACITY MINE   (in Section)
Lower Gwelo Area
125 miles north - west of Zimbabwe : 18 open stopes 900 ft long 20 - 40 ft wide

60 ft
18 m

AYRSHIRE "LAST SHOT" MINE (in Section)
Sinoia Area
210 miles north of Zimbabwe : 2 Portions : Open Stopes

60 ft
18 m

Western Portion 360 ft long   Eastern Portion 320 ft long

Note : Ancient work shaded : vertical shafts and horizontal stopes modern

Souces : Hall R.N. and Neal W.G. (1904)   Map S. Rhodesia 1 : 1 000 000 1943
          Summers R. (1969)

100   50   0   100   200   300   400   500 ft
30   20   10   0   50   100   150 m

P. Raybould delt

Roger Summers estimates a probable total of 4,000 ancient gold mines, most of them very small. The Ayrshire mine was one of the few to

must have been appalling, as fire-setting was used at the mine face and all ore and rock had to be hauled in baskets by hand to the surface. Figure 16 shows the extent of some ancient mining in relation to modern mining methods.

FAUNA

Mineral wealth was not the only gift of nature. Animals of all sorts, shapes, and sizes roamed the land in free abundance and had provided the basic life support system for humans from earliest times. But one in particular, the largest of all, the great pachyderm, the African elephant, held a special place, because of his great tusks universally in demand for fabricating cultural and luxury articles from bracelets for

become a comparatively large modern mine. Stopes varied from five feet to two feet wide, with four feet as a likely average.

Indian brides to chessmen for the Persian King of Kings.

At the other end of the size scale, three very small creatures were important: two for bad, one for good. As mentioned, the two bad were the tsetse fly and the anopheles mosquito, the first giving trypanosomiasis, or nagana, to beast and sleeping sickness to man; the second, the bearer of malaria. The two together made the coastal flatlands "the badlands" and penetrated up the deep river valleys into the interior and portions of the tableland itself. Figure 17 shows the estimated extent of the tsetse fly area from A.D. 800 to A.D. 1400, and the consequent suitable areas for early farming, together with a modern estimate of the potential of the natural resource base of the country.

The anopheles had a similar distribu-

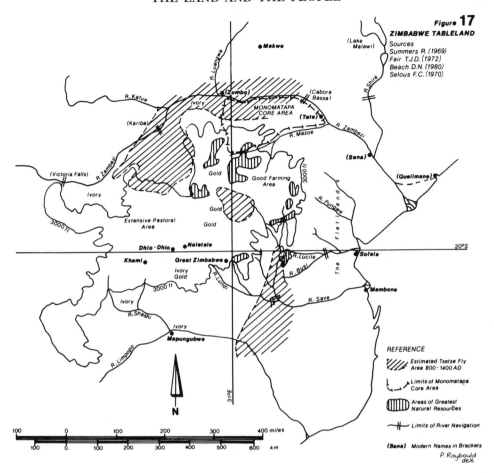

Figure 17
ZIMBABWE TABLELAND
Sources
Summers R. (1969)
Fair T.J.D. (1972)
Beach D.N. (1980)
Selous F.C. (1970)

REFERENCE

Estimated Tsetse Fly Area 800-1400 AD

Limits of Monomatapa Core Area

Areas of Greatest Natural Resources

Limits of River Navigation

(Sena) Modern Names in Brackets

P. Raybould delt

This gives the setting for the later movement to the richer north toward the Zambezi valley and the drier west round Khami and the modern Matabeleland.

tion; Caton Thompson even complained she caught a fever in the train between Gwelo and Salisbury—right in the centre of the tableland at well over 4,000 feet. But the anopheles, like all mosquitos, demands water for its life cycle, and so it was during the summer rains—which flood the rivers and make the summer the most dangerous as well as the easiest time to traverse the flatlands—that the northeastern monsoon brought down the ships from the north and made it desirable to navigate the rivers up to their head, where they issued from the eastern mountains. In this way nature tantalised man. The flooded rivers enticed him, then the mosquito and tsetse attacked him and mountains confronted him. It was a natural defence in depth that effectually stopped penetration of the interior by the unwanted visitor or invader from the coast. Yet in the end it was penetrated: the fly, the mosquito, and the mountain, never wholly beaten, were never completely victorious. Zimbabwe was drawn, willing or not, into the Indian Ocean world.

The third little creature was very industrious and, it turned out, very useful one to man—the termite ant. The huge termite mounds are a great feature of the Southern African landscape, often reaching twenty feet in height. Some may be 1,000 years old. They house great colonies so complex and integrated that the whole system has been compared to a single biological organism such as the human body. One of their essential needs is water, and to gain that they drive passages deep into the earth—sometimes up to two hundred feet—and bring back the diggings to form their mound. Again and again in the gold-bearing areas, they have brought back tiny traces of gold from the gold reefs they have dug through. If the mound-earth is panned, and gold found, the mounds become gold indicators—a very early and simple way of prospecting, and still being used today as a research tool. This useful trick of nature was probably the origin of the amazing story of Herodotus about the winning of gold in India: "Here in this desert there live amid the sand, great ants, in size somewhat less than dogs, but bigger than foxes. These ants make their dwelling underground and like the Greek ants which they very much resemble in shape throw up sand heaps as they burrow. Now the sand which they throw up is full of gold . . ."*

The story is in fact only a slight distortion of the truth. In telling second or tenth hand, the story had gotten the extra-large ants (which termites are) mixed up with the very large dogs (probably the Palegar dogs of South India) that guarded the diggings. Strabo, the Greek geographer, repeated a similar story four hundred years later about ant miners, "no smaller than foxes," who "dig holes in winter and heap up the earth at the mouth of the holes like moles: and the gold dust requires but little smelting".† Strabo may have gotten the human miners—often small people—mixed up with the ants and the dogs, but nevertheless the story has the same flavour and probably the same origin as that of Herodotus.

These rather surprising stories about

* Herodotus III. 102. Trans. G. Rawlinson (Everyman's Library no. 405, vol. 1, p. 260).
† Strabo 15.1.44. Trans. H. L. Jones (Loeb Ed., vol. 7, p. 77).

gold-digging ants are corroborated, with little doubt, by the Sanskrit phrase "paipilike swarna", "ant gold". This last name proves the great antiquity of the system, and the much greater age of gold mining than iron mining, as well as the reliability of the ancient historians, in spite of the limitation of working only from hearsay.

THE PEOPLE

Who were these people who built the ruins, and who opened up the mines—iron, copper, gold: especially gold? There are five sources to tell us: anthropology and archaeology; the actual skeletal remains found in the mines, but not found in the ruins (except for some recent burials); the written records, pre-Muslim, Muslim, and Portuguese; the living peoples met by the first hunters, explorers, and settlers coming from the south; and lastly—and most significant—the still-remembered folklore of these peoples as told to anthropologists and others in the early part of the present century, and still being recorded today.

ANTHROPOLOGY AND ARCHAEOLOGY

The San, or Bushmen

The archaeological record, correlated with the known ethnological facts of the late nineteenth and early twentieth centuries, gives a fairly clear outline of the black history of Southern Africa for the first 1,000 years of the Christian era. The basic stratum was still Paleolithic—late Stone Age man, hunting and gathering food, still today represented by the Bushmen of the Kalahari, the same Bushmen who once painted vivid pictures in caves or pecked the rock engravings. Their rock art and stone artifacts are similar from Ethiopia to the Cape of Good Hope—an immense northeast–southwest axis through Eastern and

Southern Africa. Their language included a distinctive "click", which has survived in some modern Bantu languages. The survivors of this stock are small in stature, but it is likely some were larger in the past. Their tools were flint scrapers set in wood handles, and bows and arrows with tips of wood and bone, often poisoned.

They were far closer to nature than modern man: so close they seem almost of another world, a world as old as Africa herself, a world integrated with plants and birds and beasts. There is a story of a pet baboon who got loose and stole a baby, taking it into a tree: only a Bushman, once all the white and black people had hidden themselves, was able to talk the baboon language and persuade it to come down from the tree and give up the baby. There are other true stories. A Bushman once heard a single-engine aircraft seventy-two miles away; another could hit with his arrow a buck at seventy-five yards, a third fire ten arrows in ten seconds. These skills were not wholly lost, but no doubt greatly changed by mixing with the Bantu or other visitors to Africa over the centuries. This ancient Bushman legacy has remained the base line of Southern Africa, and the famous rock paintings and engravings are its evocative memory for us today.

The Khoikhoi, or Hottentots

The second major stratum was the Hottentots. These deserve more than a passing reference, for they are the one group the whites from Europe found at the Cape with whom they could make some permanent contact but whose origins could not be and never have been fully explained. That they have some Bushman ancestry is generally accepted, as well as some other ancestry, but what ancestry is the question. That they were essentially nomadic pastoralists is clear, for it was their cattle that created their trade with the Cape settlers, to provision the ships at the "Tavern of the Seas". The routine explanation is they

represent the mixture of the Bantu iron-making farmers and pastoralists from the north with the Bushwomen, but there are some traces of legends and belief that do not seem to fit either Bantu or Bushmen. They used to worship the pleiades, for instance, and every year at their heliacal rising (the rising just before sunrise), the women used to take their children to the nearest hill-top to celebrate and worship the six sisters as they rose. They had many folk stories, like *Aesop's Fables*, of animals reflecting humans, and other stories of their gods and their very human behaviour, including the building of stone towers. Where did this come from? There seems no easy answer.

The Bantu

The third major stratum was that of the Bantu. This was a Negro group originating somewhere in the south-central Congo or western Nigeria, two to three thousand years ago, and representing the vital forward step in history—from food gathering to food producing. This new group started probably on the margins of the equatorial forest and then moved south and east. They may have been in quite small groups, but they were well fed and well organised and, having acquired a knowledge of iron, occupied land south of the Zambezi some time after the start of the Christian era. It is generally agreed it must have been these people who were primarily concerned with the building of the Great Zimbabwe.

THE SKELETAL REMAINS

So much for anthropology and archaeology. The next evidence is the skeletal remains found in the ancient gold or copper mines themselves: a total of fifteen (apart from an infant four years old), almost all of which must have been victims of the usual mining disasters, which are inseparable from mining anywhere or anytime.

Of these fifteen, four were judged to be "Bush-Boskopoid" or Khoisan stock; four pure Negroid—that is, iron-using immigrants from the north; and seven Bantu, a mixture of the other two: a proportion of roughly 25 percent to 25 percent to 50 percent—or very similar to what exists in Zimbabwe today, except that there seems at least in actual miners themselves no trace of any eastern or coastal influence. What is more interesting is that eight were female, seven male: the old story of mining everywhere—the males working at the rock face, the females fetching and carrying, underground as much as the men, and probably doing all the surface work as well. The ages ran from eighteen to forty or fifty years, with an average of twenty-eight, the height in the seven cases measurable ranging from 4'9" to 5'6", with an average of 5'1". This is short in stature for the modern Bantu male and represents no doubt both the predominance of women and deliberate selection for mining. An earlier authority, Professor Matthew Drennan, thought there were two distinct groups, based on the skeletal remains: those connected with mining—often women or children—and those not connected with mining. One other reliable report, from a find in the late 1890s, may be significant: of "a small brown man with straight black hair done in a short type of pigtail, naked except for a loincloth, in a crouching position in the bottom of an ancient stope"* on the Champion Mine, at Gwanda. The body may have been preserved by arsenic leached by water from the rocks, or by methane gas from rotting vegetation or old mine timbering. No one knows, but preserved it was. One interesting thing was that the man's brown skin and his pigtail suggested Eastern origins, perhaps Chinese; but this is not convincing, for

there is evidence the Bushmen were also known to wear pigtails on occasion.

THE WRITTEN RECORD

Pre-Muslim writers

In A.D. 100 or thereabouts, a Greek commercial traveller or Imperial Roman agent (it is not certain which) writing a report† about the Indian Ocean trade stated that all the East African ports imported iron tools from Arabia and exported ivory "in great abundance". He makes no mention of gold but states that this Arab trade (from southwest Arabia) had been going on for a long time, among ship captains and agents "who are familiar with the natives and intermarry with them and who know the whole coast and understand the language".

This shows the iron users had not penetrated to the coast by that date but that good trading relations and a flourishing ivory trade had been established for many years. The archaeological record confirms this. The early signs of iron all more or less date from the same time, the third or fourth century A.D.; are in places where penetration could have occurred from the eastern seaboard; and reflect activities of traders and explorers expanding their iron trade and so giving the emergent new Bantu food producers the tools and weapons to conquer and move south. As these people moved south, intermarriage must have taken place between the pure Negro from the north and the Bushmen and Hottentots—the Khoisan—to help form the population of Southern Africa for the next two millennia.

After this isolated record of the Periplus, a cold silence descends on the East African coast for eight centuries, broken only by casual notices. The first is from

---

* From R. Summers (1969), quoting correspondence with T.R.J. Hawkins, p. 137.

† *The Periplus of the Erythraean Sea*: see Schoff (1912).

Ptolemy, the geographer from Alexandria, with the whole weight of the classical world behind him; the second is from Cosmas Indicopleustes—the Indian sea-traveller—a Christian so twisted by theology that he was certain the world must be flat.

The knowledge of both was hearsay. Ptolemy's information carried him south of Rhapta, to Cape Prason (probably Delgado), and he had heard of "man-eating barbarians" beyond, but there was no mention of Sofala. Cosmas was more limited, mentioning only the land of Zingion, which started at the Cape of Spices (the present Guardafui); so he added almost nothing.

But the silence of this written record is accidental and misleading. For the whole period from A.D. 100 to A.D. 900 Indian, Arab, and Persian traders were extremely active, particularly about the Bab al Mandab, that bottleneck of trade between East and West. All three regimes fought for it, and when Islam broke upon the world, it was Persia who was in the seat of power in southwest Arabia, overlooking Aden and the southern gateway to the Red Sea and the West.

Muslim writers

Only the explosion of Islam cleared the air and in time produced a stable regime and a written culture. During its early years there were legends of Arab emigrants pulling up their roots for conscience' sake and settling on the East African coast. After A.D. 900 the great Arab geographic writers begin to appear and the African coast becomes visible once more.

Masudi, one of the earliest of these geographers, actually sailed (for the last time in A.D. 917) to the island Kanbalu, probably Pemba, perhaps Madagascar. He wrote a book with the romantic and appealing title *Meadows of Gold and Mines of Gems*. To him the whole coast was inhabited by the Zanj, or Zenj (possibly derived from a Persian word for black): "the sea of the Zanj reaches down to the country of Sofala [one of the earliest mentions of the famous port near the modern Beira] and of the Wak-Wak which produces gold in abundance and other marvels: its climate is warm and the soil fertile. It is there that the Zanj built their capital: then they elected a king whom they called Waklimi [who] has under him all the other Zanj kings and commands 300,000 men. Although constantly . . . hunting . . . and gathering ivory, the Zanj make no use of ivory for their own domestic purposes. They wear iron instead of gold and silver. . . ." He goes on to say that they have no code of religion but believe in a supreme god: their kings as their rulers have to follow custom, and if they "depart from the rule of justice" their subjects kill them and exclude their posterity from succession. He adds, "The Zanj speak elegantly and have orators in their own language . . . who often deliver sermons to a crowd of onlookers telling them to serve God and submit to his orders." This account, by far the fullest known, from someone who had actually visited the coast, probably reflects mainly the coastal culture, mixed with stories from inland. The most interesting statements are those telling of a customary monarchy, a built capital city, and iron more prized than any other metal. This confirms archaeology and folklore: an Iron Age people with an organised state, a capital city, and a strongly established trade well known in all the bazaars along the East African coast.

Another writer, generally referred to as Buzurg, tells of an accidental voyage to Sofala in A.D. 923 as a result of a storm. The travellers were terrified because they thought the inhabitants were canibals (as Ptolemy had said, but the reverse was found to be true. They went ashore and traded for several months and then, getting the king and his courtiers aboard, hijacked them as well as the 200 slaves already on board, and then sailed back to sell them all in Oman. Later the king was converted to Islam, found his way back to Sofala, and converted his people, only to find some years later the original Arab traders on his doorstep, again by mischance. To their immense surprise he treated them well, thanked them for giving him the opportunity of becoming a Moslem, and sent them back. This story reflects a growing sophistication and Islamic influence on the coast and, while there is no evidence of penetration inland over the mountain barrier, is proof of a profitable slave trade, if nothing else, and of ships capable of handling it.

The next evidence is from an academic Arab geographer, Idrisi, resident at Palermo in Sicily, who, somewhere between A.D. 1100 and 1150 compiled a world geography from earlier sources (and sometimes misunderstood them). All he says about Sofala and its coast was that there were two towns that looked like villages, and that the inhabitants were nomadic as the Arabs and were wretched and poor. Iron mines in the mountains were their only resource, and their only living the sale of iron, for which overseas traders found a ready market in India. Three things were significant here: the importance of iron; the lack of permanent towns, with semi-nomadic population; and the complete absence of any reference to gold. Idrisi's two last statements directly contradict Masudi's statement two centuries earlier. In view of Masudi's known reliability, this indicates clearly the unreliability of Idrisi, working probably from doubtful or out-of-date sources and not even drawing from previous well-known authors. The remaining Arab sources are silent, mostly chronicles of some of the northern coastal towns, while a famous writer such as Ibn Batuta only got as far as Kilwa and mentions "the very black complexion of the Zanj" and the fact that their faces were full of scars and they were "Kafir"—Kafirs

meaning unbelievers, non-Muslims. The prejudice of a believer towards an unbeliever seems to have coloured the stories the Italian traveler Marco Polo heard in the thirteenth century of some of the islanders on Zanzibar: "They are black and go naked, covering only their private parts. . . . They have large mouths, their noses turn up towards their forehead, their ears are long, their eyes so large and frightful that they have the aspect of demons. . . . There are in this island the most ill-favoured women in the world: with large mouths and thick noses, and ill-favoured breasts, four times as large as those of other women. They feed on flesh, milk, rice and dates".* The last remark proves he was speaking only of the coast, but the general tone probably reflects the Arab attitudes to all the Bantu, coastal and inland, and helps to explain their attitude towards the slave trade. On this coast, there was never any missionary effort by Islam: the blacks always remained "Kafir".

Portuguese writers

With the coming of the Portuguese, the records start, but they deal mainly with their military and commercial contacts on the coast. The barriers of disease, distance, and black suspicion kept all but the very exceptional out of the interior, so that no Portuguese is ever known to have seen Great Zimbabwe and only a few to have been able to describe the interior or what went on there. Vasco da Gama, on the historic first discovery of the Cape route to India in 1497, missed Sofala altogether; another Portuguese, Duarte Barbosa, writing about twenty years later, talks of Sofala and its trade "with the heathen of the Kingdom of Benametapa, who came thither laden with gold which they gave in exchange for the said cloths [Indian, from Cambay] without weighing it. . . . These

*Marco Polo (1908). *The Travels* . . . (Everyman's Library), chapter 37, pp. 395–96.

Moors [the traders at Sofala] are black and some of them tawny, some of them speak Arabic but the more part use the language of the country. . . . their food is millet, rice, flesh and fish". This again confirms inter-marriage, mentioned 1,400 years previously in the Periplus, as well as a flourishing gold trade. "Beyond this country [Sofala] towards the interior lies the great Kingdom of Benametapo [Monomotapa] pertaining to the Heathen whom the Moors [of the coast] name Cafres [Kafir]; they are black men and go naked save that they cover their private parts. . . . some are clad in skins of wild beasts and some, the most noble, wear capes of these skins with tails. . . . They leap as they go and sway their bodies so as to make these tails fly from one side to other. They also carry assagais in their hands and others carry bows and arrows. . . . They are warlike men, and some too are great traders. . . ." Later Portuguese writers—Dos Santos, Boccaro, Barreto—concentrated on the internal political system as it affected their own military and commercial operations but tell us little about the people themselves.*

THE LIVING PEOPLES FIRST MET BY MEN FROM THE SOUTH

The next useful source of information about the people is the first of the whites to come from the south—Mauch himself, the discoverer of the Great Zimbabwe. He had heard stories of gold to the north from the pioneer missionary Herr A. Merensky, coupled with stories of great ruins built by white men, and in 1870 he started on his classic journey into the interior.

But he seems to have been either unlucky or difficult to deal with: he was badly served by his carriers, recruited in the Spelonken, just south of the Limpopo;

* A publication (1980) by Dr. D. N. Beach, *The Shona and Zimbabwe, 900–1850*, has put a totally new historical light on this medieval period.

his trade goods were frequently stolen and he ended by being a virtual prisoner of the local chief, near Zimbabwe. Friendship with the old hunter, Adam Render, who had first seen the Great Zimbabwe ruins and was living nearby, alone saved Mauch. Eventually he obtained some fresh trade goods and managed to go north to the Zambezi and so to Beira and home. The picture he drew of the Karanga tribe then in control of Zimbabwe was hard and hostile: "for everybody who intends to travel in this country there is nothing else to expect than the worst he can imagine . . . where lies robbery, murder, poisoning etc. etc., are of daily occurrence as is the case here, it requires a great store of patience not to procure one's rights with a revolver continually in one's hand". Significantly, he adds, "I am blessed with a naturally stern look in my eyes . . . it is chiefly with this look I have frightened the people in this kraal so that they never dared to steal the smallest thing. . . . The one and only redeeming feature among them is the purity of the young girls . . ."

In general, Mauch's picture confirms the past records: an agricultural and pastoral people, firmly based on iron-making skills for tools and weapons, with a wide variety of food plants. A vague remnant of a monotheistic religion with one Mwali who occasionally visits the earth existed, side by side with widespread superstition and its natural companion, fraud. Mauch describes a religious feast at Zimbabwe lasting three days and including the killing of two black oxen and a heifer. The political position by this time (1870) had become quite fragmentary: there was no overlord and there was continual petty warfare. The great empire of the past based on flourishing trade in gold and other commodities had long disappeared, lost even in local memory.

No missionaries came to these parts before the pioneer settlers in 1890, but some other hunters came, Harry and Willie Posselt and the famous Frederick Selous. They confirmed Mauch's factual observation but hardly his moral condemnation. Selous saw recent goldworks (he estimated they were not more than sixty years old) in the western parts in 1884, and he mentions the artist and explorer Thomas Baines had seen some in the eastern parts in 1870, a year or two earlier than Mauch. Selous was convinced stone building had been continuous since medieval times or earlier, right up to 1820 or so, when the time of troubles started with Ngoni invasions from the south. Selous saw historical continuity in people and culture for over 1,000 years, and the chances are he was correct. He had seen at first hand "the hard grain of wood" of the people and their products more than any other man of his time, and it was Selous who led the pioneer column of Europeans up to place the British flag in future Salisbury, now Harare, near the Harare Hill, in 1890.

Only a year or two after the raising of that flag, the first archaeologist at the site, Theodore Bent, was examining the ruins and meeting at close quarters the black chief—Umgabe, or Mugabe—and his counsellors and tribesmen, resident on the hill opposite the Hill-Fortress, who considered themselves owners and rulers of the ruin. Their features and bearing are remarkable for a wide range of types and clearly show a long and varied ancestry. They had one or two things to say about the ruins, but in general they could give little or no history and certainly nothing about the original builders. But they showed a great pride in the ruins and a fierce determination to protect relics such as the soapstone birds. Posselt was hustled when taking one of the birds only a few years before Bent, and they had shown equal hostility to Mauch inspecting the ruins. To them, at the advent of the white man, the ruins still held something sacred, something to be held dear and defended as long as possible. Even Roger Summers,

writing as late as 1960, said, "all our labourers were Mugabe's people, who regard the ruins as their particular preserve. . . . future excavators would do well to . . . employ only Mugabe's people as they undoubtedly have more "feeling" for the place than anybody else. All of us had occasion at some time or other to make use of our labourers' interpretation of our finds". In Africa, tradition, in spite of all absence of the written record, dies very hard indeed—harder, perhaps, because of that absence.

When Richard Hall, the second excavator, started work at Great Zimbabwe, he was told Mugabe's tribe—the Makalanga, or Makaranga—had originally come from the lower Sabi River area only sixty to seventy years ago; but their folklore included their predecessors, the BaRotzi and Amangwa. One of them said the name Karanga meant "children of the sun", because they come from the East; and Hall consistently called them by that name. They said none of them ever occupied the ruins themselves except in times of extreme danger and then only while danger threatened; otherwise they lived in villages close by. They had no firm explanations about the ruins. Some said white men had built them, while others claimed their own ancestors were responsible. Still others said the sacred relics, which had disappeared, had been taken away by great birds out of the sky.

STILL-REMEMBERED FOLKLORE*

The last source about the people who built the ruins comes from recorded folklore of the survivors of the tribes themselves. Unfortunately, this is many times removed from the scene of the action, for it is the BaVenda tribe in South Africa, on

*The material for this section comes from Van Warmelo (1940) and Stayt (1931a & 1931b).

PLATE 20. "Umgabe and his Indunas." The
resident owners of the Great Zimbabwe in
1890; from Bent (1902, p. 66).

the southern borders of the Limpopo, and
that semi-independent tube within the
BaVenda, the BaLemba, who have Kalanga
connections and who appear most likely to
be connected with the Zimbabwe culture.
Both had preserved their folklore sufficiently well to get it set down by ethnolo-
gists in the first half of the present century.

The story they tell is of an ancient
homeland to the north from which they had
to emigrate, and of religious and political
events connected with the emigration to
their present home, the country south of
the Limpopo and stretching west from the
Maputo border for 100 miles or more. It
has still today a separate identity, Venda-
land.

Their folklore describes their homeland
as "a country of great rivers and lakes, of
dense forests and jungles, overflowing with
water and with many forests and fruits, of

bananas, of tubers and peanuts in great
variety". That was the origin of the Vha
Senzi, today called Vha Venda. They were
ruled by a king called Mwali (some relics
of the legend of a king-god), who could work
miracles with the big drum of the gods,
called *ngoma-lungundu*. The King lived in
a village of tremendous size on a mountain. "Its walls were built with huge stones;
it was impregnable. the houses were built
of shining slabs. . . . No man was permitted to see the King, they merely heard what
he spoke to the High Priest in a tremendous voice that reverberated in a terrify-
ing manner. . . . whosoever should gaze at
[the King] was immediately slain. . . . they
feared Mwali himself as if he were an
ancestor spirit."

Later the king-god Mwali died. Fighting broke out about succession, and a great
migration south started, with "cattle, sheep,

PLATE 21. Some photos of Venda men, 1935; from Van Warmelo (1940) *(By permission of the Government Printer)*

goats, dogs and others so that a tremendous herd was formed, to drive which was a great labour".

Eventually, the people cross the Limpopo and get to their present homeland. The magic drum goes with them and finally, in the valley of the Nzhelele River, they build Dzata: their new capital city, with stone walls still standing today. Another account tells how these stone towns were built: wherever the people heard the drum, "they were beside themselves with terror and by means of it the people were subjected. They came and built the walls and sleeping huts of the royal town: a great wall was built all around the town and other walls to enclose the roads and to separate the different quarters. There were two courtyards on the inside, one being only reached by stooping underneath huge slabs, its doorway being opposite a wall that surrounded the small private quarters of the queens and the council chamber. . . . In this courtyard they used to "blow tshikona [a kind of ritual dance]". The great wall and the others had loopholes through which one might look out and in times of danger, shoot arrows through them.

All these legends and stories of the Vha Venda substantiate the other evidence that they have definite connections with the Zimbabwe culture. The account in particular of how walls were built enclosing roads (that is, passageways) and spaces on which sleeping huts were built is an accurate account of both past and present planning of these towns. The legend of the Vha Lemba also corroborates this tribe's known characteristics: their refusal to become assimilated; their rigid adherence to their own law; their habit of trading and being always on the move, without fixed habitation; their striking Semitic traits—circumcision, refusal to eat the meat of animals that have not been ritually killed by throat cutting and draining of all their blood; even the ending of the prayers with "Amen". All this suggests they had an ancient Muslim or Jewish ancestry.

There were stories of another group, miners of iron, coming from the east and south, perhaps even far descendants of

PLATE 22. Photos of two Lemba men, about 1935; from Van
Warmelo (1940) *(By permission of the Government Printer)*

those earliest miners in Swaziland, who
came up and mined at Phalaborwa, hoping
for iron but finding the copper ore mixed
with iron and calling it M'sina, the "spoiler",
the thing that spoilt their iron. So, gradually, by a series of accidents finding and
mining copper, they came further and further north, almost to the Limpopo. They
were different, this group, nothing to do
with the Lemba or Venda. They did not
practice circumcision, and, most extraordinary for this time and place, they ate their
food with a wooden spoon—some brushoff
from India or Indonesia or Portugal: no one
knows.

In time this group became absorbed into
the Venda nation, so that their separate
identity was lost; but their hereditary skill
remained and was passed on. So strong was
this that these M'sina miners were still
mining copper when the white prospectors came north and found them. The
whites took over the mines with modern
techniques and called their new town
Messina. So close in time was ancient
mining to the modern that in 1920 the last
copper miner of M'sina, one Makushu Dau,

was still alive and able to be photographed.

These legends in sum total show the
remains of two races: one used to rule, with
traditions of a powerful god-king ruling over
other kings, of building towns in stone, of
skill in iron making, and of flocks and herds
and agriculture; and another race keeping
themselves ruthlessly apart, not intermar-
rying, also absorbed in iron making, but
living as itinerant traders, travelling widely
and constantly throughout this southern
part of Africa.

Whatever the truth of their connection
to the Great Zimbabwe, however strong
or weak it may be, it is certain the Venda
have still something different from their
neighbours—some sense of group identity
still articulate and still proud.

This then is the story as far as the known
facts can carry it, and the picture begins to
have an outline. It is about a land, warm
and hospitable and productive, with good
soil and a climate without excessive winter
cold or summer heat; full of elephant and
wild game and predators, but clear of the
worst diseases of man and beast once the

Vice and holed piece for wire drawing.

Makushu Dau, the last surviving copper miner of Musina.

Copper ingots from Messina, by courtesy of Dr. L. C. Thompson.

Copper ingots kept as sacred relics by Tshivhula's tribe.

Old pair of tongs.

PLATE 23. The last living survivor of African miners, Makushu Dau, 1920, with some of his tools and products; from Van Warmelo (1940) *(By permission of the Government Printer)*

coastal badlands and mountain barriers had been crossed and the highlands reached. Into this land had come most ancient man, many millenia back, and when the present story opens, some few centuries after the start of the Christian era, there is already a mixture of people—some of mixed stock with origins not yet clear; others, coming from the north; some perhaps from the sea, with skills in cattle breeding, iron making, and growing new types of food. For some reason, not yet clear, they also began building fortress hide-outs hidden among great boulders on hill-tops. The why and wherefore of all this burst of activity is the great question, and the answer may lie elsewhere than Africa in a wide sweep of history, set round the Indian Ocean. We must look at all the theories put out to date about the origins and then do a diagnosis of the buildings themselves before embarking on the quest of this Holy Grail, the answer to the riddle of the Great, the Ancient, Zimbabwe.

CHAPTER 5

Old Theories

The birth of a fact is the death of a theory and so science grows . . .
—J. J. Thomson

THE OLDEST THEORY: THE ARABS

THE oldest theories known about the origin of Zimbabwe are Arab tales first told to the early Portuguese explorers. These tales said that Sofala was the ancient Ophir, the legendary source of Solomon's gold, as recounted in the Bible in the first Book of Kings. Hiram (King of Tyre), the Hebrew writing said, "sent ships under the command of his own officers and manned by crews of experienced seamen; and these, in company with Solomon's servants, went to Ophir and brought back 450 talents of gold, which they delivered to King Solomon. . . ." And again, a few verses later, ". . . the King had a fleet of merchantmen at sea with Hiram's fleet. Once every three years this fleet of merchantmen came home, bringing gold and silver; ivory, apes and monkeys [or 'peacocks', as the earlier translations said]".* This legend of gold from Ophir and of this voyage recurring every third year has hung over the story of Zimbabwe from the beginning, but there is still no certainty where Ophir was. The legend of Solomon, originally pre-Islamic, became part of the Islamic canon by inclusion in the Koran, and so all unknowns, all wonders met with by the Arab travellers

tended to be once ascribed to Solomon, his magic, his miracle working, and otherworld supermen, the djinns. Particularly buildings: Solomon's temple at Jerusalem had become legendary through the Jewish scriptures, enhanced by the love story of Solomon and the Queen of Sheba.

So it was an Arab who told a Portuguese in 1502 that "Sofala" was Ophir and that "here there was a wonderfully rich mine to which, as they find in their books, King Solomon used to send every 3 years to draw an infinite quantity of gold".† The legend apparently grew with time, for a century later, in 1609, another Portuguese, Dos Santos, wrote: " . . . the people of these lands, and especially some old Moors who have preserved a tradition of their ancestors say that these houses [ruins of stone referred to earlier] were in older times the trading depots of the Queen of Sheba, and that from these depots they used to bring her much gold, following the rivers of Cuama [the Zambezi] down to the Ethiopian coast up to the Red Sea. . . . there they used to off-load all this gold which was brought by land to the court of the Queen of Sheba.‡

*I Kings 10:22.

†F. F. Marconnes (1935). *Native Affairs Department Annual* (Rhodesia), p. 67, quoted in B. G. Paver (1950), p. 26.
‡H. P. Junod (1938). *Bantu Heritage*, pp. 14–15 (quoted in B. G. Paver [1950], p. 27).

73

The origin of this story is almost as intriguing a question as the story itself, for it is an extremely specific statement, as it confirms the first biblical account of how gold came to Solomon—namely, by a trading middleman, Queen of Sheba herself; the gold coming from Ophir, then by land to Queen Sheba's court in South Yemen, then by land caravan through western Arabia to Jerusalem. "She arrived in Jerusalem with a very large retinue, camels laden with spices, gold in great quantity and precious stones". Solomon's alliance with Hiram* to build ships to get the gold directly himself was obviously a trader's bid to cut out the queen and her trading profit. What has not come down to us today was where the gold was mined, for it was apparently being mined in large amounts some distance away and it seems highly improbable that neither Solomon nor Sheba knew where this was. Four hundred years later, when much original knowledge could have been lost, the book of Job (28:1–11) still reflected very precise knowledge of mining methods:

*There are mines for silver
and places where men refine gold;
where iron is won from the earth
and copper smelted from the ore;
the end of the seam lies in the darkness,
and it is followed to its farthest limit.*

*Strangers cut the galleries,
they are forgotten as they drive forward far
    from men.†
While corn is springing from the earth above,
what lies beneath is raked over like a fire,
and out of its rocks comes lapis lazuli,
dusted with flecks of gold.
No bird of prey knows the way there,
and the falcon's keen eye cannot descry it;
proud beasts do not set foot on it,
and no serpent comes that way.
Man sets his hand to the granite rock
and lays bare the roots of the mountains;*

*he cuts galleries in the rocks,
and gems of every kind meet his eye;
he dams up the sources of the streams
and brings the hidden riches of the earth to
    light."‡*

Such precision suggests close contact with traders who had actually seen the mines and therefore must have known exactly where they were. Certainly, it is very far removed from the ignorance of its contemporary source, Herodotus, the "Father of History", with his wildly distorted stories of gold-digging ants "somewhat less than dogs but bigger than foxes".

What is interesting is how this knowledge got lost as it filtered down through the centuries of traders' and sailors' tales. Where did the story of Ophir being Sofala start, and why did the Arabs believe it and tell it to the Portuguese? The most reasonable explanation is that somewhere there was a misunderstanding, perhaps of place names, and that the Arabs merely equated Solomon's mines with those they got the bulk of their own gold from, and then fitted these mines into their own legends two thousand years or so later.

For Solomon, the legends said, had used his djinns, his demons, to build three palaces for the queen in her home country in the Yemen. What could be more natural than that he use his great power over distance and nature to build a temple and fortress to protect her vital interests at the other end of the world in Southern Africa? The ruins of Marib, Sheba's capital with its great dam, which only broke finally just before Mahomet's time, still existed as evidence of the greatness of the queen's kingdom. The identification of the Great Zimbabwe as part of the same tradition was inevitable. When the story is dismissed as historically impossible it is well to remember that it was those closest to these traditions, the Arabs themselves, who first suggested the connection of the Great

---

*2 Chron. 9:1.
†The Hebrew is obscure here. The Revised Bible version reads, "He breaketh open a shaft away from where men sojourn".

‡The New English Bible version (1970).

Zimbabwe with the Queen of Sheba and Solomon.

THE PORTUGUESE

Those next best placed, the Portuguese, apparently never reached Zimbabwe—indicating almost certainly that not only were its great days past, but that it may already have been a ruin. Only rumours came down to the coast from Arab and Indian traders or from someone like the prisoner taken by the Sofalans at the time of Gama's second voyage, who said he had come from the interior, "a land shut in by walls" (presumably meaning the mountain escarpment) and "producing silver and precious stones". There was obviously for very good trading reasons a conspiracy of silence, and the Portuguese learnt nothing and in the end gained very little more. The Arabs and Indians deliberately, however much or little they really knew, pulled down the curtain, and the ignorance was complete.

CARL MAUCH

But stories die hard, and the Arab stories of King Solomon's mines were picked up by the new Dutch and French settlers at the southern tip of the continent. When the time came for expansion, at the start of the nineteenth century, hunters, traders, missionaries, and serious explorers remembered these stories of wealth and cities in the interior. It was not till 1867, however, that Adam Render found the Great Zimbabwe and the German geologist-explorer Carl Mauch for the first time sketched the ruins and described them for publication in Europe. Given all this background, it is hardly surprising Mauch was certain he had found the capital of Solomon's gold-mining country. Moreover, he hunted about (avoiding a lot of native hos-

tility) till he found a man who told him in detail about the religious ceremonies held at the ruins every three or four years; he was the son of the High Priest who had last conducted the ceremonies, thirty or forty years earlier. This convinced Mauch he had the answer.

Mauch writes: "The similarity of these sacrifices to those ordained in the Israelitic cult is unmistakable. . . . Relying on this, I believe I do not err when I suppose that the ruin on the mountain is an imitation of the Solomonic temple on Mount Moria, the ruin on the plain a copy of that palace in which the Queen of Sheba dwelled during her visit to Solomon. It may well be supposed that the Queen of Sheba . . . came to the decision to have similar buildings erected with the assistance of Phoenician builders. . . . the giant twin tree that grows within the Rondeau [the Great Enclosure] may well be the kind which is known as Almugin or Algumin which was used in the Temple and has survived the ruins . . . in the beams above the entrances, I was able to cut off some pieces to bring them home".* If Solomon had used Phoenician sailors for his ships and Phoenician masons for his temple, why not the Queen of Sheba Phoenician masons for her depot? It was not only logical, it was probable. After all, Herodotus had said the Phoenicians may have circumnavigated Africa only 300 years after King Solomon's time. It was certainly good enough for the British novelist Rider Haggard sitting in England writing his best sellers, *King Solomon's Mines* and *She*, which set the seal of this romance for a generation or more, to the fury of serious historians and archaeologists.

In contrast with the Arabs the blacks themselves told a totally different story. The Portuguese Barros wrote in 1552, "there is no record but they [the people of the land] say they are the work of the devil,

*C. Mauch (1971). *Karl Mauch, African Explorer.* Ed. and trans. F. O. Bernard. Pp. 237–38.

for in comparison with their power and knowledge it does not seem possible to them that they should be the work of men".* Already in 1552 for the people actually on the spot the origins had gotten lost in mystery: the living tradition was long dead, and only superstition was left.

THEODORE BENT

The next theory came from the first man to write a book about the ruins, J. T. Bent. He was an early pioneer in archaeology, having travelled and written about the eastern Mediterranean and Middle East, particularly the island of Bahrein, which he identified as the place of origin of the Phoenicians. After his visit to Zimbabwe he went back to the Middle East and wrote about Abyssinia and the Hadramaut. To Bent a religious interpretation was the key and the religion he saw was the ancient phallic worship of pre-Islamic Arabia and Phoenicia. The Conical Tower was paralleled with a tower, representing an enormous phallus, on a coin of Byblos in Phoenicia, where a sacred cone is shown set up within a temple enclosure. He even thought the nuraghi of Sardinia and towers in Mesopotamia might be part of the same phallic worship. The Hill-Fortress to his eyes also included temples; and his surveyor, Swan, measuring angles inside the Great Enclosure, was convinced it was an astronomical observatory "fixing the limits of a tropical year and thus providing the elements of a calendar"—in spite of the fact there is not one straight line or right angle or exact circle anywhere. Bent's theories if they did anything probably reinforced Mauch's original dream of Solomon and Sheba.

*G. M. Theal (1898–1903). *Records of South-Eastern Africa*, vol. 6, p. 261 (quoted in B. Davidson [1964], p. 153).

RICHARD HALL

The next investigator was Richard Hall, a lawyer and journalist from England, who carried out the first detailed survey of the Great Enclosure and compiled and published plans of all the Valley Ruins and many other ruin sites throughout Zimbabwe. Hall's account is still the fullest description of the ruins and the relics he found, but his conclusions are not accepted today. He chose the Sabaean–Arabian culture, the home of the Queen of Sheba, as the probable source of the Zimbabwe culture, at least as a "good working hypothesis". The Sabe or Save River might be named from Sabaean merchant visitors; the Great Enclosure (called the Elliptical Temple) was "almost identical to the temple of Haram of Bilkis, Queen of Sheba near Marib, capital of the old Sabaean Kingdom of Southern Arabia". (Bent had mentioned this in his third edition). The Sabaeans were rich in gold through trade, not mining: and it was known from the Periplus account that Southern Arabia controlled the East African coast. It was also suggested the ivory and slaves of Solomon's time all came from East Africa, but the real difficulty of this theory is that the Periplus never mentions gold in East Africa.

DAVID RANDALL-MacIVER

The reaction to this rather Freudian dream of Sheba, gold, and Solomon was bound to come and it came with a bang: Randall-MacIver. This English archaeologist, trained under Flinders Petrie in the field, excavated parts of the Great Enclosure and other ruins elsewhere—Inyanaga, Dhlo-Dhlo, Naletale, and Khami. His conclusion was short and sharp—the ruins were medieval (that is A.D. 1000–1500) and showed nothing but African influence and authorship. Hall was furious, wrote another book questioning MacIver's methods and findings, and so started a controversy—African or foreign?—which three-quarters of a century later continues.

GERTRUDE CATON THOMPSON

In the next two decades important work in examining, surveying, and reconstruction of the ruins was undertaken, but no new theories were put forward till in 1929 Caton Thompson, an archaeologist also trained by Flinders Petrie, arrived to lay what was to be the foundation for all future work in the ruins, not only at Great Zimbabwe but throughout the country. After six months' work her conclusion was a modified MacIver's: ". . . all the existing evidence, gathered from every quarter, still can produce not one single item that is not in accordance with the claim of Bantu origin and Medieval date". She was as much—if not more—concerned with date as origin and saw that a foundation date (of Zimbabwe) of the eighth or ninth century fitted in with the historical record and with the evidence of Horace Beck, the bead expert, that the affinities of the Zimbabwe beads lay with South Indian and Malay beads of the same period. She saw too that the Indian trade connection was very strong—to the extent she thought it was the primary stimulus that led to the development of the indigenous Zimbabwe culture. Her assistant, Kathleen Kenyon, had established that by the tenth century A.D. there was well-established quadrangular traffic between Africa, Arabia, India, and China. She pointed out there is no evidence for pre-Muslim trade: on the contrary, all the evidence points to the start of the trade being due to the explosion of Islam in the seventh century A.D. She found no warrant for assuming Great Zimbabwe to have been the distribution centre of the

gold trade; but the later research on the gold mines and the routes to the coast had not been done when she wrote. She dismissed the idea that the ruins could have been built by Africans under foreign supervision, for such an alien race would have to have been Arab, Persian, or Indian, and nothing any of these three races built was similar to Zimbabwe. Then she makes the astonishing statement "they were all acquainted with the principle of the arch": true enough for the Arabs and Persians, but not for the non-Muslim Indians in the south, who never used the arch even in building bridges. She admits in a footnote her awareness of "buildings near Hampi" built of granite, no doubt the ruins of the great capital of the "forgotten empire" of Vijayanagar, that last Hindu stronghold of the South against the Moslems, but made no further mention of it. To her the Great Zimbabwe was essentially imitative architecture possibly the result of some black African having visited the coast and seized "with quick imitative instinct" some detail, such as a minaret, which Africans had the capacity to execute. The building style at Zimbabwe to her was "essentially the product of an infantile mind, a pre-logical mind, a mind which having discovered the way of making or doing a thing goes on childishly repeating the performance regardless of incongruity". On one point she agreed with both Bent and Hall—that the best work was the earliest and the time sequence one of deterioration in technique, not the reverse, and that the start of the culture is the difficult thing to explain, for the evidence is the advanced Bantu tribes coming south from Central Africa are not and never have been stone-building people: they learnt it for some reason after they had arrived in the country now Zimbabwe. The only reason she could suggest for this new craft was force of circumstance—ready-made granite bricks lying about, due to the natural spalling off the granite slabs from the parent rock by the action of, alternately, very hot sun and sudden cooling rain.

ROGER SUMMERS, KEITH ROBINSON, AND ANTHONY WHITTY

Broadly speaking, all later archaeologists have followed Caton Thompson's lead: the ruins were designed and built by Africans. Summers, with Keith Robinson and architect Anthony Whitty, carried out in 1958 the detailed work on the types and sequence of building already described in Chapter 1, but all served to confirm the now established canon that the work is wholly African in both conception and execution: no foreign influence need be assumed, on the principle of Occam's razor—the essentials of any subject are not to be multiplied unless necessary. The answer to this principle in the case of the Great Zimbabwe is that some multiplication is necessary in order to make any overall sense.

There was one very important exception: Summers' masterly work on the ancient gold mines. This examined in the greatest detail all aspects of the ancient mines—amount, distribution, method, labour, production, sale—and eventually came to a definite conclusion there was Indian influence, from the long established and formerly very productive gold mines of the Kolar district and elsewhere at Mysore. Summers' work also convinced him—against his previous belief—that there was a close connection between the mines and the ruins: the distribution map of both together was the evidence. At last the beginnings of some historic and economic synthesis were beginning to appear.

RECENT WRITERS

Other distinguished archaeologists and prehistorians followed Summers and Robinson, of whom two, Peter Garlake and Tom Huffman, carried Summers' work much further and deeper. Garlake visited personally no fewer than eighty-three of the ruins, including every important site, and from this deduced that there were seven distinct styles based on various combinations of five categories of architectural features, such as shape of entrances, masonry technique, type of decorative stonework, and the like. His book *Great Zimbabwe* is still today without doubt the definitive work on the subject, but it confirms in no uncertain terms his basic philosophy and interpretation of the ruins: the canonical exclusion of any foreign influence whatever.

Tom Huffman, the most recent authority on the ruins and on the pre-history of Zimbabwe generally, sees the Great Zimbabwe as a great political centre that developed only because of the Arab gold trade. He considers that its political power rose from the extra wealth created by that trade and could not have occurred otherwise. The ruins in this hypothesis were one form of conspicuous, ostentatious consumption and a means of keeping continuously employed the surplus labour that all primitive societies had to carry outside seed and harvest times. Such an hypothesis is moving away from a Pan African explanation and beginning to link this African story with the wider and more complex world beyond the African shores.

The dating of the Great Zimbabwe is a special problem, since the accepted version today, derived from normal carbon 14 interpretation of human settlement material, places the range between A.D. 1000 and A.D. 1500. But the range stands unrelated to the trading background of the western Indian Ocean, where so much of the action lay. It is this relationship that uncovers another story.

Over the last three-quarters of a century there have naturally been many others, specialists and non-specialists, putting forward other theories. One that deserves a special mention, because it stands alone, is that of Leo Frobenius, a German scholar, who visited Africa in the 1920s and saw the evidence from Zimbabwe and elsewhere forming a complex culture of its own, which he called "Erythrean", or "Red", based on the old Erythrean Sea—not the Red Sea, but the whole western Indian Ocean. It was Frobenius who guessed a link with the great kingdoms of South India, Vijayanagar and its stone-built capital Hampi—significant, perhaps, since the empire of Vijayanagar included the area in which the gold mines of Mysore had been worked.

Other writers, like James Mullan, were convinced that dissident Arabs, flying from the internal feuds of Islam, built the Great Zimbabwe. Another, Johann Van Oordt, thought that the Dravidian Indians from South India must have been responsible. The Phoenicians and the Sabaean Arabs have also been resurrected with evidence of very doubtful visual similarities, but there has been virtually nothing new.

The broad controversy still remains in simple fighting terms: black or non-black, African or foreign, make up your own minds, one way or the other. But truth, like love, has many different faces and, as Oscar Wilde once said, is never pure and rarely simple. It cannot be found ready-made, waiting to be taken; it comes only like blood from an unwilling stone. The simplistic question of African or foreign is too simple, too easy, too pure to reflect reality. To find out how impure, complicated, and unwilling is the truth about the Great Zimbabwe, that is the task of the next chapter.

CHAPTER 6

New Deductions

What song the sirens sange, or what Achilles assumed when he hid
himself among women, though puzzling questions, are not beyond
all conjecture . . .
—*Sir Thomas Browne*

THREE UNWORKED FIELDS

ALL those theories, probabilities, and assumptions—for their limited factual base really disallows any higher rating—leave several fields unexplained. Pure archaeology has for a long time been extended into wide social, political, and religious interpretations—all against a strict African background—but three other fields have been much less explored. They are the economic, the historical, and the technical, and it is these unworked fields, particularly the last, which can take us forward towards more distant horizons. Too much time has passed ever to complete the whole ancient picture, but perhaps enough evidence can be assembled to make a story coherent and sensible enough to be acceptable.

First: the economic interpretation

The building of these endless walls all over the country argues tremendous labour resources and some specially strong economic reasons to impel people to spend all that time and collective energy on such a queer thing. For it was a very queer thing to do in Africa. Soil and climate made permanent agriculture impossible, and any settlement transitory. Ten years, or less, exhausted the soil and make movement to

another new home mandatory. Survival was mobility.

The Bushmen and the Hottentots had always been on the move—it was literally their way of life. And while the Bushmen had no permanent shelter, contenting themselves at the most with a brushwood fence for their fire, the Hottentots had gotten as far as a tent which they could take to pieces and put on the back of an ox, their prime mover. The ancestors of the Bantu coming slowly south for generations were more settled, being cultivators as well as pastoralists, but they built huts good for five or ten years and then moved on. Why should they suddenly start building stone walls when they found themselves south of the Zambezi? Because they found some loose stone lying around spalled off the granite domes by alternate sun and sudden rain did they decide to build stone walls instead of a thick thorn hedge, knowing they would have to move on in a few years' time? The idea is absurd: no subsistence and pastoral farming practised by isolated groups ever needed stone walls of this height or solidity. There must have been other economic reasons to build, suddenly, stone walls of such strength in the lands south of the Zambezi.

The economic base for any trading, local or far afield, had narrow limits. Ivory, rhino horn, and tortoise shell; salt, iron, gold, and maybe a little copper or even tin; and finally some slaves. That was all. But which needed walls or had a profit to carry such a building effort? One cannot assume that men, women, and children built walls for fun or because they had nothing better to do. Elephant and rhino were caught in traps without benefit of walls; tortoises caught at the coast; salt gathered into cakes at rare salt pans and elsewhere not in ruin areas. Only the metals had any permanent location. Of them, only iron and gold had any strong correlation with the ruins. But iron, thick as the ruins themselves in an area only 50 to 100 miles west and southwest of the Great Zimbabwe, was worked on the surface by small, compact, often secret groups of generations of smiths who had no obvious need for walls and whose workings elsewhere show no sign of massive protection.

Only gold mining, and possibly slaves, remain. Both could have had need of walling, and both could have been sufficiently profitable. Slaves needed containment, and gold—and copper—mining, much of it underground and highly dangerous, could well have needed compulsion and containment for near-slave labour.

Yet none of the three indigenous groups had the slighest use for the metal. The Hottentots at some time had been smelting copper, and the Bantu were skilled iron workers; but to Bushman, Hottentot, and Bantu alike, gold was an entirely useless metal, for it could not be used for any practical purpose—to kill people, hoe ground, or cut wood. Why then go to all this trouble to dig it out of the ground in such tiny amounts and after such tremendous effort and considerable danger? The second conclusion is in this way almost equally inevitable: the initiative to mine gold must have come from outside the country.

Roger Summers's work, in showing the close parallel with Indian gold mining, gives the lead: it must have been some traders' initiative—maybe Arabs, maybe Persians, maybe Indians who had trading connections with the Indian mining bosses—that generated the enterprise. Moreover, the date is significant: the earliest date possible for the gold mines is somewhere between A.D. 600 and A.D. 800, exactly the start of the explosion of Islam. There could not be a better economic explanation. It was trade and the explosion of trade caused by Islam that created need for gold as the medium of exchange, and consequently the gold mines and the burst of stone walling. But why only gold? Surely there must have been more than that to justify all those walls? What about the trade in slaves?

Second: the historical interpretation

Is it possible that with all the activity generated by the explosive Muslim world the Great Zimbabwe played no part in the great movements of peoples and cultures, the birth and spread of major religions, and the rise and fall of empires for a thousand years after A.D. 500? It hardly seems it could have remained sterile and unknown, and if it did play a part, what was it?

An economic activity of the scale of the gold mines, and the necessity for trade on large scale to explain both the mines and ruins, argues a wide historical network of trade in both time and space. The start of the gold mines coincided with the first shockwaves of Islam upon the known world, particularly the Middle East and India, but we do not know the extent of these waves as they affected Zimbabwe, or what other waves—Persian, Indian, Indonesian, or even Chinese—may have washed its shores and left their impact. Nor do we know precisely how far afield these waves may have taken Zimbabweans, where her people may have gone or her traders have travelled.

How exactly did the trade with Zimbabweans serve the purpose of these other trading communities? How did it affect their political and religious movements? Did the great wave of Indian influence in Indonesia and the East have no counterpart in the West and Africa? Did the astonishing colonising of Madagascar by sea-gypsies from Borneo or the Celebes have no side-effects on Africa or even Zimbabwe? What can such movement of peoples have given to these long sagas of the centuries and what did it leave, if anything, in its wake?

Third: the technical interpretation

This is the biggest unworked field. The explanation given of technical aspects of the ruins does not, in spite of the very solid work outlined in Chapter 1, explain technical anomalies that occur everywhere—the things that don't make sense, to any Western mind. These are important, for in a rational enquiry about any phenomena, it is the unusual, the queer, the inexplicable that is the key to new discovery: it was so with penicillin, it was so with radar. So in this case it is the anomalies, more than anything else, that are most likely to give new clues to crack the code of the mystery.

There are four classes of technical anomalies that may help to do this: the location; the overall planning; the detailed planning; and the wall structure.

THE LOCATION: GREAT ZIMBABWE AND ITS REGION

The siting of all the ruins throughout the whole country needs examination, to see exactly what generated each particular site, what geographical control, what mining necessity justified each building effort. The siting of Great Zimbabwe itself has only been explained very casually: a position fairly central on the eastern edge of the mining area, where the soil and climate were still kind and the altitude sufficient to avoid the lowland fevers and yet pro-

vide a convenient jumping-off point for the journey to the coast. Yet that easy statement does not cover the facts accurately.

Great Zimbabwe can be said from the distribution of the ruins to be linked to the coast by two routes, one southeast through the Lundi-Sabi river system to Mambone, and one directly east over the mountains by the Busi River system to Sofala. But most of the evidence, even of the mines, suggests neither of these routes were the main route with the interior: the major river, the Zambezi, took this credit. It is thought the first ancient mining experts came up this river, that Indian and other traders followed, that on this river the Muslim geographers placed towns and Portuguese adventurers penetrated. Why then was Zimbabwe not placed on this much more obvious and better frequented route? Why later in the history did the centre of power desert Zimbabwe, move northwards towards the Zambezi valley, and later still move far inland to the west, to Khami, Dhlo-Dhlo, and Naletale, and the Matopo Hills? It is still very uncertain what prompted this first choice for the Great Zimbabwe and then its later abandonment.

OVERALL PLANNING

The planning, like the siting of the Hill-Fortress, is clear and self-evident and has similarities, if not technical links, to fortresses anywhere else in the world. Not so, however, with the Valley Ruins and the Great Enclosure. Here one feels much closer to grass-roots Africa, the Africa of tribal huts and circular enclosed cattle kraals universal over Southern Africa.

Yet on closer examination the settlement patterns in the valley, including the Great Enclosure, are not the same as the usual African hut-cattle kraal type. That type had only two basic characteristic patterns, reflecting the nature of the functional and social system of the society that built them. Firstly (the commonest): a circle of hut groups surrounding the cattle kraal in the centre, with the tribal meeting place—*khoro* in Venda—nearby, or in the kraal itself. Secondly: a circle of hut groups round the chief's hut and tribal meeting place in the centre, with the cattle kraals to one side or beyond the huts. The whole, including the cattle kraals, sometimes encircled further ground with a protecting wall for fence. This second type is, among others, the Venda type and so may have Zimbabwe connections. James Walton, the chief authority on the African village, gives a sub-type of the first type: where the cattle kraals are family kraals, so that the family huts and kraals themselves form a circle round a central meeting place, the huts and kraals forming the protective enclosure. This type occurs as far south as the Free State in South Africa. The difference between the two basic types reflects the differing importance given to the two basic functional streams in the culture: the pastoralists with their cattle (normally the men), and the cultivators with their hoes (normally the women). In the great majority of cases, the tradition of the pastoralists, with their firm belief that the wealth of cattle was their greatest asset and deserved the greatest protection, won the day and the cattle kraal remained the centre of the layout. The total result of this planning was described recently by an archaeologist as "a town planner's nightmare—but beautifully clear and logical to the social anthropologist." One thing always seemed the same whatever the layout: the refuse heaps, or middens, were well outside the settlement area, so that today they act as markers for the settlement limits.

Within these settlements the living area of each family was not the hut, but the open space (or *lelapa* in Sotho-Tswana) in front of the hut, surrounded by a low wall. Here the fire was kept, the meals were cooked and eaten, and even babies born. The hut was there only for storage, sleeping, and shelter during rains; it was never a daytime living unit. The front space might be duplicated at the back, making the front space more public, more social, the rear more private. If the family had its own small cattle kraal, it would be at the side, in which case the sequence of huts, walled spaces, and kraals might form a connected ring of enclosures giving a large protected central space—Walton's sub-group of the first and commonest type.

An examination of the valley plans shows no agreement with these patterns. There is no arrangement of huts or kraals to form a central protected space. At most, perhaps in some of the Valley Ruins a layout of huts will have the living spaces surrounded by walls, but even in these cases, the spaces are not clearly defined forecourts to the huts. Rather, it seems a collection of possible enclosures with huts somehow fitted in, without any clear relationship. Nor is there, in the Valley Ruins—the Great Enclosure apart—any clearly defined area visible today for cattle kraals that would be easily supervised, nor any surrounding wall that would enclose huts, living spaces, and kraals.

The planning of the Great Enclosure is a special case, for there are really two Great Enclosures: firstly, the internal planning without the Great Wall, which may have had an existence on its own before the Great Wall was built, and secondly, the space enclosed by the Great Wall. Neither makes much sense, for the enclosures are not the shape for either huts or their front yard, and above all, the original walls are too high—up to twelve feet or more—for the traditional yard walls. On the other hand, they are not suitably enclosed spaces for cattle; nor have the known hut positions any relationship to the other spaces that might have been used for cattle. The additional space given by the Great Wall could have held cattle, but if it was built for this purpose why the height—up to thirty feet?

The Great Wall and the space it encloses is sui generis, one-off, of its own kind, without precedent anywhere in Africa.

Two other aspects of the planning, already mentioned in Chapters 2 and 3, need bearing in mind: firstly, that the walls were never designed, or planned, to carry roofs—they were walls, plain and simple, and nothing else; and secondly, that the builders had some hydraulic knowledge and experience, particularly about the storage and drainage of water.

DETAILED PLANNING

The significance of detailed planning lies with the movement of people—with the design of passages and entrances. These points of movement always reveal most clearly the purpose of a building, for entrances and exits are where human activity becomes most concentrated, where control of movement is most easily exercised, where welcomes and warnings can most easily be given, where ceremonials of arrival or departure can be carried out.

In the case of the Great Zimbabwe in the first place, all movement was single-file. This is universal in Africa, a "road" being a footpath eighteen inches or two feet wide. Not only all people but all goods moved within these limits, loads being carried on the head. Africa never knew the wheel, so that the width of a cart or a carriage was never needed, and pack oxen were rarely, if ever, used.

This limited requirement affected all building. There is within the ruins generally an astonishing regularity of opening width, of approximately 2′, or almost the "royal cubit" of 23½″.

In the second place, certain elements of design recurred in passages and doorways. There are definite staircases, standard units of treads, and risers adjusted to some variations in stone size. There are the round-ended bastions—the low stone projections on either side of openings—and the port-cullis grooves in the bastions representing some control of movement in the narrow, two-foot openings and passages; and finally there are the "blind steps", leading apparently to raised platforms against walls that occur in several ruins and at least three of them against the west side of the inner parallel passage wall in the Great Enclosure.

All this adds up to a considerable degree of regularity, standardisation, and pre-planning, but it is not enough to make any planning objective immediately obvious.

However, a closer inspection of wall openings makes certain things clear. *Firstly,* the controlled opening with portcullis grooves and bastions occurs almost entirely in the east and south portions of the Great Enclosure and is seen as some way related to the main raised platform next the famous Conical Tower. For instance, Enclosure 8, round the Tower, has all the openings controlled with portcullis grooves.

Secondly, all bastions are always on the inside of the openings—that is, within the enclosures which the openings serve. Further, this is true of both the separate smaller enclosures—such as Enclosures 1 and 7—and of the Great Wall itself. Both the northwest and west openings have bastions on either side of the openings on their inside face.

Thirdly, for an enclosure as large as the Great Enclosure as a whole, there are a very limited number of entrances and exits: All are one-man wide and there are only three. In fact, at any one time only three people could get out simultaneously: an extraordinary arrangement when the size and the capacity of the space as a whole is considered. Moreover, only one, on the west, would have been large enough for normal-size cattle, and because of this design restriction alone the Great Enclosure could hardly ever have been intended as a cattle kraal, although Chief Umgabe said it had been used as such in the nineteenth century.

Fourthly, the only opening on to the

open countryside is the west opening. Both the other openings, the northwest and north, lead to other walled enclosures and north (generally referred to as the main entrance) to the main group of Valley Ruins. It seems therefore significant that the only opening leading to the open countryside had by far the largest bastions protecting it—on the inside, as all the other bastions.

THIS AUTHOR'S EXPERIENCE

All these characteristics are not immediately apparent on entering the Great Enclosure for the first time. As I first experienced the sensation of being inside, and as I walked slowly through the various internal enclosures, three vague but persistent impressions grumbled at the back of my mind, demanding more precise recognition.

The first and strongest was the sense of being trapped, of not having the situation under my control, of finding myself in a space that, in spite of its size and being open to the sky, it would not be easy to get out of. Why, for instance, was the Great Wall so high? None of the other walls in the valley were this height: in fact, the only other wall of equal height anywhere in the ruins was the great West Wall of the Hill-Fortress, the function of which was obvious—to control most efficiently all entrances to the Fortress. But why such a height down in the valley, with no external fortifications to it whatever? Nor was it only the height of the wall that gave me the feeling of being trapped: the internal surfaces were extremely regular and well built without any obvious toe-hold or hand-hold. Not only was the Great Wall too high to clamber over in an emergency, it was also too smooth to climb up.

The second impression, linked to the first, was that apart from the one narrow entrance on the west through which I had entered, there were no other obvious ways in or out. In fact, there were of course two

others, but they took some finding. This itself is a very queer way to design any building where the easy and simple movement of people is one of the first considerations. Was the designer deliberately making it difficult for a stranger to find his or her way around or the way out?

The third impression came as a result of looking back at the west entrance through which I had come, and after having discovered the other two entrances. In all three cases there was something unusual, almost queer, about them that at first seemed difficult to identify. The west and northwest entrances had their round-ended bastions on the inside and the north entrance had a maze of narrow walled passages all leading to it, almost shielding it. Why had these entrances—and exits—been designed in this manner?

Then suddenly something triggered a long-forgotten memory of boyhood and brought with it a sharp insistence to the very front of my awareness. It was that the Great Wall was the same height—about twenty feet—as the prison wall in my home town past which I had gone twice every day on the way to and from school. Could the wild assumption be possible that the Great Enclosure had been, at its inception, intended as a prison? Was that the reason for the height of the wall, its excellent building, and its exceptionally smooth inner face?

The more this assumption was considered, the more probable it became. For if the assumption was correct, then the narrow, limited, and hard-to-find entrances and exits made sense: the inhabitants would have been greatly discouraged from finding them easily, or getting to them too closely. Then, as suddenly as the triggering of the memory of the old prison wall, the queerness of the design of the entrances became obvious—the devices to protect the opening from attack, the round-ended bastions projecting from the wall in two cases, and the maze of passages that concentrated on the third, the north, entrance were all on the inside, not the outside, where protection from attack would normally have been required. The conclusion was almost inescapable: the entrances had been designed in the expectation they would be subject to attack from the inside and never the outside, since not only were these bastions not outside, there were no signs whatever of any fortification outside at all, particularly at the west entrance, which gave access directly to open countryside. It is noticeable that inward-turning defences at entrances in pre-historic forts elsewhere, such as in the U.K., all have strong external lines of fortificiations as well, the whole planning forming one system. No such system exists at the Great Wall. In short, the entrances had been designed to stop people trying to get out, not in, and there is only one kind of building in the world people will want to fight to get out of, and that building is a prison.

In this way, three vague impressions had crystallised to one conclusion: the Great Enclosure had been designed as a prison, whatever its use had been in later years. But such a radical conclusion demands confirmation in some detail before final acceptance.

These and other abnormalities began now to fall into place and make sense—the height of the Great Wall, its width at the top, its smooth face, its steeper batter on the inside, its exceptional visibility from the Hill-Fortress, and finally, its position in the Valley Ruins.

The height of the Great Wall as originally built varies from 17′ to 33′, with an average of 22′6″, close to the standard height of many prison walls throughout the world; the average height of nine prison walls in 1972 was 18′4″. This is no doubt due to the necessity for the wall having to be greater than a three-man height, each standing on the other's shoulders, or about 15′.

The width at the top is never less than 4′ and averages considerably more. It could

therefore have served throughout as a sentry walk, as the wall was carried through over all openings. Stores of loose stones as ammunition could always have been kept ready on the top and even the monoliths could have been used by the sentry to steady himself when taking aim.

The smooth face would be difficult to climb with bare feet, particularly if someone was throwing stones down from the top, and the *steeper batter* on the inside would increase the difficulty of climbing.

The exceptional visibility of the interior of the Great Enclosure from the southern side of the Hill-Fortress given by the lowering of the Great Wall on its northern side to about 17′ made possible direct supervision of the interior up to the inner wall of the parallel passage and the main (No. 3) platform area. The acoustic properties of the cave already mentioned above meant there could be direct verbal communication between the two centres and suggest there may have been the possibility of two-way communication if the inner wall of the parallel passage could have been used as a reflector behind the speaker. An experiment is needed to determine the optimum position; but it could have been the main platform itself, the curved wall behind the platform, acting as the reflector and amplifier, like a gigantic stone megaphone.

Finally, its position in the Valley Ruins complex seems to have been deliberately chosen to be on one side, where there is flat open country for more than half of its total circumference—from the northwest round to the southeast. On this side the ground has no defensive characteristics whatever; a queer choice of site if the Great Wall was intended as a fortification against attack. But such a siting makes excellent sense for a prison, since any attempt at escape into open country would be immediately visible and from the top of the Great Wall there is an excellent view of all the surrounding countryside. On the other sides the Wall abuts walled enclosures, where escape could be more easily controlled.

The identification of the Great Enclosure as a prison is only the first result of the analysis of abnormalities, but it is confirmed by a very important, but for some extraordinary reason a totally disregarded, source—the followers of Chief Umgabe himself. They told Hall directly that the place was a prison and Hall merely laughed and never considered the opinion seriously for a moment. Later writers have one and all completely ignored their statement. It is the more surprising since Hall stated the Great Enclosure was always called by the blacks of his day *rusingu*, "the wall", reserving the name Zimbabwe only for the Hill-Fortress. This highlights the distinction made between the two groups of ruins by the blacks themselves, and the title "the wall" reflects very well their instinctive estimation of its purpose. The presently accepted name today, the Great Enclosure, is itself both an acknowledgement of fact and a first step towards another explanation.

A PRISON—IN AFRICA?

The acceptance that the Great Enclosure was a prison only multiplies the difficulties of interpretation, of decoding the puzzle, for Africa never had prisons: they were unknown. No prisoners were ever taken in battle: fighting men were killed and all other made slaves. Indeed, when one African chief, the famous Shaka of Zululand, first heard of prisons and the European practice of incarceration he was appalled that such cruelty could be given by man to man. To him death would be infinitely kinder. Africa either killed, banished, enslaved, or merely fined her wayward children. Criminals were thrown off rocks, tied down to be eaten by ants, or just speared or clubbed to death in front of the chief. If death was not deserved they were made to leave the territory, or were enslaved or fined, with cattle generally the price; and if the criminal had no cattle, then he or his children could be sold as slaves within the tribe, but never, never imprisoned.

For African slavery was never the slavery invented by the West for their plantations in the New World during those fateful seventeenth and eighteenth centuries, when they ran the Atlantic with their human cargoes and depopulated West Africa. Nor was it the more domestic but still depersonalised slavery of the East, which at times—as we shall see—created plantation slavery as brutal as anything Rome and the Americas ever had.

The indigenous slavery of Africa was, rather, serfdom, not slavery, for it had rights and could be terminated. It was a form of adjustment of accepted social obligations in a society that had only a subsistence economy and so no surplus wealth, only labour, for the settlement of debts or disputes. The slavery outside Africa was an entirely different thing: the outright sale of the human being to a totally different culture that acknowledged no rights whatever to the person so sold. It was for this reason a prison was required.

So at the Great Zimbabwe some people must have been imprisoned by someone not African, for non-African purposes: enslavement cannot have been indigenous. Someone was dealing in slaves for other purposes and there can only be one answer: it was for sale overseas. The Great Enclosure, and perhaps also the other enclosures in the valley, were transit camps for slaves awaiting transshipment to the coast, perhaps forming part of the caravan that was needed to take ivory—and gold and iron—down to the coast in any case: a useful combination of functions. If this was so, it would have another effect upon the use of the ruins: use of them would have been seasonal. For the movement of the overseas traders was controlled by the monsoon winds: only once every year could they come down, and only once every year go back; and to do this within the same year they could only stay a short time, between the two monsoons—a matter of weeks, not months.

OVERSEAS TRADERS AND TRADITIONS—WHOSE?

If Africa was not doing this to Africans, who was? The virtual absence of all records till the great Arab geographers start writing in the tenth century makes this a difficult question to answer. But two points can give a lead: firstly, it must have been some traders with access to the Indian Ocean, for that was the only possible source of external contact; and secondly, Roger Summers's identification of the parallel between the Zimbabwean gold mines and the South Indian gold mines suggests not only that South India might be the source of the apparently abnormal building technique but also that this building technique and gold mining, both coming from the same part of the world at the same time, might themselves somehow be connected with one another.

THE WALL STRUCTURE

It is the abnormalities of the wall structure that confirm both these leads and suddenly make the abnormal completely normal. For those building techniques, so abnormal, queer, and irrational to any mind encased in Western attitudes, turn out to be entirely normal when placed in a South Indian context. Of the various abnormalities listed at the start of Chapter 3, at least four come from South India. These were stones used like brick; no mortar; no arch; and timber lintels over openings. In addi-

tion, two other characteristics could be said to be typical of South India: the use of round-ended projecting walls or bastions to protect the entrances and a knowledge of drainage and water supply.

Firstly, small, brick-like stones for building were regularly made in India by the very ancient technique of fire-setting—the heating or rock by sun and fire, followed by sudden cooling with water. Producing building stones in this way was the hereditary skill of the upper grade of a very low, even criminal class known as Wadders or Vaddas. This upper grade were the Kallu Vaddas, stone quarriers; the middle class were the Manno Vaddas, builders of earth dams for the village reservoirs of India, called "tanks"; and the lowest grade were the Uppu Vaddas, street sweepers. Malcolm Maclaren, a mining geologist, found the Kallu Vaddas making building stones by fire-setting in the early years of this century, when he was investigating the Gadag auriferous belt about 100 miles east of Goa. Dealing with the numerous doleritic and diabasic dykes that furnish the best building stone of the area, he says "the dyke rock . . . is largely worked by wandering tribes of Vaddas or Wadders who with the aid of a *small fire laid along grooves split the rock with great accuracy into rudely cubical or prismatic shapes* [emphasis added]". Nearly seventy years later, in 1973, an English traveller found the Wadders still in Mysore now on unemployment relief work, but still pursuing their hereditary profession as stone masons by repairing the famous town walls, over six miles long, of historic Bijapur.

Though this evidence is all within this century, the low caste position of the Wadders argues their great antiquity, for the caste system was firmly established long before A.D. 500 and Hindu, Moslem, and British rule did nothing to disturb it. This method of cutting building stones from a parent rock by fire-setting was an exact skill: too much or too little water, at the wrong place or the wrong time, was fatal to success. Yet so well did the Africans learn from the original Indians that in 1960 Karanga men, in eastern Zimbabwe, still possessed the skill.

The second grade of Manno Vaddas, the earth dam builders, may also have been involved with Great Zimbabwe, for their skill could well have built the earth dam or Causeway leading to the northwestern entrance to the Hill-Fortress, and they could have planned the drainage system of the Great Enclosure, telling the wall builders exactly where to place the drains in the base of the Great Wall and the Parallel Passage.

One other aspect of the masonry of Great Zimbabwe may indicate an Indian origin: the stones were cut to size at the quarry, not the site. Even in the case of the Great Wall of the Great Enclosure only small chippings were found at the base, the result of the final fitting only: at a famous temple at Madura in South India, all stone was cut at the quarry and only stone assembly took place on the site.

Secondly, no mortar was ever used in South India: all stone walling was dry-stone walling. Mortar was never even used in Greater India, the India beyond the seas in Indonesia. The whole of Angkor Vat and Borobudur, two of the greatest monuments of Indian influence ever built, are both built completely without mortar; and it is on the record of a Portuguese mason, one João della Ponti, who was sent to build a dam in about 1530 for a king of the Mysore area near Vijayanagar in Southern India, that the king laughed outright when João asked for lime to be gotten ready, for the king said, "When we build a house we do not understand how to use lime".

Thirdly, the absence of the true arch points directly to Hindu India—South India—for of all the cultures bordering the Indian Ocean it is the only one where the true arch was unknown till the Muslims introduced it in the seventeenth century

along with the techniques of arched construction they had learnt from the Persians. The Indus Vallley culture had never used the true arch and Dravidian India continued this tradition with philosophical, almost religious dislike of it on the grounds that "it never sleeps"—that is, it introduces active stresses in a building, which makes the quality of repose, of quiet, impossible: almost a symbolic contrast of the quiet, contemplative East and the restless, never-sleeping West.

The corbelled arch is another matter. This had been used from the earliest times in the Indus Valley culture and had become traditional not only in South India but in Greater India, in the great temple complexes of Angkor and Borobudur. If, as the other building abnormalities indicate, the walling technique comes from South India, then the absence of the corbelled arch can only be explained by the alternative known to the builders—timber lintels, being ready at hand and so much simpler and quicker to use.

The non-use of the corbelled arch and the apparent absence of any desire by the builders to experiment or invent may be explained too by the rigid caste system of Hindu India. Trades were passed on only from father to son and it was both a sin and practially impossible to do anything different "from that state of life unto which it has pleased God to call you". It may well be, though no evidence is known, that the wall-making Vaddas were not permitted to make a corbelled arch—that may have been the jealously guarded secret of another set of masons and these masons may not have been available for an overseas contract. The limitation and rigidity of the walling technique in general smack of very great technical limitations such as a caste system would impose. The caste system would in fact make its subjects extremely conservative, conditioned only to do one thing, and unlikely ever to experiment or innovate.

Fourthly, the use of teak timber lintels

had almost certainly been traditional in South India. Teak lintels only one and half inches thick were used to support masonry superstructure in the walls of the old capital city of Vijayanagar, near the present village of Hampi, on the northwestern limits of the Mysore area. This teak was found in "perfectly good condition" in 1881, 500 years later. This city—centre of an empire—was the last stronghold of Hindu India in the south to fall to the Muslim invaders. They reduced it to ruins in the seventeenth century and today its ruins remain one of the great historic monuments of Southern (Hindu) India. Teak from South India was also used for building purposes in the Middle East—at Ur in southern Mesopotamia as early as the seventh century B.C., and again in a Persian palace near Baghdad, built in the third century A.D. Teak in this palace was still sound in 1811, 1,200 years later.

Lastly, round-ended bastions or buttresses. Projections either side of an opening in any wall needing protection from attack are common to military engineering the world over: but the rounded end to such projections is specific and not universal. It seems to have originated in Persia or India: either could have borrowed it from the other, though the earliest cultures of the Tigris/Euphrates and Indus valleys never developed it. The Greeks never used it: all their walls and openings had square ends and the Romans only copied it from Persia, along with other borrowings such as the Mithraic religion and much of their army organisation. Wherever it may have started it was certainly Eastern, not Western, in origin and probably connected with the use of brick—the round shape is easy to build with small units like bricks, difficult with large stones. Certainly, the round-ended projections either side of a defended entrance occur again and again in the fortifications of central and southern India, antedating the Moslem influence by centuries.

CONNECTION WITH GOLD MINING

The use of small stones, and not large ones as in megalithic building (which was also practised in South India), may have been connected in some way with gold mining. This is probable, since both were directly dependent on the same technique of fire-setting—since this was practically the only way of breaking rock before the Iron Age, and even then iron still remained a precious metal and was not the complete answer. Fire-setting continued right up to—and beyond—the time when dynamite became available.

In fact, it is possible and even probable that this peculiar way of quarrying stone to produce small stones arose directly from gold-mining technique. In mining the fire was laid in narrow bands or troughs on the gold reef to loosen only the gold-bearing ore and not the surrounding rock. A small clay trough, with charcoal still in it, was found in the early days of Rhodesia in an ancient mine against the face of the reef, proving that the fire was concentrated in narrow bands, in order to break the rock in exactly the required positions. This technique could easily have been transferred to quarrying on the surface for building stone and so mining may have led indirectly to the death of the megalithic tradition in India and the start of a new era of small, instead of big, stone building.

This transfer of building technique illustrates another characteristic of Hindu architecture, which Henri Parmentier, the French authority on early Indian and Indonesian architecture, noted: the total lack of all logic or intelligence when changing from one building method to another. The stability of megalithic building depends on the combination of great weight and careful jointing: small stone—"microlithic"—building demands a substitute, such as mortar in the joints, to give it the equivalent monolithic quality. Yet no mortar was used, and the excessive thickness of the walls at Zimbabwe may be largely due to an attempt, however defective, to recapture by sheer size the monolithic quality of megalithic building. It is well known that walls in Hindu India were generally far thicker than necessary.

As the ruins as a whole have a close connection with gold mining, this identification of four and possibly six building techniques with the same area of India that produced the gold mines can hardly be accidental, for there is no other area in the east, within striking distance of Zimbabwe, that had this combination. One or even two such characteristics might be coincidence, but when the basic building techniques and the basic mining techniques come from the same area and have, moreover, a common technical base—firesetting—which is essential for both operations, then the conclusion is inescapable: it was Southern Indian technical skill that first developed both the mines and the wall building. How the indigenous peoples of Africa picked these up, developed them, and made them part of the permanent traditions to last over a thousand years is another story altogether. But they did it: for when the white man came up from the south more than one thousand years later, all the Indians had long since disappeared, but the people of Africa, in spite of appalling wars and devastation, were still using fire-setting, still mining gold, and still building walled cities.

WHY STONE WALLING?

The question remains, why walled cities, or rather walled settlements? and why so often connected with the mines? One reason may have been simply to give protection against veld fires and wild beasts, mainly lions. The miners knew the mines were permanent and not shifting like their agricultural settlements, and so they built permanent walls instead of the traditional thorn bush or log hedge. They used the technique of fire-setting they were accustomed to in the mines to make the small stone bricks above ground: they may have even used as bricks some of the waste rock brought up from the ore face itself. But the diagnosis of the Great Enclosure as a prison suggests another reason: the ruins may also have acted as forced labour camps to work the mines. For all mining experts, having seen the old shafts and stopes and knowing all work had to be carried out by hand, were appalled at the working conditions and were convinced the work in and at the mines could only have been done by compulsory serf, or even slave, labour: no one would ever willingly have gone down these shafts, lit the fires on the rock face to break the rock, hammer out the loose rock, and put up with the bad ventilation without some form of severe compulsion. A large number would be women, some would be children, both easier to control; but men would be at the rock face, and on their work everything depended. A mining geologist in India reviewing the "terrible nearly inconceivable conditions" that must have existed underground was convinced only slave labour could ever have done the work. Greek and Roman mines had the same story. The silver mines near Athens worked by chained and branded slaves; the realgar (arsenical) mines near Sinope on the Black Sea, worked by condemned criminals, as Strabo said, "doomed to a quick death by the deadly air"; the Roman mines in Spain: all were operated with slave labour. It was the same over much of Africa. The Arab writers Ya'Kubi and Ibn Batuta record Sudanese slaves working the Nubian gold mines; other slaves working the Teghaza salt mines; and slaves of both sexes working the copper mines of Takedda. Modern mining opinion, when considering the ancient workings, is that Zimbabwean mining must have led to the same working conditions. Mining has always been, next to actual war, the most dangerous game in the world, and except for a select few, always to be avoided.

AFRICAN SERFDOM

It is true that Southern African slavery for the mines may not have been so onerous as the systematised industrial slavery of North Africa or the Mediterranean, for two reasons. The first is that indigenous African slavery at least south of the equator was serfdom, not the Western idea of slavery: for as already stated it had rights and duties as an accepted part of society, and this traditional relationship may have affected the mining relationship.

The second is that mining was probably seasonal, because only during the southern spring and summer would there be sufficient water in the rivers to permit the panning and washing of the gold ores, and this would have matched the seasonal movements of the overseas traders. Nevertheless, the walls remain both as facts and symbols of compulsion, and explain another mystery of the ruins: why the original walls were never designed to have roofs. They were never designed for shelter, only for protection or containment; they may have been semi-prisons; they were in fact exactly what they appear, nothing more or less: walls, with all that that implies—to keep wild animals out, and to keep people (and maybe cattle) in.

AN ASSEMBLY POINT

However, that does not explain the Great Enclosure at Great Zimbabwe; for there were no gold mines here, only an ivory collecting and gold processing and transshipment point. This confirms the previous assumption: the Great Enclosure can

only have been built as the assembly point, a reservoir, for slaves before their selection and purchase, preparatory to their transshipment to the coast.

Platforms, parallel passages, and portcullis grooves

This functional explanation also makes clear three other things: the blind steps leading to platforms, the double parallel passages, and the portcullis grooves to some enclosures. The platforms would have been viewing platforms for the slave dealers to choose their purchases; the double parallel passages the means of getting safely from the north entrance to the viewing platforms; and the portcullis grooves the method of controlling the movement of batches of slaves as they were brought one by one for examination and purchase—or rejection (Figure 18).

The inner parallel passage gave safe and private access to platforms A and B before the Great Wall was built; the building of the Great Wall, clearly to deal with a more dangerous situation, gave completely secure access to platform C, and an equally secure escape route, in case of trouble, back to the north entrance.

The position of the portcullis grooves as control points confirms this functional pattern. Guards with wooden beams slotted into the grooves could control the movement of the slaves by letting one or two through at a time as required and making it possible to count them. In this way the bastions on the inside of the eastern entrance to Enclosure 1 could control the exit from that enclosure and the grooves in the passage just outside that exit control the sequential movement towards the viewing platforms A and B. This could have been the movement before the Great Wall was built.

Movement within the Great Enclosure

In the same way, after the Great Wall had been built, the slaves could have been

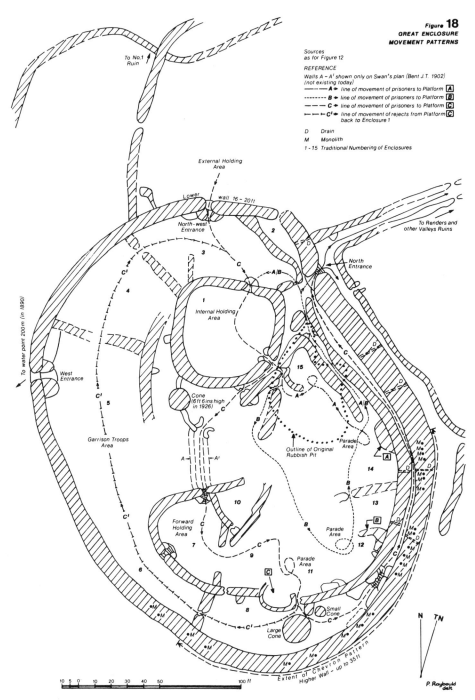

Figure **18**
GREAT ENCLOSURE
MOVEMENT PATTERNS

Sources
as for Figure 12

REFERENCE

Walls A – A¹ shown only on Swan's plan (Bent J.T. 1902)
(not existing today)

——— A ➤ line of movement of prisoners to Platform Ⓐ
‑‑‑‑‑ B ➤ line of movement of prisoners to Platform Ⓑ
— — — C ➤ line of movement of prisoners to Platform Ⓒ
├──├ C¹➤ line of movement of rejects from Platform Ⓒ
         back to Enclosure 1

D   Drain
M   Monolith
1 - 15 Traditional Numbering of Enclosures

This diagram shows the routes that could have been taken to bring prisoners to prospective foreign buyers on each of the viewing platforms, A, B, and C. The greater importance of Platform C is reflected by the provision of a private and secure passageway from the north entrance to the platform past the small and large cones. A similar but not so secure passage was given from the North Entrance to Platforms A and B. It is possible that Enclosure 15 was an earlier and discarded viewing point, to be superseded later by viewing platform A.

directed by means of these same passages to the cross-passage formed by walls A–A (see Figure 18) to discharge them into Enclosure 7, which would have served as the advanced holding area before the examination by the traders on platform C. Enclosure 8 would then have served as the holding area after purchase, the unwanted ones re-routed back to Enclosure 6 and so back to the general holding areas, Enclosures 1, 3, or 4. From Enclosure 8 the long parallel passage served a double purpose—as the exit route for the slaves purchased, to ensure no further contact with the other inmates, and as the safe exit route for their purchasers, following at their heels. Meanwhile Enclosures 5 and 6 could have been the station for the garrison troops guarding the whole operation.

One obvious question now arises: why was the Great Wall built at all? Why were the previous walls, twelve feet or so in height, not sufficient for this slave market? The answer may well be that when the bulk of the Valley Ruins were built, before the Great Wall, there was no slave market. The walls in this case were built, like the walls in the mining area, simply as protection for the foreign traders against wild beasts, which would explain the narrowness and defensive nature of many of the entrances, as well as the height of the walls—up to ten or twelve feet in many cases. But there could have been another answer: that the original prisoners were mostly women and children or at the most not older than teenagers, easily controlled and not particularly prone to escape. The later history of slave trade would suggest this possibility, in which the young were often considered the better long-term investment and the better able to stand the very severe rigours of travel and treatment.

There is also some evidence that the Africans, having sold some of themselves—even a starving father selling some of his wives and children to enable *them* to survive—would consider the sale a con-

tract that had to be honoured and so would not only not try to escape themselves but also would give the authorities—whoever they were, African or foreign—every assistance to stop others escaping.

The building of the Great Wall, however, could only have meant that the traders were now dealing either with a slave market for the first time or that they were confronted with a very different class of person, grown men in the full vigour of manhood, only too ready to revolt and make a determined effort to escape. It could even have happened it was the father of an already enslaved family that now found himself a potential slave. Such a man, realising this slavery was something very different from the slavery he was used to in African society, and realising his family had been made the victim of a trick, might become, and deservedly so, wild and dangerous. If this was the case, it was a high-risk situation and demanded measures like the building of the Great Wall and the Parallel Passages. Sir Richard Burton describes the same danger at Zanzibar in the nineteenth century, when no one could go about unarmed, even during the day, and at night gangs of starving adult slaves would roam the city hunting for food while all buildings were securely barred and shuttered.

There must have been either a sudden, unexpected demand for slaves overseas or a change in the demand away from or in addition to women and children. What this demand was, and where it came from, needs digging out of history.

Siting of the Valley Ruins: trading at arm's length

The foregoing diagnosis of the Valley Ruins and the Great Enclosure does not, however, satisfactorily explain the original siting of the Valley Ruins if they were built, as they well might have been, only for the traders' protection from wild beasts. The answer to this almost certainly lies in the plan of the Hill-Fortress: there was no room for them there. For all later evidence shows foreign traders had to travel with a considerable boydguard and such numbers could never have been accommodated in the Fortress, even if the rulers there would have tolerated such a thing.

Moreover, the traders must have come from an entirely different background and, together with their bodyguard recruited at the coast, would have created conflicts if accommodated in or near the local society clustered round the west side of the Fortress. One other aspect of these traders can be speculated on: did they use dogs as part of their bodyguard? It would have been an obvious thing to do. The origin of the Rhodesian Ridgeback, with the ridge of hair on its spine lying in the opposite direction to the rest of the coat, and often ending in two spirals at the fore-end between the shoulders, is uncertain. It may be Hottentot: but the only other known existing example is, of all unlikely places, on the island of Phu Quoc, just west of the Mekong River delta in Cambodia, where the ancient port of Oc-Eo was the main staging point of trade between India and China. The fact that this dog, famous as the lion dog, capable of keeping lions at bay, and of killing hyenas and leopards, only survives at the eastern and western extremities of the Indian trading area, certainly suggests the possibility that it was used by Indian traders as their travelling protection and was derived from some Indian prototype now possibly extinct: perhaps even the great Palegar dogs from the gold-mining area of South India.

To isolate the traders and their bodyguards would have been the obvious solution. Together with their caravans of porters—or slaves (the caravans could be either or both)—they could have been placed in some position convenient for both their journey to and from the coast and their access to the Fortress. The obvious place was where the coast road approached the Hill-Fortress: hence the Valley Ruins.

This argument, however, does not entirely explain why the Valley Ruins were not placed on the actual route from the coast on the north side of the Valley, nor why the access to the Fortress on this side, the Ancient Ascent, was so heavily defended. One reason, of course, for placing the Valley Ruins on the south side of the Valley was it was much warmer here than elsewhere, since till at least late evening it would have been free of the shadow of the hill.

But the much better visual supervision from the Fortress, given by the south side of the Valley and the heavily defended access to the Fortress on this side, suggests there was more than just convenience or a good micro-climate for the visitors. The ease of supervision and the defended access suggest there had always been nervousness, if not fear, of what went on in the Valley Ruins. Though trade rivalry, backed by force, may have been the primary cause, some trade in slaves may have been a contributory cause from the start, and this had to be kept easily visible and at arm's length. The plans of the various individual groups of ruins would fit either explanation: for in most of the individual groups of ruins it is possible to identify a small, well-protected area where the trader could have placed his shelter and another large, more extensive area in which he could have assembled his caravan of carriers, and/or slaves, under guard for his journey to the coast.

Whether slaving started later or not, the export of slaves, like a prison itself, was something unheard of, entirely new, and foreign to Africa. Did this start in the semi-slavery instituted to run the gold mines and grow into an export trade that perhaps was found more lucrative than the gold trade and so overtook it? Was it the same gold developers who developed this or some other parallel or competitive group? These questions open up wide questions of trade and commerce, of the rise and fall of markets, and of dynasties and empires. To answer them, a much wider knowledge of events in the lands and empires surrounding the Arabian Sea and the Western Indian Ocean is required. In particular, answers have to be found to at least four questions:

Can any group of peoples or nations be identified that needed grown-up slaves "in the full vigour of manhood" in such quantity and such speed as the building of the Great Enclosure suggests?

If identified, what was the place and time of such need?

Could such a place have been within a trading area that included the Great Zimbabwe?

Could such a time be possibly correlated with the chronology of the Great Zimbabwe?

In short, can a genuine historical "fit" be found to link all these events together?

CHAPTER 7

The Monsoon World and the Explosion of Islam

There is no God but one . . .

Fight in God's cause with those who fight with you. . . . Kill them wherever ye find them and drive them out from whence they drive you out; for sedition is worse than slaughter . . .
—*The Qur'an, vol. 77:II 186*, A.D. *622–32*

WIND AND WATER

To identify any group outside Africa likely to have needed slaves of the quality (and the quantity) kept, presumably, at the Great Zimbabwe, it is necessary to consider natural constraints and the trading pattern of the Western Indian Ocean, which was the only sea route by which the Great Zimbabwe could be reached.

The seas that sweep the coast nearest to the Great Zimbabwe, at Sofala, lead only north. To the east lies the thousand-mile-long bulk of Madagascar and to the south lay the terror of those unknown seas that "curve round towards the sunset" and from which no traveller had ever been known to return.

In contrast the northern sea route led to the oldest civilisations on earth, to Egypt, Arabia, Mesopotamia, and India, all with ports on the long coasts of this circulating sea. For it was a very special kind of sea, the sea of the monsoon winds, the "seasonal sea" of Arabia, with such a strong regularity of wind and water that it drew to itself men and ships from the earliest times who grew to understand it, trust it, and sail on it. Across its face in time there was thus built up a whole network of contacts and trade that became catalysts of a common culture, the first of the great historic cultures of the world.

The monsoon winds, dry in the northern winter, blew from the northeast to send the ships in November down to Southern India and South-East Africa; and the opposite, southwest monsoon blew the ships back again in the northern summer, picking up moisture as it went and depositing torrential rain on the Western Ghats in India, to close all ports on the western shore for nearly half the year.

THE UNKNOWN SOUTH

But there was a snag, as far as the Zimbabwe country was concerned, about the beautiful regularity of these monsoon winds:

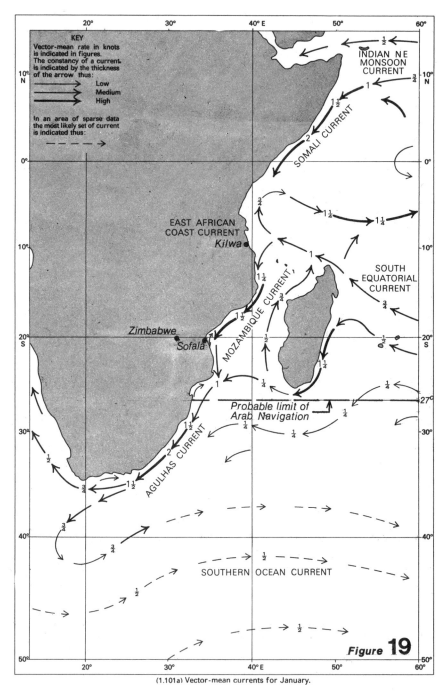

Figure 19

(1.101a) Vector-mean currents for January.

Northeast monsoon winds. The currents reinforce the seasonal rhythm of the winds. Note how the probable southern limit of Arab navigation, at 27°, agrees with the southern limit of northward-flowing currents at all times of the year and that Sofala itself is divorced from all northward currents.

Produced from portion of *BA African Pilot*, vol. 3, 13th ed. (1980), with the sanction of the Controller, HM Stationery Office, and of the Hydrographer of the Navy. (Kilwa, Sofala, Zimbabwe, and limits of Arab navigation added by author).

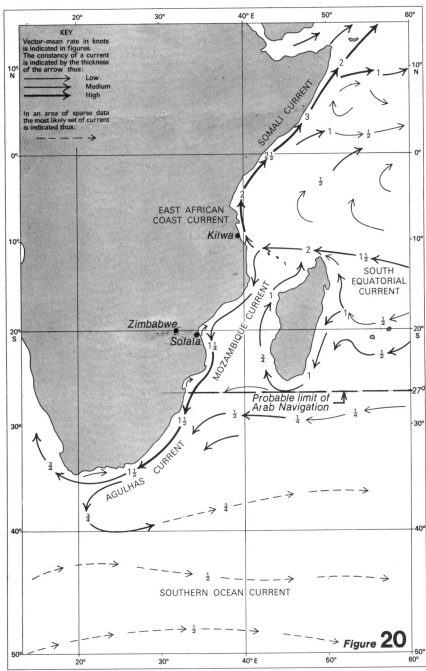

(1.101b) Vector-mean currents for July.

Southwest monsoon winds (See also notes to Figure 19)

Produced from portion of *BA African Pilot*, vol. 3, 13th ed. (1980), with the sanction of the Controller, HM Stationery Office, and of the Hydrographer of the Navy. (Kilwa, Sofala, Zimbabwe, and limits of Arab navigation added by author).

they stopped short about 10 degrees south of the equator, at Cape Delgado, probably the Cape Prason of the ancient Greeks. This was the turning point where the long East African coast begins to veer southwest and enter the dangerous channel between Madascar and the mainland (formerly the Moçambique channel), where the current against the African coast runs always to the south and northward winds are absent the whole year round.

Sofala, just south of the modern port of Beira, lies in the westernmost recess of this coast towards the southern end of this channel, at 20°10′ South, while the later known limit of Arab navigation was at 27° South, just past the southern tip of Madagascar and level with the modern Maputo (formerly Lourenço Marques). It was this remoteness in the far south that had for so long protected the land of Zimbabwe from foreign curiosity. It lay at the end of a long and dangerous sea road and in that had lain her safety and integrity.

All this was unknown country to the Greeks and Romans at least up to A.D. 200, if not later. Who broke this barrier of ignorance and pioneered and route to Sofala and then, having gotten there, found the way back seems at first sight almost anyone's guess. Certainly it was known by A.D. 900 when Masudi visited Zanzibar and spoke of "gold and other marvels further south". Someone in that interval had discovered the secret—to sail back up the *east* side of the channel, avoiding the navigation hazards in the centre and taking advantage of the on- and off-shore breezes from the west coast of Madagascar as well as some weak northbound currents and intermittent winds. Who found this secret that brought Zimbabwe into the trade area of India and Islam will be discussed later.

BAGGALAS AND GHANJAHS

The ships that sailed these seas and carried all the trade were built of local timber—mostly teak, sissoo, or sal from the Western Ghat forests of India—and all, without exception, were sewn together with coir thread, from the husk of the coconut, without any trace of iron nails anywhere. These sewn boats, with ropes and rigging all of the same coir thread, were universal throughout the Indian Ocean, Indonesia, and the Pacific islands: even in 1939 a new one was being built in the Gilbert Islands. Marco Polo thought them so dangerous he preferred the Gobi Desert for his journey to China but they were the boats that took Sinbad on his legendary voyages and must have carried all the traders and their goods to Sofala for their journey inland to the Great Zimbabwe.

There were variations in size and shape but all were built on much the same pattern—long, raking prow; high, raised stern; and great triangular lateen sails on one or two masts. The big baggalas or booms from the Persian Gulf ran up to 300 tons but their capacity was measured in the 180-pound packages of Basra dates, half a camel load and the limit of what one man could carry. Twenty thousand to thirty thousand such packages were normal, with a passenger (or slave) capacity of 150 to 200. The boom Alan Villiers sailed on in 1939 carried over 150 people apart from crew and one thousand years earlier a slaving ship had sailed from Sofala back to Arabia with 200 slaves on board; and nineteenth-century slave dhows seem to have been much the same.

A smaller version, the sambuk, operated on the African coast, particularly between Kilwa (in Tanzania) and Sofala while the dungiyah, or ghanjah, was a product of the northwest Indian ports in the Gulf of Cambay, built with a shallow draft to deal with the dangerous and shifting hazards of that gulf. Such ships would have been particularly suitable for the African rivers when in flood and increase the likelihood of the Indian connection with Zimbabwe. The only known ship to have

Sambuk: the commonest; coastal trader, Arabia and Africa

Boom: from Kuwait; most seaworthy, long-distance

Baggala: from Sur; the largest, and near extinction; long-distance for ivory and slaves

Lamu Dhow: successor to mtepe; the "African workhorse" with coconut matting above rails as protection in rough seas

Ghanjah, or Dungiyah: Indian, from Cutch and Cambay of great antiquity

PLATE 24. The chief types of Arab and Indian dhows. *(By courtesy of the* National Geographic *magazine from "The Twilight of the Arab Dhow" by Marion Kaplan, September 1974. © 1974 National Geographic Society)*

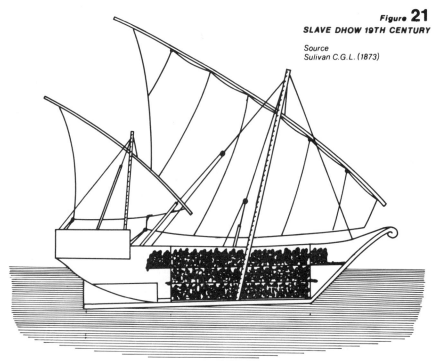

P. Raybould
delt

Sulivan says, "The poor creatures are stowed sometimes in two, sometimes in three tiers on extemporised bamboo decks, not sufficiently distant from each other to allow them to sit upright . . ." It would seem 200 slaves was an

average capacity: Buzurg gives this figure in A.D. 923 (G. F. Hourani [1971], p. 82) and Alan Villiers estimated 250 could have been taken "at a pinch" on the boom *Triumph of Righteousness* in 1939 (A. Villiers [1969], p. 71).

been built on the African coast was the mtepe or Lamu dhow, a much smaller version of the Arab and Indian ships. The ghanjah and the sambuk could have come to Sofala and sailed up the rivers when in flood to their navigation heads.

UP THE RIVERS AND OVERLAND

The last leg of the long haul for any trader to the Great Zimbabwe was a safari journey of over 300 miles through the fevered flatlands, through the mountains, and across the eastern plateau. There seem to have been two routes, a southern and a northern. The southern route started at Mam-

bone, a small port sixty miles south of Sofala (Sofala originally was the name of a stretch of coast rather than an actual port). This was at the mouth of the river Save (or Sabi) and the route happens to have followed that river, on water or land, for 200 miles till its junction with the river Lundi at the southern end of the Chimanimani mountain barrier. At this junction of the rivers at a place called Marhumbini a small dock leading from the river has been found, 750 feet long and 120 feet wide, sufficient to take a number of these smaller ships where they could have been cleaned, re-oiled (with fish-oil, to protect against the sea worm), and repaired, if need be, with timber from the nearby mountains. As the river

PLATE 25. Marhumbini dock, air view (1982). Note: 1) the narrowing at the northeast end, with the possibility of some dock gate, between the main dock and a smaller introductory dock beyond; 2) the slope into the dry donga stream bed at the southwest end (see R. Summers [1969], pp. 206–7). This would have enabled ships to be pulled out, cleaned, and repaired. *(By permission of the Surveyor-General, Zimbabwe. Copyright reserved.)*

floods coincided with the northeast monsoon bringing the ships south, river navigation up to the navigation head was inherently possible, if not probable.

From this dock a journey of 160 miles along the Lundi valley brought the traders to the iron district to Belingwe, 50 miles west of the Great Zimbabwe; alternatively a journey of 130 miles along the Mtilikwe valley brought them to the Great Zim-

babwe itself. These journeys would have given totals of 360 or 330 miles in all for this southern route, or a little over two weeks travelling at 20 to 25 miles a day.

The northern route was a little shorter, and probably safer, but not immediately obvious to an exploring stranger, since the rivers that led to it were not as large as the Save. This route led up the river valley of the Busi from Sofala to its navigation head

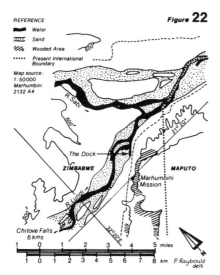

REFERENCE
- Water
- Sand
- Wooded Area
- Present International Boundary

Map source:
1:50000
Marhumbini
2132 A4

Figure 22

There are falls a short distance upstream in both the Sabi and Lundi rivers, making this a natural place for a dock; and in addition, timber for repairs could be obtained from the wooded area nearby or floated downstream from the Chiamanimani forests further up the Sabi valley.

at the present Dombo on a tributary, the Lucile. Here at the foothills there may have been another dockyard from which the route could have crossed the big mountain barrier in an area of several ruins near the present Melsetter. From here it would have crossed the upper waters of the Sabi slightly north of the Birchenough Bridge to continue straight westward, calling at the hill-fort of Chibvumani on the way to the Great Zimbabwe. This route would have been a total of 280 to 300 miles, but its advantage was not only its minimal distance (100 miles, or 4 to 5 days travelling) over the fevered flatlands, but by crossing the Sabi at the point mentioned it avoided the tsetse fever area of the middle Sabi above its junction with the Lundi. These were serious considerations for an age without cures for malaria or sleeping sickness. It is to be noted that the site of the Great Zimbabwe lies on a direct line from the Belingwe area to the sea at Sofala, which suggests it was the iron deposits, not gold, that first determined the site.

Such, then, were the constraints of wind and water, sea and land that helped or hindered the invading trader in reaching the Great Zimbabwe. Who were these traders, and wherefore, whence, and when did they come?

THE TRADING CENTRES

The land had four main commodities for export, probably in this historical sequence: ivory, iron, gold, and slaves. To find who needed these goods and the where and when of the markets requires a careful examination of the whole coastline of this rhythmic monsoon sea, from the southernmost point, Cape Galle in Sri Lanka, to the northernmost limit of the Red Sea at Suez and Eilat.

In any such enquiry it is the ports that are the indicators of trade, for it is at the ports that the land and sea routes meet with maximum profit to both. Sheltered anchorages that were near the critical mountain passes leading to a rich hinterland; ports at the delta mouths of major rivers to which the produce of the rivers' catchment areas could naturally gravitate; terminal points of navigation where one type of ship had to hand over to another type: these were the points where goods changed hands, payments were made, and old and new loans were argued about, written off, or recovered. Such places, where fortunes could be made or lost, gave their name to the products they handled, regardless of their origin. Indian gold became Ophir gold, from Ophir or Sophira (Indian Suppara), just north of Bombay; Indian cotton cloth, Calico from Calicut or Cambay from Cambay; Iraqi dates, Basra dates; and Zimbabwe gold, Sofala gold. The name of the port, not the place of origin, set the branded value for the market. It is the ports, in short, with their productive hinterlands, that can unlock the trading background to the Great Zimbabwe.

Round this long coastline four main groups of trading ports can be identified as having firmly established themselves over the centuries, even millenia.

1. The South-West, and Western, Indian ports. These were equally famous as the pepper, ginger, and gold ports and as the mixing points of east and west. The pepper and ginger ports were the southerly ones, with the shrub forests just behind them in the Western Ghats, and with the transshipment routes through the Ghats to the eastern ports on the Bay of Bengal. Ships from the east, having rounded Sri Lanka, and ships from the west, having sailed the open sea route from Arabia, all found their terminal points in Muziris, Quilon (or Male), and the other southerly ports on the Malabar coast.

The more northerly ports on the west coast, such as Goa, were nearer to the goldfields of Hubli and the Dharwar region, while Supara, originally Supparacha, and later Sophira or Sophir (just north of Bombay), was, in earlier Hindu times, one of the most famous ports in India, with legendary master mariners who never knew shipwreck. This must have been Solomon's Ophir (for in Egypt Sophir meant India and the local Indian dialect often omitted the initial "S"), in which case the Hubli-Mysore gold would probably have been shipped locally from ports further south to Sophira, which for some reason had become the terminal point for ships from Arabian and Red Sea ports.

How much did these ports take in Zimbabwe products? In the first place, it must

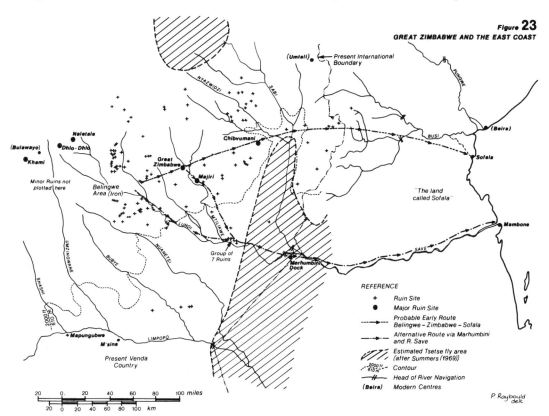

Figure 23
GREAT ZIMBABWE AND THE EAST COAST

REFERENCE
+ Ruin Site
● Major Ruin Site
- - - ▶ Probable Early Route
         Belingwe – Zimbabwe – Sofala
- - - ▶ Alternative Route via Marhumbini
         and R. Save
///// Estimated Tsetse fly area
         (after Summers (1969))
- - - Contour
       2000 ft
       610 m.-
- H - Head of River Navigation
(Beira) Modern Centres

P. Raybould
delt.

The more northerly route helps to explain the siting of the Great Zimbabwe: a collecting point for the iron area of Belingwe, en route to the coast by avoiding the tsetse fly area of the middle Sabi valley, and taking one of the tributaries of the Busi to Sofala.

have been traders and mining experts from these ports that first developed the Zimbabwe gold mines, for these miners came from this region and no other region: and having found the gold they would no doubt have brought it home once their own mines were running dry, as is thought, about A.D. 300, for gold was needed to finance both trade and war.

But ivory and iron were also needed in India: African ivory, softer and more workable than the Indian, was popular for the bracelets demanded by Indian brides, and African iron, with a 60 percent *Fe* content compared to a 30 percent *Fe* content of Orissa iron, was used for the tough wootz steel of India. This not only went to the armaments industry serving the incessant internecine wars of Southern India but also travelled much further afield, for the famous Damascene steel blades are thought to have been in origin Indian steel.

But for these Indian ports there is little evidence or probability of a slave trade, since there was no major demand. There may have been some slave transshipment, for black Zanj slaves appear in Java and even in China before A.D. 1000, but all the Indian evidence suggest most Indian slavery was indigenous and domestic, serfdom rather than slavery, except for the rare industries, such as pearl fishing off the Manaar coast of Sri Lanka, manned by condemned criminals. Indian agriculture was intensive, small-scale village production: it had no need of the massed manpower that could have explained the Great Enclosure's purpose.

2. The North-West Indian ports. These were all centred on the Gulf of Cambay and in origin went back to the earliest, pre-Aryan civilisation of the Indus Valley, for the earliest port, Lothal, was a southern outpost of that civilisation. This was a planned city and had a planned dockyard of some sophistication, capable, it is said, of holding fifty ships, in 2000 B.C. Queerly enough this dock, 719 feet long and 121 feet wide, was almost the identical size and shape as that dock three thousand miles away and three thousand years later at Marhumbini at the junction of the Save and the Lundi. Was this just coincidence or did Indian shipping skills both build and use it, so unchanging and conservative was Indian maritime technology? Even 700 years later than the possible date of Marhumbini—in the eighteenth century—it was said by the British that the Cambay Gulf ships built at Surat were the best in the whole of the East and could last a hundred years.

This gulf had another connection with Zimbabwe. It was the source of the two main export staples that formed the basis of Zimbabwe trade: beads and cotton cloth. The beads, agate and carnelian, came from the gravels of the Narbada River, the second most sacred river of all India, which discharged into the gulf at the most famous medieval port, Bharukachchha to the Indians, Barygaza to the Greeks, and Broach today. The cotton goods were manufactured at the head of the gulf at the town Cambay itself, long after it had silted up as a port; and the raw cotton was grown up-country in north-central India. Cotton had been grown and woven in the Indus Valley in 2000 B.C. or earlier, so that the cotton goods trade with the Great Zimbabwe in A.D. 1000 was already three thousand years old, another indication of the immense survival strength of early technology.

Against these never-ending exports of beads and cotton goods, what did this gulf import? The Periplus mentions a host of things, from tin, lead, and gold coin to cloth and perfumes, and adds slaves from the Persian Gulf and Oman and particularly female slaves for the king's harem. But there is no mention where these females came from: perhaps Abysinnia, famous for its attractive women, or from Somalia, where the Periplus mentions "slaves of the better sort" and a modern traveller notes "the golden-skinned Somali women, the most beautiful in Africa". There is no

mention of the bulk supply of male slaves from Africa, or anywhere else. Nor is it to be expected, for the labour needs of North India were the same as for South India: small-scale village agriculture, fed by "tanks" or local reservoirs filled by local rains, with no need of large-scale irrigation for plantation agriculture.

3. The Persian and Oman Gulf ports. The Oman Gulf ports, guarding the entrance to the Persian Gulf,were at the crossroads of this northern sea: the sea-road from Egypt and the West to India, and the sea-road from Africa to Persia and Mesopotamia. They had no hinterland beyond their own backdrop of mountains, which with monsoon rains produced a local food supply but nothing for export. So they survived only on location and became great transshipment ports for the slave trade. It was from some Oman port the first recorded slaving ship came to Sofala in A.D. 923— and how many were unrecorded?—and it was to Oman ports such as Sur and Muscat the slaving dhows made for in the nineteenth century, when evading the British anti-slavery cruisers. Even if only transshipment points in the slave trade, the trail to find the ultimate market for adult African slaves is getting hotter.

The Persian Gulf ports, by contrast, were all terminal points. They served either the inland valleys and highlands of Persia or, at the mouths of the twin rivers Tigris and Euphrates, the great productive lowlands of Mesopotamia. Persia had a limited economic capacity: it bred famous horses exported to South India for the cavalry of those southern kingdoms, but its agriculture was "patchy", with, even in 1960, four-fifths of all holdings less than twenty-four acres in extent, growing only for local consumption, a pattern that had apparently existed for centuries.

Water was short but irrigation was mainly local, the well-known underground *qanāts* bringing mountain water to the nearby valleys. But there was one very important exception: large-scale irrigation for sugar cane in the province of Khuzestan, in the valley of the river Karun, which reaches the sea at the Tigris delta. This had been introduced by the early Sassanian kings; and while the actual infrastructure of dams and canals was probably built by the Roman Army engineers captured in the defeat of the Roman Emperor Valerian in A.D. 260, the cultivation of the cane was undertaken by imported agriculturists from Gujarat, the Jats, specialists in sugar cane culture although on village scale. The Jats were never slaves, but they were the first step towards using immigrant massed manpower for large-scale agricultural production.

The ports for Mesopotamia were al-Ubullah (the Greek Apologos) at the eastern mouth of the delta and Basra at its head. In these fifty miles of delta land were the largest and finest date-palm forests in the world, the basic food of Mesopotamia and one of the main exports. But its cultivation demanded massive manpower. Each tree, "with its feet in water and its head in fire", had to be 20 feet apart, with water channels every 40 feet serving two rows of trees. This gave 80 trees and 800 feet of channels to every acre, or 512,000 feet (or 97 miles) of channels to every square mile. Air photos suggest there may have been once well over 100 square miles of such cultivation. As the urban population grew, so did the manpower need grow to produce the food for the cities.

Up-country from the delta, the land between the twin rivers was virtually rainless and its food production completely dependent on large-scale irrigation from the rivers. Similar to Egypt it needed serf—or slave—labour on a massive scale, combined with strict, centralised control of the water supply, to keep the system going. For this reason, from earliest Sumerian days, slavery had been endemic in Mesopotamia: the code of Hammurabi, about 1800 B.C., specifically made the third or lowest class a servile class, able to be bought and sold like cattle or sheep or any other object. The technical requirements of this sytem of production, servile at base and centralised at top, have been said to have created the political system known as Oriental despotism, which became traditional in the Middle East not only for centuries but for millenia, the caliphs of Baghdad dispensing instant justice with their executioners at their side in A.D. 800 just as Hammurabi must have done two thousand years earlier. Here, in Mesopotamia, and only here, can be found that massed slave manpower market we have been looking for that could explain the Great Enclosure of the Great Zimbabwe. For we know that here, in Abbasid times, sometime between A.D. 700 and A.D. 900, very large numbers of black Zanj slaves from the east coast of Africa were imported for this large-scale irrigated cultivation of both the date-palm and the sugar cane. Just how and when it was done is shown in the next section of historical perspectives.

4. South-West Arabian ports. These ports, and the sequence of supporting empires in their mountainous Yemenite hinterland—Minaean, Sabaean, Himyarite—controlled not only the gateway on the land and sea routes up Arabia and the Red Sea to Egypt and the West but also the turning point of the sea route from India to eastern Africa. Their wealth consisted in both transshipment traffic and the control of the produce of the frankincense and myrrh forests of the Hadramaut. This produce was gathered by slave and criminal labour, but the harvests were seasonal and this labour appears to have been home-grown.

SOME HISTORICAL PERSPECTIVES

If Mesopotamia was the place, what was the time, and how was this market supplied?

The ivory trade from Africa went back to several centuries before the Christian era, dominated by Yemenite traders, and iron manufacture was appearing in Southern Africa in the early centuries of that era. But it was the wars of Alexander the Great, his successor generals, and then the ubiquitous Roman Army that acted as a forced draught on the iron industry and guaranteed the success of an iron manufactury such as Meroe in the Sudan, 120 miles north of the present Khartoum. Alexander's political shake-up did another thing: it took the West to north India to govern and to south India to trade; and—for our investigation more important—it brought Indians to Egypt, the Sudan, and eventually Abyssinia, but more especially to Meroe.

THE INDIAN CONNECTION

There was Indian penetration of the Indian Ocean from the earliest times. Indians from the Indus Valley as early as 2000 B.C. had taken to the sea and gained the trading initiative with Mesopotamian Sumer by establishing an outpost on Bahrein Island halfway up the Persian Gulf. From Bahrein it is probable the same traders went west in the time of troubles, about 1500 B.C., to found the Phoenician cities, with old names such as Sur and Arad re-used, on the Mediterranean Levant.

INDIAN PLACE NAMES

Later, other Indians speaking Sanskrit left their mark in place names in the west: Dvipa Sukhaddra, "the island Abode of Bliss" in terms of their religion, shortened to Dioskorides by the Greeks and Socotra by the Arabs; navigation islets Hindi Kebir and Hindi Seil in the Red Sea, marking the critical turning point to the entrance channel to Suakin, the port for Meroe; and even more extraordinary, far to the south,

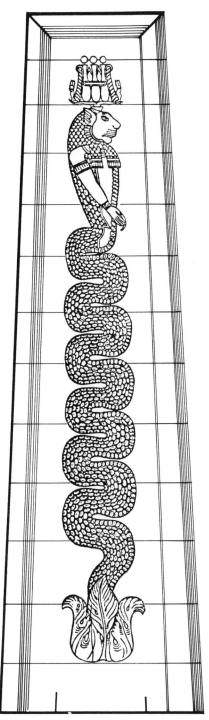

and east of Madagascar, Indian names for the Mascarene Islands, Dina Margubim, Dina Arobi, Dina Muraze—Dina being a corruption of the Sanskrit Dvipa, an island. To have reached these islands Indian navigators must have of necessity sailed down the African coast, and this is confirmed by the legends of Debuli traders (from the port Debul on the Indus delta) on the coast near Zanzibar.

There was every reason why in the first early centuries of the Christian era Indians should be searching for new sources of raw materials, particularly iron and gold, for iron was in constant demand through their incessant internal wars and, their own gold mines becoming exhausted by A.D. 300, gold must have been getting short for both war and trade.

INDIANS AT MEROE AND AXUM

The kingdom of Meroe on the Nile might have supplied both, though its primary product was iron. But the presence of Indians there at a high level, now firmly established through the existence of a syncretic culture showing lion-snake gods and kings riding elephants, appears due almost

FIGURE 24. Snake-God: Musowwarat-es-Sofra. The lion-god with the body of a snake, another instance of Indian influence. From P. L. Shinnie (1967). *(By permission of P. L. Shinnie)*

FIGURE 25. A king riding an elephant, from the elephant training camp Musowwarat-es-Sofra. From P. L. Shinnie (1967). *(By permission of P. L. Shinnie)*

FIGURE 26. Plan of probable elephant training camp at Musowwarat-es-Sofra. From P. L. Shinnie (1967). *(By permission of P. L. Shinnie)*

0 10 20 30 40 50

METERS

to an accident—the need to catch and train elephants for the army of the Egyptian kings Ptolemy II and III in the years 230–280 B.C. Ptolemy I when in India under Alexander had been impressed with the military force of elephants—the "armour" of that day.

One such training ground has been found near Meroe at Musawwarat-es-Sofra and has been dated about 230 B.C. The plan reflects the Indian system of elephant training described by Strabo; what is especially interesting are the long, walled-in passages joining temple enclosures and staff quarters with the training enclosures, reminiscent of the walled-in parallel passages of the Great Enclosure, as if elephants-in-training or adult male slaves were equally dangerous and their respective keepers needed equal protection.

SOUTHWARD TO ZIMBABWE

After the kingdom of Meroe had failed about the second century A.D. and the centre of power had moved to the Axumite kingdom in northern Ethiopia, the Indian influence again appears. It is here that the Indian connection with the Zimbabwe country may have started. Ezana, a king of Axum about A.D. 350, must have been a strong personality, for he corresponded with a Roman emperor, became a Christian, and started exploring the east coast of Africa. The Indians at his court may have suggested the exploration, for having lost the iron supply of Meroe they must have been keen to find an alternative source. It may not be coincidence that some of the earliest Iron Age sites in East Africa are very near the coast. Examples are Kwale,

a coastal village with a good anchorage and water supply, and sites in the Pare mountains only 50 to 100 miles inland from Kwale—both localities easily found by maritime explorers on the look-out for the metal. But as agents of Ezana they may also have been looking out for something more profitable and sinister—slaves, since the slave trade was endemic in Ethiopia and Ezana's men may have wanted fresh supplies. The coast became known as "Ezana's coast"—Azania—and if they developed a slave trade their product may have been called "Ezana's men", which could have been shortened in the trade to the nickname Zanj (the name has never been satisfactorily explained). Hence, perhaps, the very early appearance of the Zanj in Islamic history in the revolt near Basra in A.D. 694.

Tales from the interior further south may have reached the coast and whetted these explorers' appetite, till one day some trader, greedier and bolder than the rest, braved the seas beyond Cape Prason, sailed through the channel between Madagascar and the mainland, found the Sofalan coast, and went inland. The return journey may not have been a problem for such Indians, for they could have tried the direct passage home to India across the ocean from the southern end of the channel, south of Madagascar, and so found the Mascarene islands; or, more probably, found the west coast of Madagascar with its on- and off-shore breezes and used them as they had used for centuries the breezes of the west coast of India for all north-bound voyages.

THE DISCOVERY OF ZIMBABWE

News follows trade very fast. The southwest and northwest traders would soon have been alerted to new sources of iron and once in the Zimbabwe country they would have recognised the similarity between the landscape of big granite outcrops and their own Dharwar landscape of the gold-mining country between Hubli and Mysore. With the experience of Indian "ant gold" they may well have noted the huge termite mounds as well and then panned both the rivers and the mounds for gold—and found it in both. Their market sense would have been aroused when they realised that at least three products, ivory, iron, and gold, were all available at one source—a traders' paradise. Zimbabwe's isolation was thus finally broken and from now on the country would be permanently caught up in the trading world beyond her borders. The tsetse fly, the shallow rivers, the sand bars of the river mouths, the mountains, none of these could any longer protect her from that other and wider world.

TRADING TO THE EAST

This Indian influence in the West was only part of a much wider movement of Indian expansion. Buddhist missionaries, Hindu priests, Brahman State Advisers, merchants, and sea captains like Sinbad had all gone East to create what has been called "a greater India beyond India" but was, rather, a new, syncretic culture both on the Asian mainland and on the islands—the culture that produced the architectural masterpieces of Angkor and Borobudur.

It is an historical anomaly that this success of Indian cultural export in the East was never duplicated in the West. Africa proved too tough, too remote, too resistant, just too different for the Indian culture to take root and flourish. Africa remained obstinately herself. The success of India in the East became a failure in the West.

THE INDONESIANS

Yet one Eastern influence did settle in the West and survive satisfactorily—the

Indonesians. How and when and why they chose to colonise and occupy Madagascar is still largely unknown, but one thing is becoming clear: they must have had some time in Africa before finally settling in Madagascar and part of that time may have been, as we shall see, in the Great Zimbabwe.

THE ISLAMIC EXPLOSION

Sometime, then, between A.D. 350 and A.D. 600, the route to Sofala had been found and trading in Zimbabwean iron and gold started. Then in A.D. 622 a world-shaking explosion occurred—the explosion of Islam. Its effect on Zimbabwe was sudden and catastrophic.

The new religion of the One and Only God may have released, on a continental scale, the hoarded energy of the desert tribes, which would explain their astonishingly rapid military successes; but the new Islamic world they set up was the very opposite of their desert home. It was essentially an urban world, based on trade, and the new towns Islam created were the taxing nodes in a trading network. This suddenly expanded urban world made two urgent demands upon the existing trading economy.

Gold shortage

The first was gold, as the essential lubricant of trade and sinews of government and war. Only two home-grown sources were available—the treasuries of the Sassanian kings in Persia and the tombs of the Pharaohs in Egypt. The Sassanian treasuries became Islamic by right of conquest: the tombs by right of robbery. But these supplies were short-term: other, more permanent sources had to be found and only five sources capable of exploitation were known. These were: Central Asia (Urals, Siberia, Tibet); Nubia, accessible from Egypt and the Red Sea, mined since Phar-

aonic times; India in the Hubli-Mysore area; West Africa, the famous Wangara country; and finally South East Africa, the new-found mines of Zimbabwe. Of these the Central Asian sources were unreliable owing to continual political instability; Nubia gave limited amounts, and was very old and probably nearing exhaustion; India was already exhausted; and the West Africa country was very distant and its production absorbed by Mediterranean markets. Only the Zimbabwe mines remained and their great productive wealth must have been a godsend to Islam. There can be little doubt that the bulk of Zimbabwe gold was absorbed by the Islamic Middle East and the remainder by the warring states of Southern India. It is well known that Southern (Hindu) India has been one of the greatest hoarders of gold in history.

Manpower shortage

The second demand was for manpower—in that day and age, slaves. Islam had inherited from Persia her large-scale irrigated sugar cane culture manned by the Jats (called Zotts by the Arabs), originally immigrants from Gujarat in northwest India.

This was, as already stated, in the valley of the Karun in Khuzistan province, but there were also the great date-palm forests of the delta along the Shatt-al-Arab between Basra and the sea. Both these were the base food supplies for the urban populations and both needed massive manpower. When the new towns of Basra, Wasit, and Kufa were set up in lower Mesopotamia after the first wave of Arab conquests, the peasants, including no doubt the Jats, began flocking to the towns and by becoming *mawali*, Islamic converts, claimed all the Islamic privileges—including not doing any agricultural work. Al-Hajjaj, the greatest of the Islamic governors, sent them all packing back to the fields on pain of death and almost at once, in A.D. 695, the peasants revolted and were joined by some black

Zanj slaves from East Africa led by some-one calling himself Shir-l-Zanj, the "Lion of the Negro slaves". The revolt was abor-tive and crushed by the Basra citizens themselves, but what is significant is that this sudden appearance of the Zanj in recorded history proves the trade in black slave manpower from somewhere in East Africa had already started before A.D. 700.

THE LOSS OF THE JATS

The Abbasid revolution in A.D. 750 that shifted the centre of power from Damas-cus to the new capital, Baghdad, vastly increased the need for more manpower, since there were whole new towns to be fed. The period, as Toynbee said, was "pock-marked with revolts", and in 833 the Jats finally revolted and were deported to the Byzantine Empire to become the gyp-sies of the west.

This created a major crisis. If other manpower was not found fast, the cities would starve. Three of the standard sources of slaves were not really suitable. The Turks from Central Asia were nomadic fighters suitable for the army and the caliph's bodyguard; slaves from Eastern Europe for servants in the home and in the state; West Africans, for the Mediterranean markets and too remote for the Middle East. Only the East African black was left, for unskilled manual labour; and perhaps some Islamic official thought new untried slaves without a strong common identity would be less of a security risk. The passing of time was to put any such easy assumption to an acid test.

A ZANJ INVASION

Whatever the reasoning, an untold number of Zanj slaves—possibly 300,000—were shipped from East Africa to the Basra region in the period from 833, when the Jats were deported, to 869, when the great Zanj revolt started. They must have come up like raw army recruits without the slightest idea of what would happen to them. They could not understand, much less speak, Arabic and as social outcasts had no other company, no women, no future, and no hope. The labour conditions in the delta heat were appalling, with malaria and heatstroke endemic, and the need to expand date-palm and sugar cane cultiva-tion meant digging up the nitrous soil to expose the better soil underneath. If ever there was an explosive human situation, this was it.

The explosion came, the Arab historians tell us, on September 10, A.D. 869, and was led not by any black but by an Islamic fanatic, of the Kharijite sect, whose motto was a verse of the Qur'an (9:112): "Verily, God hath bought of the believers their persons and their wealth, for the paradise they are to have; they shall fight in the way of God, and they shall slay and be slain: promised in truth, in the law and gospel and the Qur'an;—and who is more faithful to His covenant than God?"

The revolt spread like wildfire. The Zanj defeated the government forces sent from Baghdad, many of the latter, themselves slaves, deserting to the Zanj with their arms. The Zanj then built a capital city—Moktara, the "City of the Saints"—in their own area, the marshes below Basra, close to the Shatt-el-Arab; and with command of this tidal waterway held to ransom the food supply of Basra and Baghdad. Official troops were again defeated and the Zanj replied by taking Basra, murdering the males and selling the women and children as slaves to the highest bidder among themselves.

They went on to take Ahwaz, on the Persian borderland, as well as the military post of Wasit on the Tigris only seventy miles from Baghdad. Finally, thirteen years after the start of the revolt, a new gen-eral—the future Caliph Mutadid—with new ships and new men, including "nap-

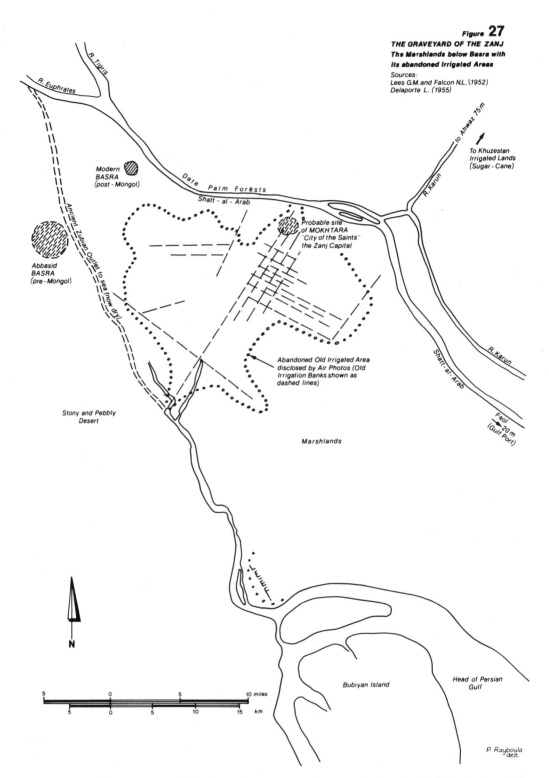

Figure 27
THE GRAVEYARD OF THE ZANJ
**The Marshlands below Basra with
its abandoned Irrigated Areas**
Sources:
Lees G.M. and Falcon N.L. (1952)
Delaporte L. (1955)

R. Tigris

R. Euphrates

to Ahwaz 75 m

To Khuzestan
Irrigated Lands
(Sugar - Cane)

R. Karun

Date Palm Forests

Modern
BASRA
(post - Mongol)

Shatt - al - Arab

Probable site
of MOKHTARA
"City of the Saints"
the Zanj Capital

Ancient Zubian Outlet to sea (now dry)

Abbasid
BASRA
(pre - Mongol)

Shatt - al - Arab

R. Karun

Abandoned Old Irrigated Area
disclosed by Air Photos (Old
Irrigation Banks shown as
dashed lines)

Faol 20 m
(Gulf Port)

Stony and Pebbly
Desert

Marshlands

N

5   0   5   10 miles

5   0   5   10   15   km

Bubiyan Island

Head of Persian
Gulf

P. Rayboula
delt.

The lines of old irrigation, probably dating from Abbasid times, have been disclosed by air photos. This was the heartland of the Zanj revolt and where their last stand was made.

tha-men" with Greek fire, started to invest and then attack Moktara. For a year the City of the Saints held out and then in 883 at a third and last assault, after hand-to-hand street fighting, it was taken, the leader Ali Ibn Mohammed killed, and his head, stuck on a pole, brought in triumph to Baghdad. The Zanj revolt had held out, against all the forces of the time, for fourteen years.

THE ZANJ ACHIEVEMENT

This Zanj state, for all the abuse contemporary Islamic and nineteenth-century European historians have heaped on it, was by any objective standard a very considerable achievement. An extraordinary combination of Arab fanaticism and black despair had immobilised a major centre of the Islamic world, threatened their capital city with starvation, and controlled for a time some of their major cities and one of their premier provinces. It was the first known outburst of blacks from the unknown darkness of Africa into the broad daylight of world history. They, the non-Moslems, had demanded the quality of treatment only given to Moslems: an idea to Islam of that day totally unintelligible, uncontrollable, and unacceptable.

It was called all the abusive names the culture of the day could invent—and in abuse that culture was highly inventive—and traditional historians of the nineteenth century followed that example: "Islam's greatest traitor"; "the revolt of the scum of the earth"; "the servile war in the East".

Yet regarded in the cold light of history, after all the passions have disappeared, it is a remarkable record of solid determination, committed energy, and inspired leadership. There must also have been a sufficiently strong and lasting community spirit and belief in a self-determination of some kind, to have enabled the movement to have continued to exist, to fight, and to organise a capital city capable of withstanding a set siege and eventually hand-to-hand street fighting. Such a state of mind is the raw material of a developing political consciousness; and in full retrospect it is not an exaggeration to say the whole movement could be given the title, never known before to history, of "the first black republic". The uprooted blacks from Southern Africa had proved themselves to be a time bomb under Islam.

CHAPTER 8

Zimbabwe and After

God alone knows all truth . . .
—*The Chronicle of Kilwa, about* A.D. *1520*

THE HISTORICAL FIT

IT is submitted that the answers to the questions given at the end of Chapter 6 can now be answered, as follows:

Firstly: it was the Abbasid caliphate that, after the disappearance of the Jat cultivators in A.D. 833, were faced with a major manpower problem for their basic food supply of the state and imported black Zanj slaves from somewhere in eastern Africa to fill the gap. An enormous number were imported, and at top speed, since—a probable exaggeration—there were said to be 300,000 black slaves involved in the revolt. Thus the need for a collecting point such as the Great Enclosure.

Secondly: the place was the Mesopotamian delta and parts of the river Karun irrigation area, inherited from the Persians; the time, between A.D. 833 and A.D. 869.

Thirdly: by A.D. 833 the Great Zimbabwe had been brought into the Western Indian Ocean trading area. The gold mines had started in response to Indian and Islamic demand and in 923, less than 100 years later, there is a record of a slaving ship travelling from Sofala to Oman.

Fourthly: there is a possible correlation with a revised chronology of the Great Zimbabwe but a conflict with the presently accepted chronology. This aspect will be dealt with later.

REASONS FOR THIS HISTORICAL FIT

The reasons for this identification of Abbasid demand with Great Zimbabwe supply are as follows:

(1) Very great numbers of slaves were transshipped from East Africa to the plantations in Mesopotamia between the years 833 and 869. Three hundred thousand are said to have been involved in the great Zanj revolt, and although, as mentioned, this is likely to have been a gross exaggeration, that number may have actually been imported, to cover the enormous wastage of slaves that was likely to have occurred during the voyage and in the plantations.

(2) Fifty dhows a year, with two hundred slaves each, could have transported ten thousand each year from Sofala to the Middle East. This conservative estimate compares well with the trans-Saharan trade all through the Middle Ages. Here twenty thousand slaves were driven on foot every year across the desert from West Africa to Mediterranean depots.

(3) Numbers such as ten thousand coupled with the shortage of buying time enforced by the monsoon made warehousing essential. Its need is proved by the existence a thousand years later of the barracoon warehouses at the coast used by the slave traders of the nineteenth century,

holding at times over a thousand people. General Rigby, British consulate at Zanzibar in the mid-nineteenth century, also reported it was common practice to march captured slaves in the interior to an assembly point till a caravan large enough for the journey to the coast had been collected.

(4) No other known structure from this Iron Age in Africa could have fulfilled this function. On arrival at the ship, whether up-river or at the coast, the ship became the warehouse.

(5) Some group of traders—Indian, Arab, or Parsees—must have organised the trade in conjunction with perhaps the gold-mining bosses and with expert fire-setting and building skills imported from South India.

(6) If ten cubic feet of walling represented one man-day of labour, the Great Wall of the Great Enclosure could have been built by fifty men in one year. If, however, only one cubic foot of walling represented one man-day of labour—a safer assumption—then the Great Wall could still have been built in ten years; or with one hundred men, in five years. If started soon after the Zott (or Jat) revolt of 833 it could have been completed between 840 and 845, depending on the amount and quality of labour available.

(7) If completed in 840 there would have been twenty-nine years to ship men to the Middle East, and at the rate of ten thousand a year, a total of three hundred thousand in that period is feasible. Given the high wastage in the marshes of the existing labour force and the known wastage on the voyage, these high figures of new intake are not unlikely; an appalling thought, which alone could explain the explosive revolt.

(8) If the Great Wall could have been built in five to ten years, then all the Great Zimbabwe walling including the Hill-Fortress could have been built well within a century. The whole complex could then have been started between 700 and 750, just after the first Zott peasant revolt in the marshes near Basra, at the period when al-Hajjaj—the ablest administrator Islam ever produced—was taking over Mesopotamia. It could have been at that date, when labour problems were first beginning to plague Islam, that the trade in Zanj slaves started.

Great Zimbabwe, in short, may have been started in response to Indian and other pre-Islamic demand for iron and gold, but its major development was due to Islam's general need for gold and manpower and in particular the Abbasides' frenetic need for manpower after the departure of the Zotts in 833. Viewed in this light, if it was a cataclysm out of Arabia that started Islam, it was a cataclysm out of Africa that shattered the Abbasides.

This then is the logic on which the theme of this book has been based. It is an attempt to see the Great Zimbabwe comprehensively, in its total context of time and space, and as a very unusual artifact requiring very unusual explanations. In spite of the nonconformity of this explanation to existing ones, it is inherently reasonable, being derived from an analysis of the ruins coupled with known historical facts that fit the analysis. The only thing it does not fit is the latest chronology constructed from the most recent archaeological interpretations. This is dealt with towards the end of the chapter.

SOME LEFTOVER THREADS

Trading aspects

The way the traders already involved in Zimbabwe responded to this demand of Islam, to ensure the provision of food and services for the new and growing city life, could have been almost an accident. A trader might have been offered by a local chief a few individuals who had become serfs through some mischance and who happened to have become of no particular use to him. The trader could have bought them with some cotton cloth and maybe beads and then sold them at very high profit in the markets up north. Such news would spread quickly in the suks, the markets of the Middle East, and as a result other traders could have invented other methods.

One such method could have been hijacking their ivory porters on arrival at the coast by offering them food or foreign goods to come aboard ship—as Al Ismailiyah had done to the Sofala king in 923, not so long after the Zanj revolt.

Another method could have been by taking the labour on the gold mines. All Indian and African evidence indicates some form of serfdom, if not slavery, of men, women, and children was essential for gold mining, though it may not have been as drastic as it is known to have been in the Nubian gold mines in Egypt: the workers, both sexes, naked, shackled, and continually flogged by armed guards. Mine labour in Zimbabwe, being used only seasonally when the rains made water available, may have on occasion also been taken overseas for sale in the markets of Oman or Sīrāf or Basra.

But the bulk of the people taken as slaves came probably from the serf class always present in African society as in every other contemporary society. Such people would have accepted the customary obligation to a superior and their change of masters after purchase would have merely transferred this obligation, as some form of debt to society that had to be paid off. This would be especially the case if many of these people were women and young children or teen-agers, as was often the case in later slavery, and this would explain why so much of the walling at the mines and at the Great Zimbabwe Valley Ruins is so minimal, only ten or twelve feet high. Such enclosures would have been ample control for such groups resigned to their fate and making little or no attempt to escape. Sentries could still walk along the summit of the walls and monitor all movement within.

But the sudden demand in 833 for able-bodied adult manpower was a totally different matter. Such men required entirely different constraints from those required for women and children and it was for these new requirements the Great Wall of the Great Enclosure was built, over double the hieght of everything else in the Valley and as great a deterrent to unwanted movement as the main West Wall defending all entrances to the Hill-Fortress.

"To do business"—but what business?

This new demand may also have changed the relationship between African and foreign trader very much for the worse. Even without overtones from slave trading, the foreign traders who came up "to do business" must have been under very grave suspicion from the start. "What kind of business?" must have been in everybody's mind. They would have been under a double suspicion in any case. They came from a completely unknown land, across a waste of waters of which Africa knew nothing, and they were, as well, completely un-African in appearance, stature, habits, and speech. Once slaving had started and become known, everyone would have been on guard. There must have been a knife-edge tension during the traders' stay, only made barely tolerable by the prospect of prestige for the chief and his chosen followers given by exotic beads and Cambay cloth.

This fear of foreign merchants was endemic in early societies. Homer's Greeks feared the Phoenicians—with good reason—as good traders and sly slavers; and Harun al-Rashid, with a similar fear that foreign traders were potential spies and saboteurs, expelled all of them from their planned quarters in Baghdad's famous Round City.

Such fear and suspicion on both sides seems the only explanation of the extraordinary lengths the designers of the Hill-Fortress went to in the planning of entrances and internal passages. This almost fierce control of movement is reminiscent of the design of Indian strongholds where precautions for security were taken to the most ingenious and complex lengths, equalled only by the ferocity and ruthlessness with which they fought.

This sense of suspicion and danger may also explain the relative lack of visitors' accommodation in the Hill-Fortress and the clear separation of the Valley Ruins from the Fortress. For in the valley visitors could be housed under full supervision from the Fortress and the planning of the Valley Ruins as a whole suggests such an arm's-length relationship. Some of the larger, very ruinous enclosures on the higher ground between Ridge Ruins and Mauch Ruin, and between No. 1 Ruin and the Great Enclosure, could have been general holding areas for people destined for sale. But in addition, at the centre of each group of ruins there is a small, compact area and a larger, more roomy area. The first could have been the traders' private area and, as the traders must have come with armed escorts, the second could have been for their escorts and the assembly of the caravan in preparation for the journey back to the coast. All areas, private and more public, could be very clearly seen from the Hill.

Saivism

It would be strange if foreign traders, far from home, at risk of seeming even more foreign, did not cling at all costs to their religion as a lifeline. The great number— over 100—of miniature stones identified by Bent and Hall as phalli and found in both the Great Enclosure and the Hill-Fortress suggests at once the revived Hindu religion of Saivism current in both North and South India in the latter half of the first millenium A.D. At that time the great revolutionary religions, Buddhism and Jainism, were declining, Jainism to wither and almost die, Buddhism to find a new home in Indonesia and China. The revived Hin-

duism became concentrated upon Siva, both destroyer and re-creator, lord of death and re-birth, symbolised by the phallus or linga as the generative principle of all life. A figure of Siva mounted on a linga has been found in a village near the Kolar goldfields in South India, and one of the Hindu sacred writings promises great prosperity to all who worship constantly the linga of the great god—a strong incentive to any serious trader.

The great numbers of phalli found suggest occasional losses from frequent, everyday use. They could have been carried about the owner's person as a form of worry beads, ready to be fingered and prayed to in times of stress. The largest found was only seven and a half inches high and the smallest seven-eighths of an inch— the latter a suitable size for a neck amulet, at once a charm and a reminder of the god's presence.

The interest in this possible existence of Saivism amongst some of the traders is that it might offer an explanation of the Conical Towers in the Valley Ruins. Except for the one built into the wall of the Outspan Ruins, all are freestanding and near entrances through walls and all are part of the best Q-type walling. This suggests they were all built at the same time by the same masons for the same group of people—those who engineered the Great Wall, the Philips and the Posselt ruins, the only places where the towers occur today.

For the followers of Saivism these towers could be very large and crude lingas, very rough copies of the sikharas, or stone towers over Hindu temple shrines, which in northern India often were conical in form, with convex, curved sides and a decorative finial, or *kalasa*, on top. The Zimbabwe tower conforms to this profile and the chevron pattern that was originally at its summit could have been an attempt at a *kalasa*. The Zimbabwe towers, being all freestanding (except one), could have been cult objects round which one could walk as one walked round Indian temples or as devout Muslims still walk round the sacred Kaaba at Mecca.

If this explanation is correct—and another will be discussed later—then the famous, mysterious, and apparently useless Conical Tower becomes merely the greatest linga of all time, built by the Vaddas as an act of celebration to their God and perhaps as some form of benedictory cult object for the traders to walk round after the completion of their business. The small towers in the Posselt or Philips ruins could also have been used in the same way.

In spite of these possible religious overtones, the foreign traders seem to have made no attempt to proselytize or colonize. They left no other traces anywhere of Buddhism or Hinduism or their many variations. Their visits remained rather like trading forays, smart commando raids for quick profits. Africa, in return, took from these raiders what she wanted, learnt their skills, and in the long run in spite of almost endless exploitation managed somehow to survive and remain firmly African.

Technical aspects

The walling tradition. Most of the technical explanation has been told. It is possible that some traditions of building had survived among the Dravidian people during their movement southward from the Indus Valley and was married to the quite distinct megalithic tradition of building with very large stones, without mortar, already existing in south India and later employed in Cambodia and Java. The result of this mingling of traditions was small stones used like bricks.

The extent of Indian participation in the actual building process of the Great Zimbabwe was probably minimal: the bulk of the labour must have been African, and only a few skilled masons would have been needed to teach the Africans dressing and laying of the stones and to supervise the work. In fact, from a purely technical point of view the whole of the Great Zim-

babwe—the Hill-Fortress and all the Valley Ruins—could easily have been built as one operation.

The differences in the quality of walling could have been due simply and solely to differences in the quality of labour and the degree of skilled supervision—the usual story every architect knows on any construction job. Even the butt-ending of one wall against another without bonding in a T-junction, used as a criterion for the sequence of operations, could have been simultaneous: it may have been simply the standard way of making walls meet in T-junctions. In short, the variations in walling are possible, but by no means certain, evidence for any time sequence of actual building.

What is remarkable is the way in which Africa accepted this method of wall building and made it her own. The skills in walling once implanted never left Zimbabwe and spread from there throughout Southern Africa to the extent set out in Chapter 1. The full story of the stone walls of this part of Africa is a long and absorbing one. It seems, after the Great Zimbabwe had been built, it set a pattern that anyone who aspired to be anyone had to follow. It was developed in a very different manner in the "status" palaces in western Zimbabwe, already mentioned, with the much greater use of patterned stonework and differently coloured stone; it was used in a much simpler and rougher way in the new capital the Venda built at Dzata and other sites further west after they had crossed the Limpopo and settled on the green valley of the Nzhelele River.

A living example

But perhaps the most significant example of the African survival strength of a tradition once started is a small garden wall built not more than fifty years ago in Mafikeng, the traditional home of the Ba-Rolong tribe, next the modern town built by the British to serve their railway from Cape Town to the north.

In this little wall standing today four Zimbabwe techniques clearly survive: (1) regular stone courses, of approximately equal height; (2) alternate dark and light stone courses; (3) incorporation of large rock outcrops in the wall at its base; and (4) an upright support at the end of the wall where there is an opening. One could almost say, "Zimbabwe is alive and well and living at Mafikeng". That wall is a triumph of African persistence.

The planning for storage

It is generally agreed the Africans of the Iron Age used their rare hill-fortresses only occasionally, in times of danger and for religious festivals or in other special circumstances. One such time would have been the traders' short annual visit, enforced on them by the rhythm of monsoon sailing, and which necessitated some storage planning in advance. Such assembly points in the interior for caravans due for the coast were still being used in the nineteenth century and it is known kings and their court followers had the habit of continually moving from one site to another, so that it could have been part of an annual routine to hold court at the Great Zimbabwe during the trading season, when stocks of trading goods would have been accumulated. For the rest of the year a minimal caretaking garrison would have been sufficient for the purpose of storing trade goods in preparation for the annual visit. The need for protection of these goods during storage to prevent theft when the king and his court were not in residence would also help to explain the extreme security measures incorporated into the design of the Fortress, particularly the entrances. At least four types of goods required storage: gold, iron, ivory, and manpower.

Gold storage. Gold dust was carried, it is said, in porcupine quills, but sometimes nuggets may have been found and some larger container would have been required. The legend of the *fuko-ya-nebandge*, the hollow zoomorphic pot, which was said to have contained yellow beads that glistened, that moved about on its own legs and would close its mouth on any hand that tried to steal its contents (the relic mentioned in Chapter 3), seems the obvious candidate for gold storage.

The yellow beads that glistened suggest gold rather than precious stones, since gems were not a product of Zimbabwe, though when not used for gold, the foreign beads, purchased from traders and kept as tribal heirlooms, may well have been stored in the pot as well. The legend of the pot continually moving about on its own suggests it moved in secret with the chief whenever he moved, always being kept close to him. The legend that it would seize any hand that attempted to steal its contents suggests that chiefs had adopted the simple Arab punishment for any convicted thief, chopping off the right hand. And as for the name *fuko-ya-nebandge*—what better name for the national bank where the bullion was stored than "the king's favourite adviser"? He would only have to consult the contents to know exactly what his trade balance was to trim his conduct with the traders on their annual visit.

It would have held up to 1,000 cubic centimeters, or 16,000 grams or 570 ounces, about one-twenty-eighth of the average total annual production of all gold mines in Zimbabwe as calculated by Summers; but still a reasonable amount for one year's trading purposes—say a value at current trading of $350 per ounce, or $199,500. As there was also a legend about a sister or duplicate, there may have been more than one such pot, so the total gold available for trade might have been double or more in value, up to $400,000.

Iron storage. There is no evidence as to how iron might have been stored. All that is known is that in Africa it was a precious commodity and that the Indians prized it very greatly, and subjected it to their own processes to produce a very superior article, including their wootz steel. They would

PLATE 26. *A:* The Zimbabwe tradition, 1980.

B: Tswana walling at Mafikeng—The Place of Stones *(Photos by G. le Roux)*

This sunken passage has no apparent purpose, except for storage of ivory and perhaps iron—always major articles of trade.

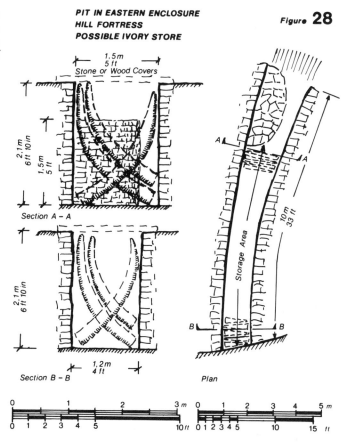

**PIT IN EASTERN ENCLOSURE
HILL FORTRESS
POSSIBLE IVORY STORE**

Figure **28**

1.5 m
5 ft
Stone or Wood Covers

2.1 m
6 ft 10 in

1.5 m
5 ft

Section A – A

2.1 m
6 ft 10 in

1.2 m
4 ft

Section B – B

A

A

Storage Area

10 m
33 ft

B

B

Plan

0   1   2   3 m   0   1   2   3   4   5 m
0 1 2 3 4 5   10 ft   0 1 2 3 4 5   10   15   ft

therefore not have bought finished articles like hoes or spearheads, but unwrought iron straight from the furnace. At the same time the traders must have obtained the iron from a central point such as the Great Zimbabwe: they would hardly have roamed about where they wanted in order to deal with the original producers on the spot. The most likely container for such a load would be an animal skin—of a bullock, for example—which could be carried on a pole between two bearers down to the coast. Such a container would leave no traces and explain the absence of evidence.

Ivory storage. Ivory was the great staple trade of East Africa for many centuries and would have had to be treated seriously. The first tusk that touched the ground when the animal was killed was always the chief's. Tusks can be large—up to 7 or 8 feet long—

and heavy—up to 150 pounds—and can easily be damaged; for instance, ivory will crack if subjected to rapid changes in temperature.

To store ivory, therefore, some fairly large and safe place, not subject to rapid changes of temperature, and yet easily accessible for traders' inspection, was required. Some underground chamber would give a steady temperature range throughout the year, and a central position where the chief and his court would normally function and where guards would be on duty for most if not all the time would be the obvious solution. The unexplained "sunken passage" in the Eastern Enclosure in the Hill-Fortress, described in Chapter 2, complies with all these requirements. Figure 28 shows its size, shape, and capacity for up to 25 or 30 tusks if stored in a single rank, or double that number if stored double, one rank on top of the other. It would seem unlikely that more than 60 tusks—over one a week—would ever be collected in one season by African trappers. The whole store could be covered with wooden logs if stones were not used (owing to the great lengths of stone required—7'10" to 8'0") and only one or two logs were needed to be moved to get at individual tusks during a sale.

The storage if ivory would also explain the variation in width: it would allow the tusks to be graded, the shorter at the narrower end, the longest at the wider end. This grading would then be obvious in the length of logs covering the trench, so that only those logs need be removed where the required length of tusk was stored. For this purpose the position of the passage/trench was ideal—directly under the personal surveillance of the monarch and his court, and directly available for inspection by traders while all three—the traders, the chief, and his courtiers—were still in the audience chamber.

Manpower storage. This has already been explained. The upper Valley Ruins, on the ridge and immediately north of the Great Enclosure—groups A and B in Chapter 1—would have been sufficient for the early stages of the slave trade, limited to women and children. The sudden demand for able-bodied men in the prime of life was dealt with by the Great Wall, turning the smaller internal enclosures into the Great Enclosure, and so providing the facilities for viewing and selecting the manpower material as already described in Chapter 6.

The timing of storage. As African conditions never permitted the construction of a definite calendar, this accuracy of timing appears almost miraculous, till the great respect paid to rain-makers is remembered. Then it becomes obvious that these wise men must have known the passage of time—if only the number of moons in their memory—to foretell the annual return of the rains, and this could be related to the annual coming of the traders to the coast. In this way the necessary action for storage of all trade goods could have been taken in good time. What is absolutely certain is that, unless this timing was correct, there would have been no trade, for the traders had no option whatever about their own arrival and departure times. The swollen rivers in December or January, later than the first rains, would have been the signal for the traders' arrival. If the rains were late, the rain-making priests would have known this by the number of moons since the last rains and could have been ready for the traders if the traders have decided to come overland and not wait for the floods to use the rivers for navigation.

THE CONTROVERSIAL FINDS AND RELICS

To the five relics mentioned in Chapter 3 that have added to the mystery of the Great Zimbabwe must be added the greatest enigma of all—the Conical Tower—making six objects, all of very definite character, that need relating if possible to the theme of this book.

The Conical Tower

As stated, this may have been the greatest linga of all time: but it might also have been designed and used for a much more practical purpose. When the Great Enclosure was full of prisoners awaiting transshipment to the coast, supervision would have been essential. Day supervision from the top of the Great Wall and from lookout points in the Hill-Fortress was straightforward: but at night, when there was no moon, some light would have been almost essential. The Conical Tower could have been used as fire tower to give that light—a phallus with a fire on top. The tower would have lit up most of the interior, and most of the exterior surroundings not attached to other enclosures. It could have been used, with some pre-arranged code, to signal to the Hill-Fortress.

The idea of using the Conical Tower as fire tower would also apply to the smaller towers in the Valley Ruins and Outspan Ruins, used as markers at night and as protection to any strangers, such as traders, using the ruins as temporary encampments, whether they were Saivish, Muslims, or adherents of any other religion. With the tensions that must have existed on the part of everyone at the time of trading, some lighting obviously would have been desirable. The position of the towers in the Posselt and Philips ruins is next the entrances to the smaller and more private enclosures in each case, where the trader himself would have encamped. A fire on a tower in this position would have been ideal for his personal protection, from either man or beast, and could have been kept going by his guards all night.

The hollow pots

The possible explanation of the *fuko-ya-nebandge* has already been given. The legend of the sister pot that has disappeared gives a slight but possible linkage to the Sakalava legend that the ancestors of the Maroserana landed somewhere on the west coast of Madagascar with a shipload of gold. (The name Maroserana has been linked with the word *mari*, said to be the word for gold in Zimbabwe.) Further, it was said white men—meaning, presumably, not African blacks; was it Arab traders or Indonesian immigrants?—were at the Great Zimbabwe for a time and stole the gold. If the legends are correct—there are more than one—they stole much more than one pot, for it was said there were four containers, each requiring four men to carry. If a man's load was 60 pounds, then the total weight would have been 960 pounds or 11,520 gold ounces, over two-thirds of the estimated average total annual production of 16,000 ounces. Such figures

if true imply residence and collection of the metal over some years and increase the probability of an Indonesian presence at the Great Zimbabwe. If gold there was in Madagascar, certainly it was Zimbabwean gold, stolen or not.

As regards the other hollow animals, the stone wild hog in Madagascar and the wooden buffalo in Botswana, there seems no evidence to connect them to the Great Zimbabwe and they remain mysteries for others to solve.

The zodiacal bowl

There is little doubt the damaged zodiacal bowl with its divining symbols found near the Great Zimbabwe and the very similar divining bowls of the Venda are both in some way connected to the Zimbabwean culture, and probably in some semi-religious sense; but the fact that not all the signs are there shows that the bowl must be at the far end of a long and much-forgotten tradition, when both the totality and the individual meanings had been lost. Of the ultimate source of these signs there is no doubt; it is Babylonia, 2000 B.C. or earlier. From this centre of star lore it spread throughout the Middle East, the Mediterranean, and, eventually, European culture. Further, one of the vehicles of this dispersion was the Mithraic religion, famous as the religion of the Roman Army but equally popular with traders in its insistence on the sanctity of contracts. Mithraism was beaten in the West by Christianity, largely because it excluded women completely, but it survived in the East, in the form of its successor, Manichaeism, for many centuries, including an appearance in South India in the fifteenth century, close to the Saint Thomas Christians. It would seem therefore that traders, Persian or Indian in origin, and Mithraic or Manichaean in loyalty, could have brought the use of the zodiac to Southern Africa and left its astrological magic to be mingled in time with African divination, to finish in the BaVenda bowl, without any zodiacal signs whatever.

The soapstone birds

The bird that really needs explanation, as mentioned, is the finest of them all, the one with a carved crocodile (or lizard?) crawling up the pole and which is still the national emblem of the country Zimbabwe. All the other soapstone birds look like weak and altered memories of this first one. The one clue that has come out of the historical record is a possible Indonesian connection, for Malagasy historians have suggested that not only were the Indonesians resident for some considerable time in Africa, but may have been in some kind of authority or at least influence at the Great Zimbabwe, for two reasons: first, the legend of a hoard of gold being taken to Madagascar just described; and second, the habit of carving birds on the top of poles on their ancestors' graves and also on the ridge-pieces of their houses as if they were family, household items.

This possibility is increased appreciably by the fact that the Bugis of the Celebes—the group that probably gave the African name of Bouki to Madagascar—were in the habit of fishing off the north coast of New Guinea into which the river Sepik flows. It was in the Sepik River culture that the lizard and a bird were the inseparable "home companions" or permanent domestic guests—part of the family, so to speak: the lizard representing the male and the bird the female principle. The Bugis may have borrowed from the Sepik culture the lizard-bird combination. The Melanesians, just east of New Guinea, also worshipped birds; in the Solomon Islands, one of the Melanesian group, the frigate-bird was sacred. They also put birds in their star map for navigational purposes: East, for instance, was a "Big Bird". If this was so, not only does it explain the Great Zimbabwe bird, but it also suggests the Bugis were at the Great Zimbabwe in some

strength, either as very influential traders, or later perhaps sharing power with the Zimbabwe rulers. The fact that the finest soapstone bird was found in the Philips Ruin, almost certainly a traders' camp, suggests that it was as influential traders the Indonesians first established themselves. It could very well be it was still in that capacity that they obtained possession of the gold hoard—in one of the hollow pots—and went off with it to Madagascar.

This explanation of the famous soapstone bird may seem farfetched and a long shot in the dark, but it is perfectly feasible for great navigators to have taken a bird such as the frigate bird for their totem; and the shot is no longer and no darker than the colonisation of Madagascar—with a preliminary stop-over in Africa or not—3,000 miles away from home in the Celebes or another island group. And that colonisation is an established fact.

The stone door

As stated in Chapter 3, no stone door was found in Africa, but one still exists in Madagascar. This is the stone disc weighing twelve tons forming the main entrance to the sacred walled village of Ambohimanga, twelve miles north of the Malagasy capital in the central highlands. The disc is called in Malagasy vato-kodia, "stone wheel", and is designed to be simply rolled over to block the entrance. This is pure megalithic tradition and must surely be Indonesian in origin, for the stonework in the adjoining town walls has no resemblance whatever to the Great Zimbabwe walling, and there was a long-standing megalthic building tradition in Indonesia. Moreover, the stonework of the walls of Ambohimanga—a mixture of big and very small stones—is very similar to the walling in some of the forts in the Inyanga terraced hillside area mentioned in Chapter 1. If there is any truth in the assumption the Indonesians spent time in this part of Africa before settling in Madagascar, the

FIGURE 29. The sacred city of Ambohimanga, central Madagascar: the Town Wall with stone disc as entrance door (after H. Deschamps, 1972). A remarkable example of megalithic mechanical invention unique enough to suggest the work of some creative individual, never to be imitated again. (*Drawing by G. le Roux*)

stonework and stone door would be another indication the Indonesians could have been involved in the Southern African story—in trade, or politics, or both.

The fabled inscription

If the inscription ever existed—and it probably did, as discussed in Chapter 3—then it must have been on the wooden lintels over the entrances, which would explain its disappearance. The fact that the "learned Moors" could not recognise the script suggests it was one of the scripts of Southern India, the home of the stone Vaddas or their trading bosses. This may not have been sufficiently known to foreign traders at the coast: perhaps some script of Tamil or Telugu. It is of course intriguing to guess what the inscription said—a votive thanks to their great god Siva, the Great Linga, or some sardonic Indian equivalent of Dante's welcome to the *Inferno:* "All hope abandon, ye who enter here"?—or, much more likely, a simple statement of the chief's name and perhaps a date of the Arab or Indian calendar.

THE GENERAL INCONCLUSIVENESS

The general lack of firm conclusions in the planning and design and the almost total lack of rectangularity prove beyond doubt the foreign traders who stimulated all this development brought with them no continuous long-term plan and were not of the correct social class to introduce new religious concepts or transform the political structure. The traders who managed to reach the Great Zimbabwe had taken much greater risks and must have been born gamblers, playing for high stakes, and always ready, like any deeply committed gambler, to change their plans and tactics at a moment's notice in order to survive in highly volatile situations.

With tactics such as these, it was natural that beginnings without conclusions and conclusions without beginnings would occur all the time, and that is the way Zimbabwe was built: an immediate, direct, pragmatic adaptation to changing circumstance in order to survive in a violently changing world in which whole new markets could suddenly appear—as in 833, when the disappearance of the Zotts left a labour vacuum—or equally suddenly fade—as in Canton in 878, when all the foreign merchants were massacred and the China trade practically came to a standstill.

THE LATER HISTORY

A trading watershed

The years that followed the great Zanj revolt—A.D. 900 onwards—marked a watershed in the history of both western and eastern Indian Oceans. The Arab Mappilah, or Moplah, traders had become firmly established in the southwestern ports of India from Calicut to Quilon, and the trade of the western ocean gravitated to them and their Muslim compatriots in the north, in Arabia, Mesopotamia, and Persia.

Indian interests gravitated to the trade with Indonesia and China and to a consolidation of their share in that trade. After years of incessant war between the small kingdoms of South India, one dynasty, the Chola, became the dominant power and gained control of the ports of both coasts and so of the highly profitable east-west trade. To ensure the eastern and southern seaways were open for shipping, they successfully attacked the Maldives, Sri Lanka, and even the empire of Shrivijava on Sumatra in order to free the Malacca straits,

the gateway to Indonesia and China. Significantly, however, the Cholas accepted the west coast Moplah traders and even gave a charter to a long-established Jewish trading community in Cochin. The Cholas decided to capitalise on this existing position, accepted it, and no doubt obtained handsome royalties on all passing trade.

Trade with the Great Zimbabwe after A.D. 900 must be seen against this background of Muslim maritime dominance. At the same time the encouragement of east-west trade by the Cholas and their opening of the eastern seas to their ships must have helped to bring eastern products to Great Zimbabwe and East Africa in general. For this was the period that saw the foundation of the Muslim city-states on the East African coast: Mogadisho, Mombasa, Zanzibar, Kilwa, and the rest—no less, it is said, than thirty-seven in all. This was the beginning of another world and was marked by the trading power firstly of Mogadisho and later of Kilwa, the southern end of monsoon navigation. Kilwa in time came to dominate the gold trade from Zimbabwe and special ships, sambucs, were used for most of the trade between Kilwa and Sofala. The history of the medieval trade with Zimbabwe is the history of these coastal towns headed by Kilwa.

Later Great Zimbabwe

The immediate effect on the Great Zimbabwe of this change in the power structure of the western Indian Ocean seems to have been indirect. The trade in staples—iron, gold, ivory, and slaves—must have continued in exchange for beads and cotton goods, but there is one remarkable fact: no Arab writer even mentions its existence, let alone records a visit. The nearest was the remark of Ibn Batuta that gold came to Sofala from Yufi in the land of the Limiin, one month's march away. But this was only hearsay from another merchant; no one has yet identified either Yufi or Limiin, and the Great Zimbabwe was only two weeks away from Sofala. Two earlier writers talk of Sofala but place it 500 miles north of its real position. One can only infer either that trade with the Great Zimbabwe was too far south to be bothered with when Arab historians had the whole of Islam for their field, or that it was already fading into insignificance when they were writing, from A.D. 1000 to A.D. 1400.

The archaeological evidence, however, suggests the Great Zimbabwe continued after 900 to be a growing and active centre with a physical extension after a century or two so great that, as usual in Africa, it overtaxed the environment and, having destroyed its living base, was forced to move elsewhere.

Whatever the cause and whenever the time, certainly it is known power moved away from the Great Zimbabwe to the north and west. By 1500, when the Portuguese came to the coast and found Sofala, the Great Zimbabwe was almost certainly deserted and probably in ruins.

The movement to the north

The movement to the north was to the area of the northern gold mines, with a northern boundary on the Zambezi itself, called by one king "the enemy" because it blocked further northward expansion. This area was the territory of the *Mwene Mutapa*, the "master pillager", corrupted for medieval legend into Monomotapa, the great Central African empire that, it was said later, stretched from the Congo to the Cape. What is significant for the present story is no northern stone walled Zimbabwe has survived—if it was ever built. The site of its capital city is not even known. The nearest indication is the capital the first Portuguese explorer, one Antonio Fernandes, found in 1513, which he called Camanhaia, "a newly constructed fortress of stone without mortar", where he said "the Monomotapa is always to be found, the greatest of all these kings, and all obeyed him as far as Sofala". The Great

Zimbabwe tradition of walling was clearly still alive and well in 1513 but nothing has survived. Why was this? Was it that the "fortress" was only some walls six or seven feet high and the rest normal African huts or was it that Camanhaia, like other previous capital cities built in the same way, not as strongly as the Great Zimbabwe, was destroyed by the incessant warfare that the Portuguese records are always describing? What is certain is that the centre of power, in moving north, occupied some of the best farming land between the Zambezi and the Limpopo.

The movement to the west

The movement to the west seems to have been of an entirely different character, different both from the movement to the north and from Great Zimbabwe itself. It differed from the north for an unusual reason, hard to understand: the land had less resources and less rainfall, yet it has left architectural monuments of considerable skill and extent—Naletale, Dhlo-Dhlo, Khami—whereas the north has left nothing of equal consequence.

Moreover, these western monuments—the "status" palaces mentioned in Chapter 1—are in an entirely different tradition from the Great Zimbabwe. The only common element is the use of small stones like bricks, but the way they are employed is radically different. Here there are no enormous, blank, forbidding walls dominating from a height, no tiny slit entrances or fortresses from which, once inside, it would be difficult to escape. On the contrary, the great west front of Naletale is an exercise in flamboyant virtuosity in its exuberant use of almost every pattern that could be made with small, identically shaped stones; and the main entrance to Khami is a wide-open, welcoming flight of shallow steps.

This western development is in fact another world, just as the development of the Muslim towns on the east coast rep-

PLATE 27. Naletale, west front *(Photo by courtesy of the Zimbabwe Tourist Board)*

PLATE 28. The main entrance to Khami Ruin: "Wide, open and inviting"; from Fagan, *Southern Arabia*, Thames and Hudson *(Photo C. K. Cooke)*

resented another world in maritime power. These two worlds could have been contemporary in their prime and it is tempting to see some connection between the two, for the decorative effects of a front wall like that at Naletale are immediately reminiscent of the geometric decoration of Muslim architecture, where representation of the human figure was forbidden and all decorative effects had to be achieved through abstract geometric forms alone. Had some Muslim trader given some idea or had some African architect actually visited Kilwa or another east coast town?

The atmosphere generated by these monuments must have had its origin in very different social, economic, or political conditions. It would seem that the great need for defensive planning which so dominates the Hill-Fortress at the Great Zimbabwe had disappeared forever. Had the relationship with Muslim traders improved so much that foreign traders were no longer under suspicion and had become if not actual friends at least neutral agents, and no longer potential enemies? Had the enslaving operation disappeared altogether in the west while still active in the north? Or was it that Khami and other western centres were now so far inland that no trader ever penetrated so far? Had external trade evaporated or changed to such an extent that security for the storage of trade goods was no longer required?

It seems impossible to find an answer to these questions in the present state of knowledge, but the known character of both the northern and western developments make one primary fact abundantly clear— the essential uniqueness of the Great Zimbabwe. Whatever explanation is accepted to solve the mystery of the Great Zimbabwe it has to explain the astonishing fact that nothing else like it was ever made, either in extent or character, anywhere else. It stands alone, and this loneliness can only have been the product of a one-off situation, the result of accidental circumstances that historically could not be repeated.

Hence the argument of this book.

Finale

THERE are a thousand and one other loose threads left hanging from the Great Zimbabwe story that when gathered up with far more research and study can give a fuller, richer, and more rightful place to the past of Southern Africa in world history. Stories of the High God Mwali, or Mlimo, his rites of worship at the Great Zimbabwe, and his bitter ending in the Matopo Hills; stories of the legendary founders of Malawi, the bringers of fire and flame to that country; stories of Afro-Shirazi colonisation on the coast and the Comoro Islands; stories of Persian traders or prospectors, pictured in rock paintings near the Zoutpan, fifty miles south of the Mapungubwe fortress next the Limpopo; stories of Indonesian navigation across 3,000 miles of ocean in multi-hulled catamarans of thirty tons to colonise and dominate Madagascar; stories of Sinbad and Sheherazade; a thousand and one folklore stories, keys to the unrecorded history of the East and Africa. All must wait for another time.

CONFLICT IN CHRONOLOGY

There is still the apparent conflict in chronology between the assumption of this book and the presently accepted chronology. The answer to the conflict is that different disciplines produce different results. The historical and technical approach used here produces a date sequence for the first period of A.D. 700–900 in order to correlate the building of the Great Zimbabwe

with world events, and then another period of 500 to 600 years of prosperity followed by decline and eclipse. Archaeology on the other hand produces a date sequence of 1100–1300 for the earlier period and 1300–1500 for the later period, in which it is assumed most of the walls were built. In other words, the accepted chronology places the building of the walls completely in the later Iron Age after A.D. 1000, while the story of this book places all the wall building in the early Iron Age before A.D. 1000. The conflict therefore consists solely concerning the date of origin, when the walls were built, but this conflict is more apparent than real, because archaeology in this very unusual case of the Great Zimbabwe has suffered from three major constraints.

The first is that the site of the Great Zimbabwe was ransacked thoroughly before any control was imposed upon investigators, and in this way an untold amount of evidence was permanently lost. The evidence left for archaeological analysis is thus largely accidental and dangerously limited as a base for an historical sequence.

The second constraint is the almost automatic and unquestioned assumption that walling equals settlement and therefore that the date of settlement is the date of the walls. But the walls were only walls, never dwellings, and their existence cannot pre-suppose dwellings. In the case of the Great Zimbabwe there is good reason to believe that in its origins it did not. Economic, historical, and technical considerations all strongly point to the conclusion it was originally designed as a seasonal trading depot to be fully used only for a maximum of one to two months every year. Such temporary use, without the undestructible equipment, such as pottery, of a permanent settlement, would tend by its nature to leave no trace of its transitory existence.

The third constraint is the nature of the walling itself. Built without mortar and without foundations, they could be built, unbuilt, and re-built without leaving the slightest trace of previous construction. Alterations to a wall become almost impossible to identify with certainty for the same reason. An example is the wooden lintel in a drain through the wall of the Inner Parallel Passage in the Great Enclosure. This provided the first carbon 14 date for the Great Zimbabwe, later revised to a date six to seven hundred years later. The date of the lintel has been assumed to be the date of the wall, and while there are strong reasons why this may not be so, it is impossible to obtain proof either way.* Any deductions about building sequences and dating from the character or state of the walling are very hazardous and represent only one option in a wide range of many.

The cumulative effect of all these constraints and other considerations suggested in previous chapters imposes limitations against which the historical framework constructed from archaeological data—mainly pottery sequences and some carbon 14 dates—must be assessed. The fact, for instance, that many traces of settlement appear to be much later than the story given by this book may itself be a confirmation of the story.

For it was after the decline of the Abbasid caliphate consequent upon the Zanj revolt, from A.D. 900 onwards, that there must have been a drastic lessening of demand for Zanj slaves by the Abbasid rulers for

---

*See notes to this chapter for discussion of the lintel.

the reclamation of the marshlands below Basra. This would have destroyed one of the original reasons for the existence of the Great Zimbabwe, and though trading in other goods would have continued and accommodation for traders, their escorts, and their caravan assemblies would still have been required, the frenetic demand for able-bodied adult Zanj would have disappeared.

Slowly Great Zimbabwe began to be converted to other uses, and like the common fate of most buildings the world over, it was eventually put to uses for which it was never designed. It became the settled base for a permanent society with a growing population engaged in their usual agricultural, pastoral, and, no doubt, warlike pursuits, so successfully and for so long, it is thought, that it eventually destroyed its own environment.

There may therefore be no real conflict between the dates suggested in this book and the presently accepted dates, since the two sets deal with two separate and distinct sets of events—the origins in the demands of Islam, and the later development as an African capital city. It can be added that the dates for origins suggested by Caton Thompson and Beck in 1929 and accepted by Robinson in 1958 largely agree with those suggested in this book.

The problem of constructing a chronology for any historical period without written records of any kind can only be solved by combining and balancing, one against the other, all the factors that make history. Economic, social, political, religious, technical, and other aspects, with their changes over time, must also be included if the result is to make historical sense. Archaeology, within the self-imposed limits of its own discipline, is the best equipped of all disciplines to start the historical ball rolling: but by its nature it cannot finish the picture. That can only come by taking its findings and matching and adjusting them to the findings of all the other disciplines. Multi-disciplinary work of this nature is always difficult and generally slow, but without it the full thousand-year saga of the Great Zimbabwe will never be fully or truthfully known.

ONE LAST LOOSE THREAD

One last subject needs mentioning to give a clear finish to the present story. The fact that the builders of the Great Zimbabwe might have been involved in an enslaving operation may appear an insult to those faraway founders of the state.

The reverse, however, is much nearer the truth. The indigenous African serfdom from which came the external trade in manpower that caused the Zanj revolt was a form of social adjustment to internal tensions that could only be resolved in this way—by enforced labour for payment of some kind of social debt or crime. The fact that the forces of external trade and overseas demand turned this domestic serfdom into chattel slavery was no fault of Africa: it was her misfortune that world forces happened to impinge on her at this moment of her history, forces against which she had no defence of any depth.

She had no defence because just as her internal serfdom was a necessary condition of her own internal survival, so was the external chattel slavery necessary to the world of that age for its survival. The system of growing urban life and culture and the parallel extension of agricultural production to keep the cities going demanded large amounts of additional manpower. This had to be obtained somewhere and the newly discovered resources of Africa provided an easy answer. It was an easy answer because to that world slavery was a fate, not a stigma. It was a misfortune similar to proverty, and poverty was considered the greater misfortune, whereas slavery was accepted as inevitable, even natural. It was only the growing productivity of the early

Industrial Revolution in Western Europe that made slavery in the west obsolete and therefore increasingly obnoxious. Till then, like smallpox or any other endemic disease, it was merely part of life to be accepted as the will of God.

In this light, so far from being an insult to the memory of those faraway founders, the story of the Great Zimbabwe and of those untold thousands who passed through its walls is a story of the greatest courage and resolution in a major crisis, a crisis played out in a foreign hell, thousands of miles from home at the other end of the world. The story of the first black republic is the story of the Great Zimbabwe uprooted, exiled, lost: but still firmly African, independent, and undefeated in spirit till the end. It is worth remembering that had the Great Zimbabwe never been built the first black republic would never have occurred, to leave its permanent mark on history and bring to an inglorious end the golden age of Islam.

A RETROSPECT

The story of the Great Zimbabwe becomes in retrospect the story of that forgotten segment of humanity, the ordinary person, the common man. It was not built by a highly limited elite aristocracy floating like cream on the top of a vast labouring mass; it was not planned to represent a cosmic picture of the universe with some god-king at the centre ruling all; it produced no architectural masterpieces, no Angkor Vat, no Borobudur, no Versailles, no Saint Peter's, no Peking Summer Palace. It was built only by simple, straightforward people for simple, straightforward purposes, with no thought of egocentric gradeur, no megalomanic desire for celestial glory; and so it had no Babylonian towers to challenge God.

It remains impressive because it is in this

way unique in the world, wholly functional, wholly direct, wholly devoid of deliberate personal expression. It is this starkness that gives it a monumentality that is of the spirit even more than of the eye. For it combines with this monumental quality a queer humility. It accepts with ease, even gratitude, the far greater monumentality of nature; and the towering rocks that guard the innermost heart of the Hill-Fortress from one of the most impressive compositions in all southern Africa.

The greatness of the Great Zimbabwe is the greatness of omission. There are only the rocks, the sunlight, the shadow, and the walls: nothing else; and yet the effect is overpowering. There is no victory over nature, only an acceptance: a fundamental simplicity of purpose, an absolute directness of intention. It is a plain statement of the human spirit, naked and unashamed; and by that very virtue of stark asceticism it will always survive as the greatest of monuments to its builders.

Appendix

Since the text was completed, a metallic object has come to light that was found by H. H. McNeil in the Great Zimbabwe ruins in 1914—almost certainly on the Hill-Fortress, but where exactly is not on record. Plate 29 shows it full-size: cylindrical in shape tapering to a rough cone at one end, with a diameter of 85 mm. (3½"), a height of 170 mm. (6⅔") and a weight of 3.5 kg. (7¼ lbs). It is now in the possession of Hugh A. McNeil of Johannesburg.

It has been analysed in detail by Dr. A. Koursaris of the Department of Metallurgy of the University of the Witwatersrand, who concluded that the artifact is made of almost pure zinc and that it appears that the manufacturing process involved reduction of zinc oxide and consolidation of small particles of zinc.

Pure zinc does not occur in nature and can only be obtained by gasifying one of the zinc ores and then condensing the gases in a separate container. This process was unknown in the West till the eighteenth century A.D., for Roman and medieval brass was made by liquifying a zinc ore with metallic copper, not by first obtaining pure zinc. But the process of obtaining pure zinc was known in China by the ninth century A.D. and had probably filtered through to India and the Middle East in the succeeding centuries. Marco Polo in about 1272 describes a process of gases solidifying on iron bars set close together above a furnace to produce "tutty", which was almost certainly zinc, at the town of Cobiam (the present Shah-Dad) in eastern Persia. Cobiam lies in a metalliferous area and on the route from Hormuz, in the Persian Gulf, to the Central Asian silk route to China; knowledge of the process may have come by that route. The Persian product was exported to India for a constituent of ointments and possibly re-exported through the Cambay Gulf ports.

Mardo Polo's description of the manufacturing process agrees with the composition of this metallic object—formed "by the consolidation

PLATE 29. Metallic object found at the Great Zimbabwe in 1914 (*Photo by City-Lab [Pty.] Ltd, Johannesburg*)

of small particles". The possibility of a Persian origin is supported by the undoubted portrayal of four Persian traders in a cave painting in the western end of the Soutpansberg Mountains, 230 miles southwest from the Great Zimbabwe. Their beards, their headgear (three with the pointed Persian caps, the fourth with the aristocratic gathered headdress), their baggy trousers, and the cummerbund or girdle, all proclaim them unmistakably Persian. One further detail may be even more significant: at least two of the figures, including the aristocrat, are shown with a single strand of hair hanging down from the neck. This could be the *kakul*, the long lock worn by every good Moslem to enable the prophet Mahomet to draw up the true believer into Paradise after death. If this interpretation is correct, these Persian figures are Mawali, Persian converts to Islam: precisely the class that run the Abbasid Civil Service and could have been the landowners running the date palm and sugar cane plantations below Basra.

The procession is shown presenting a goat— no doubt to the local chief of the Salt Pan, an important trading centre, nearby. This Salt Pan lies on a direct line from the Great Zimbabwe—230 miles away to the northeast—to the prehistoric Rooiberg tin mines, 170 miles further to the southwest. The well-known Lundi ruins, 60 miles from the Great Zimbabwe, the prehistoric copper mines at Messina, two groups of ruins (the Machemma and the Verdun) between Messina and the Salt Pan, and a little-known group of ruins 40 miles from Rooiberg, all lie on the same, almost straight, line. Was this an ancient trade route to get tin and copper, and did Persian traders pioneer and develop it? The network of trading contacts that supported and was controlled by the Great Zimbabwe may have been much wider than has been assumed, and needs much greater investigation.

Certainly that lump of zinc must have come with some trader from the East, to be abandoned as useless by either the trader or his local customer. The extraordinary thing is that it ever arrived at the Great Zimbabwe at all: somebody had made a very great miscalculation of trading opportunities, for in the correct market that lump of scarce metal must have had considerable value. It could be that the trader concerned was, in fact, an inexperienced pioneer, and that he paid a heavy price for his inexperience.

Notes to the Appendix

BOSHIER, A. & BEAMONT, P. (1972) "Mining in Southern Africa and the Emergence of Modern Man". *Optima.* 22, no. 1 (March): 2–17 (for the cave painting near the Salt Pan).

FORBES, R. J. (1950) *Metallurgy in Antiquity.* Leiden. Pp. 274–84.

KOURSARIS, A. (1982) "Examination of an Artifact from Zimbabwe Ruins". Unpublished. Johannesburg.

MARCO POLO (1908) *The Travels of Marco Polo the Venetian.* (Everyman Ed.) London. Chap. 20, p. 71.

MORGAN, S.W.K. (1973) Article "Zinc" in *Encyclopedia Britannica*, vol. 23, p. 968.

NEEDHAM, J. S. et al. (1945–80) *History of Science and Technology in China.* Cambridge. 5 vols. Vol. 5, pt. 2, p. 214.

Notes

These notes give the chief sources used for each chapter, but they also include any comments on specific items considered too detailed to merit inclusion in the main text. It is hoped these references will assist any who wish to pursue or evaluate any of the arguments in the text. The full list of all sources used, however slightly, follows the notes.

In general, sources have been taken at their face value. The objective was not to assess or add to the sources but to make some connected sense out of the mass of material that was found to be available: in short, to construct an overview. It is very obvious that much more study is needed to give any such overview the sharp focus it needs if the real history of the Great Zimbabwe is ever to be known in full.

Prologue

The quotation at the head of the Prologue is from *Africa Awake* by W.E.B. Du Bois (1958), quoted in *W.E.B. Du Bois Speaks*, ed. P. S. Foner (New York, 1970), in turn quoted by L. D. Hutchinson in *Out of Africa* (Washington, D.C., 1979).

The analysis of Africa is largely personal, based on general reading on African development, started while working with Dr. L. P. Green and Professor T.J.D. Fair on their book *Development in Africa* (1962). Other sources were E. W. Fitzgerald (1950), L. D. Stamp (1953), G. P. Murdock (1959), and A. T. Grove (1967).

Indian Ocean: A. Toussaint (1961) and A. J. Villiers (1952). The note about the spider is from a recent press report (1980).

Chapter 1

Quotation from Edward Thomas: from "The Pilgrim's Way", published in a collection of English essays. London, n.d.

Stone ruins in Zimbabwe: from the official list of the National Monuments Commission, Bulawayo, given through the kindness of the

director of the commission, Mr. C. R. Cooke.

Other ruins: from published work—J. Walton (1956), R. J. Mason (1962 and 1973*b*), T. M. O'C Maggs (1976), R. Summers (1971).

Ruins in Botswana: personal communication from Dr. A. C. Campbell, director, the National Museum, Gaberone, Botswana, whose help is gratefully acknowledged.

European megalithic: G. Daniel (1963) and F. Niel (1961).

Rock shelter at Makwe: D. W. Phillipson (1976).

Inyanga terraces: R. Summers (1958), P. S. Garlake (1966 and 1973).

Telford Edwards: quotation from R. N. Hall and W. G. Neal (1904).

The BaVenda: H. A. Stayt (1931*a* and 1931*b*), N. J. Van Warmelo (1940), Van Warmelo and W.W.D. Phophi (1948), G. P. Lestrade (1927).

Chapter 2

Quotation from Sir Thomas Browne: from "Urn Burial".

Description of ruins: primarily from personal observation, supported by all main sources—K. Mauch (1969 and 1971), J. T. Bent (1902), J. C. Willoughby (1893), R. N. Hall (1907), D. Randall-MacIver (1906), G. Caton Thompson (1971), R. Summers et al. (1961), R. Summers (1971), P. S. Garlake (1973).

Base map: Surveyor General, 1:5,000-scale series, sheets TN 8056, 8058, 8456, 8458.

Time to build the Great Wall: A. R. Willcox (1976).

Belief in a square earth and circular heaven: Aristotle's *Physics*, summarised by T. V. Smith, ed. (1956). This idea goes back to Babylonian concepts: see "Some Cosmological Patterns in Babylonian Religion" by E. Burrows, in *The Labyrinth*, ed. S. H. Hooke (London, 1935), pp. 45–70. The same concept of a circular heaven and a square earth was current in China: see J. Needham, *Science and Civilisation in China* (Cambridge, 1962), vol. 4, p. 262.

Chapter 3

Quotation from Sir Thomas Browne: from "Urn Burial".

Much of this chapter is from personal observation, and from the sources given for Chapter 2.

Variations in masonry technique: R. Summers et al. (1961).

Timber lintels: it seems uncertain whether the stone lintels to the central entrance of the West Wall of the Hill-Fortress were original or part of the rebuilding of that portion of the wall sometime after 1915.

BaVenda bowls: H. A. Stayt (1931*a*), G. Caton Thompson (1971).

Wooden buffalo: information by courtesy of Dr. A. C. Campbell.

Stone wild hog: H. Deschamps (1972).

Barros: quoted by E. Axelson (1973).

Stone door: R. N. Hall and W. G. Neal (1904), H. Deschamps (1972), M. Brown (1978).

Chapter 4

Quotation: from G. Kay (1970).

Generally: G. Kay (1970). Data also derived from professional work with Professor T.J.D. Fair at Bulawayo, 1972–74, and at Harare (formerly Salisbury), 1969–74.

Hematite mine in Swaziland: A. Boshier and P. Beaumont (1972).

Specularite mine in Botswana: personal visit, and data from Dr. A. C. Campbell.

Gold mining: R. Summers (1969).

Tsetse: J. Ford (1971) and R. Summers (1969).

Herodotus. Book III, chap. 102. (Everyman Ed.), vol. 1, pp. 259–60.

Strabo. Book 15, chap. 1, sect. 44.

Termite ant as indicator (in use today): *Signature,* the journal of Diners Club International (1975); as a colony, E. N. Marais (1970).

San and Khoikhoi: M. Wilson and L. Thompson (1960).

Hottentot tales: W.H.I. Bleek (1864). The "great basket" could of course be the folk-memory of a sewn boat.

Skeletal remains: R. Summers (1969).

The Periplus: W. H. Schoff (1912), J. W. McCrindle (1882), G. Mathew (1975).

Masudi: trans. C. B. de Maynard and P. de Courteille (1861–73); quotation from B. Davidson (1964).

Buzurg: G. F. Hourani (1951).

Idrisi: al-Sharif al-Idrisi (1960).

Marco Polo: The Travels of Marco Polo the Venetian (1908).

Duarte Barbosa: quoted by B. Davidson (1964).

Mauch: C. Mauch (1969 and 1971).

Selous: F. C. Selous (1893 and 1899).

Chapter 5

Quotation from J. J. Thomson: source unknown.

Other quotations: from B. G. Paver (1950) and *New English Bible* (1970).

Solomon and Sheba background: J. B. Pritchard (1974).

"A land shut in by walls": Calcoen (1874).

All other sources: as listed in notes for Chapter 2; also J. E. Mullan (n.d.), J. E. Van Oordt (1907 and 1909), H. K. Silberberg (1978).

For Sabaean theory: R. Gayre of Gayre (1973).

Chapter 6

Quotation from Sir Thomas Browne: from "Urn Burial".

General economic background: R. Gray and D. Birmingham, eds. (1970)—particularly Chapter 1 (by the editors) and Chapter 2 (by B. M. Fagan); also B. M. Fagan (1965).

Gold mining: R. Summers (1969).

African settlement patterns: J. Walton (1956), E.W.N. Mallows (1963), R. J. Mason (1968 and 1973*b*), T. M. O'C Maggs (1976).

Inward-turning entrances in pre-historic forts: two well-documented examples are The Wrekin and the fort at Old Oswestry, in the U.K. In both cases (in frontier country, near the Welsh border) the main ramparts turn inwards at the main entrance, but they are heavily defended externally by a series of ditches and ramparts hindering access to the main wall itself (personal communication, by courtesy of Mr. Michael Law, county planning officer, Salop, whose help is most gratefully acknowledged). No such external defences of any kind protect the Great Wall of the Great Enclosure.

The height of the Great Wall: twenty-one measurements taken from Hall's external measurements (owing to uncertainty of internal ground surfaces).

The average of these was $\dfrac{473'8''}{21} = 22'6''$ (D. N. Hall, 1907).

The height of the prison walls: the nine walls are:

1. Horsham	U.K.	19'7"	
2. Norfolk	U.S.	22'7'	
3. Everthorpe	U.K.	18'2"	
4. Wandsworth	U.K.	19'0"	(press cutting)
5. Low Norton	U.K.	17'0"	

6. Channing-wood	U.K.	17'0"	
7. Ringe	Denmark	16'5"	(press cutting)
8. Proposed (1975)	?	19'0"	
9. Proposed (1976)	?	16'5"	
Average of nine		$\frac{165'2''}{9} = 18'4''$	

Source: L. Fairweather (1975).

Chief Umgabe's followers' opinion: R. N. Hall (1907).

African slavery: E. Berlioux (1872), A.J.H. Goodwin (1927), M. Meltzer (1972), E. A. Alpers (1975), R. W. Beachy (1976), S. Miers, I. Kopytoff (1977).

The Vaddas: J. M. Maclaren (1907) *Vaddas* (1907), J. Wiles (1974).

Indian building technique (corbelled arch, etc.): Sir Banister Fletcher (1961), P. Brown (1956).

Angkor Vat: G. Coedes (1963).

Borobudur: F. Grenade (1978).

Teak lintels in Indian and Persian buildings: Encyclopedia Britannica (1910)—art, teak, vol. 26/484, no. 1.

Vijayanagar Empire: R. Sewell (1900).

Temple at Madura: S. Lewandowski (1980).

Round-ended buttresses in Indian forts and Indian strongholds generally: S. Toy (1957 and 1965).

Classical slavery: W. L. Westermann (1955).

Realgar mines: Strabo. Book 12, chap. 3, sect. 40, p. 451.

West African mines: E. W. Bovill (1968), R. Mauny (1961).

Rhodesian Ridgeback: T. C. Hawley (1957).

Note: W. Phillips (1967), citing R. Reusch's *History of East Africa* (Stuttgart, 1954) states that Suleiman and Said (of the Azd tribe from Oman), who settled in East Africa about A.D. 700, became "the first slave-hunters on a large scale". This would agree approximately with the probable start of the slave trading at the Great Zimbabwe, and might have been due to the same demand for slave labour in Mesopotamia.

Chapter 7

Quotation: from E. H. Palmer's translation.

Climate and navigation: U.K. hydrographer to the Navy (1961, 1967, 1967a, 1967b, 1971, 1973).

Northward sailing in Moçambique (Maputo) Channel: R. Summers (1969).

Indian Ocean: A. Toussaint (1961), A. J. Villiers (1952).

Earliest sail: V. G. Childe (n.d.).

Boats, A.D. 1950: W. Thesiger (1967).

Ship-building tools: A. J. Villiers (1969).

Sewn boats: Tim Severin has built such a boat and sailed her successfully from Arabia to Canton, on Sinbad's legendary route. See T. Severin (1982).

Pacific sewn boats: D. Lewis (1972).

Typology of the sail and the ship: J. Poujade (1946), J. Hornell (1946), M. Kaplan (1974).

Orang-Laut: D. E. Sopher (1965). This thesis is important for the Indonesian maritime background.

Indian and Arab navigation: J. Hornell (1946), G. Ferrand (1921–28), J. Prinsep (1836), G. F. Hourani (1951), W. Tomascheck and M. Bittner (1897), G. R. Tibbets (1971).

Polynesian navigation: D. Lewis (1972 and 1978).

River travel: F. Balsan (1970).

Marhumbini dock: R. Summers (1969).

Mud-dock: G. Ferrand (1921–28).

One reason why river travel would have been preferred by any visiting foreigner was that there were no made roads in Southern Africa, only single-file tracks. This compares sharply with the 10,000 miles or so of roads, many of them stone-paved, built by the Incas in South America; a reminder of Africa's much simpler technology and much less developed political systems (V. W. Von Hagen[1957]).

Geographical background: India—O.H.K. Spate et al. (1967); Middle East—P. Beaumont et al. (1976).

Indian history and background: R. Thapar (1966), E. Thurston (1966 and 1909), B. Allchin and R. Allchin (1968), A. L. Basham (1967), *Cambridge History of India* (1922–1953), R. H. Major (1857), D. N. Majumdar (1961), L. Mouton (1970), M.S.P. Pillai (1963), V. K. Pillai (1904), K.A.N. Sastri (1966), V. A. Smith (1924), M. Wheeler (1954 and 1966).

H. Brownrigg (1982) makes clear the age-old passion of Hindu India—that is, South India—for hoarding gold. Pliny the Elder, in the first century A.D., Francois Bernier in the seventeenth century and J. M. Keynes in this century all emphasize this characteristic. It made South India an almost inexhaustible market for the metal.

Dock at Lothal: Indian Archaeology—A Review (1954–1960), S. R. Rao (1969), B. Allchin and R. Allchin (1968), M. Wheeler (1966).

Seagoing merchants at Ur: R. L. Oppenheim (1954).

Bahrein: G. Bibby (1972).

Docks at Ur: L. Wooley (1954), W. J. Elliot and T. G. Elliot (1950).

Phoenicians: D. Harden (1971), G. Contenau (1949).

Post-Alexander period: W. W. Tarn (1938), W. W. Tarn and G. T. Griffiths (1952), E. Bevan (1927—for elephant training).

Indian place names: J. W. McCrindle (1882; A. Toussaint (1974); U. K. Hydrographer of the Navy (1967), charts 81 and 138; and W. Tomaschek (1897).

Meroe: P. L. Shinnie (1967), A. J. Arkell (1951, 1961, and 1966).

The Axumite power: R. Oliver and B. M. Fagan (1975). The story of Axumites exploring the East African coast comes from Cosmas Indicopleustes, who was at the Axumite port of Adulis at the time of the Axumite invasion and conquest of Yemen. He therefore had good opportunities to know about any exploration down the east coast of Africa.

The Axumites built without mortar and had no knowledge of arches or domes, both Indian characteristics. This suggests that although they were in touch with the Byzantine Empire, technically the Indian and not the Byzantine influence was dominant. The great Axum monolith, seventy feet high, was described by Ferguson as an Indian temple converted into a monolith: a series of identical, but diminishing, façades superimposed on one another.

The hypothesis that Azania is connected with Ezana conflicts with the mention of Azania in the Periplus, but the date of the Periplus is not absolutely certain and it could have been, like Ptolemy's *Geography*, a compilation over a period. The name Ezana could also have been a dynastic name, or the name of a previous unrecorded king.

Kwale and Pare: R. Oliver and B. M. Fagan (1975), U. K. Hydrographer of the Navy (1967).

Mascarene Islands: A. Toussaint (1961 and 1974—latter for Cantino map, 1502), M. Lombard (1975—for map of Indian Ocean).

India and the East: H. G. Quaritch-Wales (1961), D.G.E. Hall (1968), O. W. Wolters (1967).

The Qur'an: trans. E. H. Palmer (London, 1928).

Islam in general: P. M. Holt et al., eds. (1970), T. W. Arnold (1913), M. A. Shaban (1970 and 1971).

Economic background: M. Lombard (1975).

Geographical background: P. Beaumont et al. (1976).

Persia and Sassanids: A. Christiansen (1944), E. G. Browne (1929, vol. 1).

The caliphate: M. J. De Goeje (1910a and 1910b), G. Le Strange (1905 and 1924).

Persian navigation: H. Hasan (1928).

East African Coast: L. M. Devic (1975), G.S.P. Freeman-Grenville (1962), R. Coupland (1938).

African slavery: as noted for Chapter 6.

Classical slavery: W. L. Westermann (1942 and 1955).

Oriental despotism: K. A. Wittfogel (1957). The story of the Indian Zotts or Jats eventually becoming the *tsiganes*, or gypsies, of Europe is an extraordinary story that has to be pieced together from many sources—Indian, Persian, Arabian; but it has been known since the end of the eighteenth century that the base of the gypsy language was Indian.

The story of the Zanj revolt is based almost completely on T. Noldecke (1963). A. Masudi (1861–77), available in French, also deals with it, but modern histories give no more than a passing reference. The most detailed modern outline of the background to the revolt is in four long notes (nos. 3, 4, 5, and 6) to the article "The Arab Geographers and the East African Coast" by J. S. Trimingham, in H. N. Chittick and R. I. Rotberg (1975), pp. 115–46.

The area irrigated during Abbasid times, and the heartland of the revolt: G. M. Lees and N. L. Falcon (1952), with air photos and map.

For the general economic background of Islam in the Middle East see M. Lombard (1975). Lombard also makes clear that the Iraq marshes and the Khuzestan lowlands were the dominant slave markets of the Middle East, while the *Cambridge History of Iran* (vol. 4, ed. R. N. Frye, 1975) points out that these large private estates or *latifundia* were quite exceptional.

Chapter 8

Quotation from the Chronicle of Kilwas: from G.S.P. Freeman-Grenville (1962), p. 35.

Trans-Saharan slave traffic: E. W. Bovill (1969), R. Mauny (1961).

Barracoon warehouses: R. W. Beachy (1976), p. 14 (quoting W.F.W. Owen [1833, p. 296]), p. 18 (at Quelimane in 1843), p. 19 ("barracoons, large sheds encompassed by a stake kraal, capable of holding 4,000–5,000 slaves" [Angoche area]), p. 32, p. 35, p. 54, p. 59. For an opinion that *all* the Zimbabwe stone ruins were virtually barracoons for either gold-mine labour or holding areas for ivory porters or slaves en route to the coast, see A. T. Bryant (1965), chap. 16, particularly pp. 313–15.

General Rigby's report (on slave assembly points in the interior): C.E.B. Russell (1935).

Estimate of ten cubic feet equals one man-day of labour: A. R. Willcox (1976). As this author is an experienced professional quantity surveyor, his estimate must be respected.

Capacity of dhows: G. F. Hourani (1951), p. 82 (quoting Buzurg). Alan Villiers estimated the capacity of the *Triumph of Righteousness* was not far short of 200. The sketch section of a slaving dhow showing the three crowded slave decks in C.G.L. Sulivan (1873) suggests the same.

Saivism: P. Banerjee (1973), R. C. Majumdar and A. D. Pulsalker (1953–54), vol. 2, pp. 459–61.

Indian wootz steel: P. Neoghi (1914).

Ivory storage: the existence of a buttress controlling the east end of the "sunken passage" is queer. It suggests the passage might also have been used as manpower storage, as a holding place for prisoners brought to the king's court for judgment.

Sakalava legend: R. K. Kent (1970).

Zodiacal bowl: for Mithraism, F. Cumont (1903 and 1956). Mithraism spread very widely—in Britain as well as South India.

The lizard-bird combination and Sepik River culture: J. Guiart (1963 and 1968).

Melanesians: B. Malinowski (1922), R. H. Codrington (1891), C. G. Seligman (1910), W. H. R. Rivers (1914). The old Malgache word *lakato*, meaning "true outrigger people" (R. K. Kent [1970], p. 263), would seem to have, without doubt, a direct connection with *laka-toi*, the multi-hulled catamaran of the Motu in Southeast New Guinea. In Motu *laka* means canoe with its sides heightened by planks; *toi* means three, originally, presumably, a triple-hulled catamaran. In Antalote, the dialect spoken in the Comoros in 1870, *laka* also meant "canoe": see A. Gevrey (1870), p. 113.

Polynesian navigation: D. Lewis (1972 and 1978). There can be little doubt that Madagascar and, probably before Madagascar, East Africa, were invaded and settled by Indonesians of many different origins, at many different times, for short or long periods: Maanjan of Borneo, Bugis from the Celebes, and other island inhabitants as far east as New Guinea or Melanesia.

It is surprising how little attention has, as yet, been given to the question of Indonesian settlement in East Africa, in view of arguments as set forth by R. K. Kent (1973). A reasoned criticism of Kent's argument is given by Adrian Southall in his "The Problem of Malagasy Origins" (in H. N. Chittick and R. I. Rotberg [1975], pp. 214–15). Southall suggests African settlement was after, not before, settlement on Madagascar, but a glance at any map of the Indian Ocean, with its currents, suggests at once the final land fall must have been the east coast of Africa, since the most southerly likely starting point for any westerly voyage from Indonesia—the Sunda Strait—would take any ship (using the south equatorial current, and sailing on the Sunda Strait latitude of 6° S.) direct to Zanzibar. This is 5°, or 300 nautical miles, north of the most northerly point of the Comoro Islands or Madagascar. It is, therefore, on technical navigational grounds, in the highest degree improbable any ship from Indonesia would hit Madagascar before Africa. The settlement on Africa first is far more probable. Where, and for how long, needs further study.

Ambohimanga stone door: H. Deschamps (1972), p. 113; M. Brown (1978).

Fernandes and Camanhaia: E. Axelson (1973); reassessment, R. W. Dickenson (1971).

Great Zimbabwe chronology: T. N. Huffman (1972), P. S. Garlake (1970).

The dating of the drain lintel: This was originally dated by carbon 14 methods to between A.D. 598 and A.D. 700 and then, much later, revised to about A.D. 1350—an enormous change in interpretation, which hardly increases one's respect for this particular scientific method. But much more important is the unreliability of the assumption that the date of the lintel is the date of the wall—that is, that the wooden lintels (there were two) were built into the wall when the wall was first built.

But the published evidence suggests the contrary. The cross-section of the wall and drain showing the two lintels in place (R. Summers [1955]) suggests strongly, by the relative positions of the stones, that this (western) portion of the wall over the drain had collapsed and the two lintels had been inserted to repair the collapsed portion. Otherwise, why were not wooden lintels used throughout the whole length of this drain? The eastern portion of the drain appears in good condition, covered, as other drains elsewhere, with stone lintels. The change in material from stone to wood argues another set of builders and another time.

The use of tambuti *(Spirostachys africanus)*, however, gives another twist to the puzzle: it suggests foreign builders. Today, at least, all

African blacks have a fear amounting almost to a taboo for this wood and would in normal circumstances never touch it. Its milky latex is used to poison fish and arrowheads; if used as fuel its smell causes vomiting and its smoke taints all food (K. C. Palgrave et al. [1977]). It must have been an emergency if African blacks used it, or were made to use it, which adds to the likelihood of foreign direction, and the possibility of a wall collapse that needed immediate action.

In short, the details of these two lintels illustrate the difficulties, if not the impossibility, of dating any of the walls precisely by such a method. The date of the wooden lintel remains the date of the wooden lintel and very little else, except that at some unspecified time someone—probably not African—used it to repair the wall.

Dates of origin suggested originally by Caton Thompson and Beck: Caton Thompson (1971), pp. 188–89—Beck (in Appendix), p. 237—"A Foundation date of the 8th to 9th Century . . . fits in well with the historical record".

*Medieval slave trade (post-*A.D. *1000) in East Africa:* R. W. Beachey (1976), Chapter 1. As Beachey says, a "blanket of silence" has fallen on the slave trade on the East African coast. But what evidence there is suggests it was continuous, and Beachey, quoting Barros, thinks it probably increased with the coming of Islam. Three stories suggest continuity. The *first* is that of the Chinese traveller, Cheng-Shih, who died in 863: "They [almost certainly, from the habits described, the Masai] kidnap their women and sell them to strangers at prices many times more than they would fetch at home. The Arabs are continually making raids on them". The *second*, already quoted, is of one Al Ismailiyah at Sofala, who with 200 slaves already on board kidnapped the local king and his courtiers and sold them all at Oman. This was in 923. Four hundred years later the most celebrated Arab traveller of all time, Ibn Batuta, repeats much the same story of Kilwa. "The people are engaged in a holy war for their country lies beside that of the pagan Zanj. . . . The Sultan frequently makes raids into the Zanj country, attacks them and carries off booty, of which he retains a fifth". The booty in that African hinterland can only have been ivory and slaves and—significantly—the Zanj are labelled pagan (and therefore available for slavery) and there is no talk of conversion to Islam.

A further, and significant, indicator of the permanence of the slave trade is the stability of the price. Buzurg in 933 gives an estimate of twenty-three to thirty dinars for an adult male; Ibn Batuta paid twenty-five dinars (considered excessive) for an educated female in West Africa in 1353; Leo Africanus twenty dinars for a male slave in Morocco in about 1512; and Willis, a British traveller to Persian in 1880, said a "Bombasi [presumably from Mombasa] chosen merely for physical strength" could be bought for fourteen pounds (twenty-eight dinars, say, at 1900 values). All these are astonishingly stable prices over immense periods of time, and argue strongly for the stability of both supply and demand, and the regularity of the trade.

References

ABRAHAM, D. P. (1959) "The Monomotapa Dynasty". *Native Affairs Department Annual* 36: 58–84.

ABRAHAM, D. P. (1962) "The Early Political History of the Kingdom of Mwene Mutapa, 850–1589". In "Historians in Tropical Africa". Proceedings Leverhulme Inter-collegiate History Conference September 1960. Salisbury.

ALLCHIN, B. & ALLCHIN, R. (1968) *The Birth of Indian Civilisation.* Harmondsworth.

ALPERS, E. A. (1970) "Dynasties of the Mutapa-Rozwi Complex". *Journal of African History* 11(2): 203–20.

ALPERS, E. A. (1975) *Ivory and Slaves in East Central Africa.* London.

ARKELL, A. J. (1951) "Meroe and India". In *Aspects of Archaeology in Britain and Beyond,* ed. W. F. Grimes. London.

ARKELL, A. J. (1961) (2nd Ed.) *A History of the Sudan to 821.* London.

ARKELL, A. J. (1966) "The Iron Age in the Sudan." *Current Anthropology* 7(4): 468–81. (Reprinted in Z. A. Koczacki and J. M. Koczacki [1977]).

ARNOLD, T. W. (1913) *The Preaching of Islam.* Lahore.

ATKINSON, T.J.C. (1960) *Stonehenge.* Harmondsworth.

AXELSON, E. (1960) *Portuguese in South East Africa, 1600–1700.* Johannesburg.

AXELSON, E. (1973) *Portuguese in South East Africa, 1488–1600.* Johannesburg.

BAINES, T. (1877) *The Gold Regions of South Eastern Africa.* London.

BALADHURI, AL- (1924) *The Origins of the Islamic State.* Part II. Trans. F. C. Murgotten. New York.

BALANDIER, G. (1969) *Ambiguous Africa: Cultures in Collision.* New York.

BALSAN, F. (1970) "Ancient Gold Routes of the Monomatapa Kingdom". *The Geographical Journal* 136(2): 240–46.

BANERJEE, P. (1973) *Early Indian Religions.* Delhi.

BANISTER-FLETCHER, SIR (1969) (17th Ed.) *A History of Architecture on the Comparative Method.* London.

BARBOUR, K. M. (1973) "The Geographic Knowledge of the Medieval Islamic World". Department of Geography, University College of London. Occasional Paper 22.

BARNES, A. C. (1974) *The Sugar Cane.* Aylesbury.

BARTHOLOMEW, J. (1973a) World Travel Map: Indian Subcontinent. Scale 1:4,000,000. Edinburgh.

BARTHOLOMEW, J. (1973b) World Travel Map: Middle East. Scale: 1:4,000,000. Edinburgh.

BARTHOLOMEW, J. (1975) World Travel May: Africa, Central and Southern. Scale: 1:5,000,000. Edinburgh.

BASCH, L. (1969) "Phoenician Oared Ships". *Mariner's Mirror* 55 (2): 139–62 and (3): 227–45.

BASHAM, A. L. (1967) (3rd Ed.) *The Wonder That was India.* London.

BATES, M. (1963) *African One-Party States.* Ithaca.

BAUMANN, H. & WESTERMANN, D. (1962) *Les Peuples et les Civilisations de l'Afrique suivi de les langues et l'éducation.* Trans. L. Homburger. Paris.

BEACH, D. N. (1980) *The Shona and Zimbabwe, 900–1850: An Outline of Shona History.* Gwelo.

BEACHEY, R. W. (1976) *The Slave Trade of Eastern Africa.* London.

BEAUMONT, P., BLAKE, G. H., & WAGSTAFF, J. M. (1976) *The Middle East: A Geographical Study.* London.

BECK, H. (1971) "Rhodesian Beads". Appendix 1 in G. Caton Thompson (1971), pp. 229–43.

BELGRAVE, C. (1972) *The Pirate Coast.* Beirut.

BENT, J. T. (1902) (3rd Ed.) *The Ruined Cit-*

ies of Mashonaland: Being a Record of Excavation and Exploration in 1891. London.

BERLIOUX, E. F. (1872) *The Slave Trade in Africa in 1872*. London.

BEVAN, E. (1927) *A History of Egypt under the Ptolemaic Dynasty*. London.

BHATTACHARYA, S. (1967) *A Dictionary of Indian History*. Calcutta.

BIBBY, G. (1972) *Looking for Dilmun*. Harmondsworth.

BIBLE, THE (1970) *The New English Bible*. Oxford and Cambridge.

BLEEK, W.H.I. (1864) *Reynard the Fox in South Africa, or Hottentot Fables and Tales*. London.

BLOOMHILL, G. (1962) *Witchcraft in Africa*. Cape Town.

BOSHIER, A. & BEAUMONT, P. (1972) "Mining in Southern Africa and the Emergence of Modern Man". *Optima* 22(1) (March): 2–17.

BOTTING, D. (1958) "The Oxford University Expedition to Socotra". *The Geographical Journal* 124(2): 200–9.

BOVILL, E. W. (1969) (2nd Ed.) *The Golden Trade of the Moors*. London.

BOXHALL, P. G. (1966) "Socotra: 'Island of Bliss'. *The Geographical Journal* 130(2): 213–24.

BOYLE, V. C. (1940) "Boat-building on the Euphrates". *Mariner's Mirror* 26: 216–17.

BREUTZ, P. L. (1959) *The Tribes of the Vryburg District*. Pretoria. (Ethnological Publications 46.)

BREUTZ, P. L. (1968) *The Tribes of the Districts of Taung and Herbert*. Pretoria. (Ethnological Publications 51.)

BRIGGS, M. (1937) "Muslim Architecture in India". In *The Legacy of India*, ed. G. T. Carratt, pp. 223–55. Oxford.

BROHIER, R. L. & PAULUSZ, J.H.O. (1950) *Land Maps and Surveys: A Review of the Evidence of Land Surveying As Practised in Ceylon from Earliest Known Periods and the Story of the Ceylon Survey Department from 1800 to 1950*. Columbo. (Vol. 2, Descriptive Catalogue of Historical Maps in the Surveyor General's office, Columbo.)

BROWN, M. (1978) *Madagascar Rediscovered*. London.

BROWN, P. (1956) *Indian Architecture* (Buddhist and Hindu periods). Bombay.

BROWNE, E. G. (1929) *A Literary History of Persia*. 4 vols. Cambridge.

BROWNRIGG, H. (1982) "The Place of Gold in Indian Society" *Optima*, 31(1) (October), pp. 18–29.

BRYANT, A. T. (1965) *Bantu Origins: The People and Their Language*. Cape Town.

BULLOCK, C. (1927) *The Mashona*. Johannesburg.

BULLOCK, C. (1950) *The Mashona and Matabele*. Cape Town.

CAMBRIDGE HISTORY OF AFRICA (1977 and on) 8 vols. Cambridge.

Cambridge History of India (1922–1953) 6 vols. Cambridge.

Cambridge History of Iran (1968 and on) 8 vols. Cambridge.

Cambridge History of Islam (1970) 2 vols. Cambridge.

CASALIS, E. (1965) *The Basutos, or Twenty Years in South Africa*. Cape Town (reprint).

CAIRNS, H.A.C. (1965) *Prelude to Imperialism: British Reactions to Central African Society, 1840–1890*. London.

CALCOEN (1874) *A Dutch Narrative of the Second Voyage of Vasco da Gama to Calicut*. Printed at Antwerp circa 1504. Intro. and trans. J. P. Bergeau. London.

CAMERON, I. (1965) *Lodestone and Evening Star*. London.

CAMPBELL, L. A. (1968) *Mithraic Iconography and Ideology*. Leiden.

CARY, M. & HAARHOFF, T. J. (1961) *Life and Thought in the Greek and Roman World*. London.

CARY, M. & WARMINGTON, E. H. (1963) *The Ancient Explorers*. Harmondsworth.

CASSON, L. (1971) *Ships and Seamanship in the Ancient World*. Princeton.

CATON THOMPSON, G. (1971) (2nd Ed.) *The Zimbabwe Culture: Ruins and Reactions*. London.

CHAPLIN, J. H. (1967) "Vernacular Month Names from Zambia". *African Studies* 26(3): 145–69.

CHITTICK, H. N. & ROTBERG, R. I. (1975) *East Africa and the Orient: Cultural Syntheses in Pre-Colonial Times*. New York.

CHILDE, V. G. (n.d.) (4th Ed.) *New Light on the Most Ancient East*. New York.

CHRISTENSEN, A. (1944) (2nd Ed.) *L'Iran sous les Sassanides*. Copenhagen.

CLARK, G. (1969) (2nd Ed.) *World Prehistory: A New Outline*. Cambridge.

CLARK, J. D., ed. (1957) *Proceedings of the 3rd Pan-African Congress on Pre-history* (Livingston, 1955). London.

CLARK, J. D. (1959) *The Pre-history of Southern Africa*. Harmondsworth.

CODRINGTON, R. H. (1891) *The Melanesians: Studies in Their Anthropology and Folklore*. Oxford.

COEDES, G. (1963) *Angkor: An introduction.* Hong Kong.

COLLEDGE, M.A.R. (1967) *The Parthians.* London.

CONTENAU, G. (1949) *La Civilisation Phénicienne.* Paris.

COOKE, C. R., ed. (1971) (4th Ed.) *A Guide to the Zimbabwe Ruins.* Bulawayo.

COUPLAND, R. (1938) *East Africa and Its Invaders: From the Earliest Times to the Death of Seyyid Said in 1856.* Oxford.

CRESSWELL, R.A.C. (1958) *A Short Account of Early Muslim Architecture.* Harmondsworth.

CULICAN, W. (1966) *The First Merchant Adventurers: The Ancient Levant in History and Commerce.* London.

CUMONT, F. (1903) *The Mysteries of Mithra.* Chicago.

CUMONT, F. (1956) *The Oriental Religions in Roman Paganism.* New York.

DAHL, O. C. (1951) *Malgache et Maanjan.* Oslo.

DALES, G. F. (1962) *A History of Building Materials.* London.

DAMES, M. L. ed. (1918) *The Book of Duarte Barbosa.* London.

DANIEL, G. (1963) *The Megalith Builders of Western Europe.* Harmondsworth.

DART, R. A. (1954) *The Oriental Horizons of Africa.* Johannesburg.

DAVIDSON, B. (1964) *The African Past: Chronicles from Antiquity to Modern Times.* London.

DAVIDSON, B. (1968) *Africa in History.* London.

DAVIDSON, B. (1970) *Old Africa Rediscovered.* London.

DAVIES, J.N.P. (1979) *Pestilence and Disease in the History of Africa.* Johannesburg.

DEERR, N. (1949) *The History of Sugar.* 2 vols. London.

DEVIC, L.-MARCEL (1975) *Le Pays des Zendjs ou la Côte Orientale d'Afrique au Moyen-Âge.* Amsterdam. (Reprint Paris ed. 1883).

DESCHAMPS, H. (1972) (4th Ed.) *Histoire de Madagascar.* Paris.

DIETERLEN, G. (1965) *Textes Sacrés d'Afrique Noire.* Unesco.

DODO, E. (1972) *Polynesian Seafaring . . .* Lymington.

DOE, R. (1971) *Southern Arabia.* London.

DELAPORTE, L. et al. (1955) *Atlas Historique, I: Antiquité.* Paris.

DIKSHITAR, V.R.R. (1970) *Origin and Spread of the Tamils.* Madras.

DU BOIS, W.E.B. (1958) *Africa Awake.* New York.

DRENNAN, M. R. (1939) "Summary of My Findings in Prehistoric Skeletal Material from Rhodesia. *Rhodesian Science Association Proceedings* 37:167–69.

DICKENSON, R. W. (1968) "Sofala, Gateway to the Gold of Monomotapa". *Rhodesiana* 16 (December): 33–47.

DICKENSON, R. W. (1970) "Sofala and the S.E. African Iron Age". *Rhodesiana* 22 (July): 20–27.

DICKENSON, R. W. (1971) "Antonio Fernández: A reassessment". *Rhodesiana* 25 (December): 45–52.

DICKENSON, R. W. (1975) "The Archaeology of the Sofala Coast". *South African Archaeology Bulletin* 30:84–104.

DICKENSON, R. W. (1976) *Surface Survey of Archeological Sites on Angoche Island.* Supplement Central African Historical Association. Local Series no. 31. University of Rhodesia. Salisbury.

EDYE, J. (1833) "Description of the various classes of vessels . . . of the coasts of Coromandel, Malabar and . . . Ceylon . . ." *Journal of the Royal Asiatic Society*, article 1, pp. 1–14, plates 1–14.

EDWARDS, I.E.S. (1961) (Rev. Ed.) *The Pyramids of Egypt.* Harmondsworth.

ELIOT, W. H. & ELIOT, T. G. (1950) *Excavations in Mesopotamia and Western Iran.* Cambridge, Massachusetts.

EPSTEIN, T. S. (1973) *South India: Yesterday, Today and Tomorrow.* London.

FAGAN, B. (1965) *Southern Africa During the Iron Age.* London.

FAGAN, B. (1970) "Early Trade and Raw Materials in South Central Africa." in R. Gray and D. Birmingham, eds. (1970), pp. 24–38.

FAGE, J. D. (1955) *An Introduction to the History of West Africa.* Cambridge.

FAIR, T.J.D. (1972) "Present and Future Economic Base of Bulawayo." (Report "A", City of Bulawayo Development Plan, unpublished). Johannesburg.

FAIRWEATHER, L. (1975) *Prison Architecture.* London.

FAULKNER, R. O. (1941) Egyptian Seagoing Ships. *Journal of Egyptian Archaeology* 26: 3–9.

FERGUSSON, J. (1899) *History of Indian and Eastern Architecture.* London.

FERRAND, G. (1905) "Les Migrations Musulmanes et Juives à Madagascar". *Revue de l'histoire des religions* 52: 381–417.

FERRAND, G. (1910) "Les Voyages des Javanais à Madagascar". *Journal Asiatique* 10th Séries, 15 (2): 281–330.

FERRAND, G. (1919) "Le K'ouen-Louen et les Anciennes Navigations interocéaniques dans les mers du Sud". *Journal Asiatique* vols. 13 & 14, Séries 12.

FERRAND, G. (1921–28) *Instructions Nautiques et Routiers Arabes et Portugais des XVe et XVIe Siécles.* 3 vols (vols. 1 and 2 Arabic texts only). Paris.

FERRAND, G. (1922) *L'Empire Sumatranais de Crīvijaya.* Paris.

FERRAND, G., trans. (1922) *Voyage du Marchand Arabe Sulaymân en Inde et en Chine.* Paris.

FERRAND, G. (1924) "L'élément Persan dans les Textes Nautiques Arabes des XV et XVI Siècles". *Journal Asiatique* Avril-Juin: 193–257. Paris.

FILESI, T. (1972) *China and Africa in the Middle Ages*, trans. D. L. Morison. London.

FITZGERALD, E. W. (1950) (2nd Ed.) *Africa.* London.

FITZPATRICK, J. P. (1973) *Through Mashonaland with Pick and Pen.* Ed. A. P. Cartwright. Johannesburg.

FOOTE, R. B. (1888) "The Dharwar System, the Chief Auriferous Rock Series in Southern India". *Recordings of the Geological Survey of India* 21, 2: 40–56.

FORBES, R. J. (1955) Studies in Ancient Technology. Vols. 1 & 2. Leiden.

Ford, J. (1971) *The Role of the Typanosomiases in African Ecology: A Study of the Tsetse Fly Problem.* Oxford.

FREEMAN-GRENVILLE, G.S.P. (1962) *The East African Coast: Select Documents.* Oxford.

FREEMAN-GRENVILLE, G.S.P. (1973) *Chronology of African History.* London.

FUGGLE, R. F. (1971) "Relationships between Micro-climate Parameters and Basuto Dwelling Sites in the Marakabei Basin, Lesotho". *South African Journal of Science* 67: 443–50.

GARCON,, M. (1963) "Le Commerce du Bois d'Ébène". *La Revue de Paris* 5(70): 1–12.

GARLAKE, P. S. (1966) *A Guide to the Antiquities of Inyanga.* Bulawayo.

GARLAKE, P. S. (1970) "Rhodesian Ruins, A Preliminary Assessment of Their Styles and Chronology". *Journal of African History* 11 (4): 495–513.

GARLAKE, P. S. (1971) "Majiri Ruins". in C. R. Cooke, ed. (1971), pp. 35–36.

GARLAKE, P. S. (1973) *Great Zimbabwe.* London.

GAYRE OF GAYRE, R. (1972) *The Origin of the Zimbabwean Civilisation.* Salisbury.

GELFAND, M. (1956) *Medicine and Magic of the Mashona.* Cape Town.

GELFAND, M. (1973) *The Genuine Shona: Survival Values of an African Culture.* Gwelo.

GEVREY, A. (1870) *Essai sur Les Comores.* Pondicherry.

GHAIDAN, U. (1974) "Lamu: A Case Study of the Swahili Town". *Town Planning Review*, 51 (1) (January): 84–90.

GHIRSHMAN, R. (1954) *Iran: From the Earliest Times to the Islamic Conquest.* Harmondsworth.

GLANVILLE, S.R.K. (1942) *The Legacy of Egypt.* Oxford.

GOEJE, M. J. DE (1910a) "The Caliphate". In *Encyclopedia Britannica*, 11th ed., vol. 5, pp. 23–54.

GOEJE, M. J. DE (1910b) "Thousand and One Nights". In *Encyclopedia Britannica*, 11th ed., vol. 26, pp. 883–85.

GOODRICH, L. C. (1948) *A Short history of the Chinese People.* London.

GOODWIN, A.J.H. (1927) "The Conception of Slavery in Africa". *South African Journal of Science* 24: 537–48.

GRAY, R. & BIRMINGHAM, D., eds. (1970) *Pre-Colonial African Trade: Essays on Trade in Central and Eastern Africa before 1900.* London.

GREEN, L. P. & FAIR, T.J.D. (1962) *Development in Africa.* Johannesburg.

GREENLAW, J. P. (1976) *The Coral Buildings of Suakin.* Stocksfield.

GRENADE, F. (1978) "Boroudur". *L'Oeil* 278 (Mai).

GROSLIER, B. P. (1966) *Indochina.* Trans. J. Hogarth. Cleveland, Ohio.

GROVE, A. T. (1967) *Africa South of the Sahara.*

GUIART, J. (1963) *Océanie.* Paris.

GUIART, J. (1972) "Multiple Levels of Meaning in Myth". In *Mythology: Selected Readings*, ed. P. Miranda, pp. 111–126. Harmondsworth.

GUYOT, A-L. (1942) *Origine des Plantes Cultivées.* Paris.

GWYNNE, M. E. (1967) "The Possible Origin of the Dwarf Cattle of Socotra". *The Geographical Journal* 133(1): 39–42.

HAIGHT, M.V.J. (1967) *European Powers and South-East Africa.* London.

HALL, D.G.E. (1968) (3rd Ed.) *A History of South East Asia*. London.

HALL, R. N. &. NEAL, W. G. (1904) (2nd Ed.) *The Ancient Ruins of Rhodesia*. Bulawayo.

HALL, R. N. (1907) *Great Zimbabwe*. London.

HALL, R. N. (1909) *Pre-historic Rhodesia*. London.

HALLETT, R. (1970) *Africa to 1875: A modern history*. Ann Arbor, Michigan.

HARDEN, D. (1971) *The Phoenicians*. Harmondsworth.

HARRIS, J. E. (1971) *The African Presence in Asia*. Evanston, Illinois.

HASAN, H. (1928) *A History of Persian Navigation*. London.

HAVELL, E. B. (1915) *The Ancient and Medival Architecture of India*. London.

HAWLEY, T. C. (1957) *The Rhodesian Ridgeback: The Origin, History and Standard of the Breed*. Johannesburg.

HERODOTUS (1910) *The History*. Trans. G. Rawlinson. 2 vols. London.

HAZELTINE, N. (1971) *Madagascar*. London.

HITTI, P. K. (1964) (8th Ed.) *History of the Arabs*. London.

HOGBEN, L. (1973) *Maps, Mirrors and Mechanics*. London.

HORNELL, J. (1934) "Indonesian Influence on East African Culture". *Journal of the Royal Anthropological Institute* 64: 305–32 and plates 38–42.

HORNELL, J. (1946) *Water Transport Origins and Early Evolution*. Cambridge.

HOURANI, G. F. (1951) *Arab Seafaring in the Indian Ocean in Ancient and Early Medieval Times*. Princeton.

HOYT, E. E. (1926) *Primitive Trade*. London.

HUFFMAN, T. N. (1970) "The Early Iron Age and the Spread of the Bantu". *South African Archaeological Bulletin* 25: 3–21.

HUFFMAN, T. N. (1972) "The Rise and Fall of Zimbabwe". *Journal of African History* 13(3): 353–66.

HUFFMAN, T. N. (1973) "Radio-Carbon Dates and Bibliography of the Rhodesian Iron Age". *Rhodesian Pre-History* 11 (December).

HUFFMAN, T. N. (1976a) *A Radio-Carbon Date from Regina Ruins*. Rhodesia.

HUFFMAN, T. N. (1976b) *A Guide to the Great Zimbabwe Ruins*. Salisbury.

HUFFMAN, T. N. (1981) "Snakes and Birds: Expressive Space at Great Zimbabwe". *African Studies* 40 (2): 1–20.

HUFFMAN, T. N. & VOGEL, J. C. (1979) *The Controversial Lintels from Great Zimbabwe*. Antiquity. Pp. 55–57.

HULL, R. W. (1976) *African Cities and Towns before the European Conquest*. New York.

HODGES, R. E. (1971) "Tours of the Ruins Area". In *Guide to the Zimbabwe Ruins*. Historical Monuments Commission. Bulawayo.

IDRISI, AL-SHARIF (1960) *India and the Neighbouring Territories*. Trans. S. M. Ahmad. Leiden.

INDIAN ARCHAEOLOGY—A REVIEW Excavation at Lothal. 1954–55: 12, and plates 13–17; 1955–56: 6–7; 1956–57: 15–16, and plates 10–15; 1957–58: 11–13; 1958–59: 13–15, and plates 12–20; 1959–60: 16–18, and plates 11–17.

INGRAMS, W. H. (1931) *Zanzibar: Its History and Its People*. London.

INGRAMS, W. H. (1942) *Arabia and the Isles*. London.

JACQUES, A. A. (1931) "Notes on the Lemba Tribe of the Northern Transvaal". *Anthropos* 26: 245–51.

JEFFREYS, M.D.W. (1938) *The Cowry Shell*, vol. 15. Nigeria.

JEFFREYS, M.D.W. (1963) "Mumbo Jumbo or Mambo the Heart Easter". *Native Affairs Department Annual* 40: 74–83.

JEFFREYS, M.D.W. (1968) "Some Semitic Influences in Hottentot Culture". 4th Raymond Dart Lecture. Johannesburg.

JONES, W. (1799) "Remarks on the Preceding Essay (Wilford, 1799) by the President of the Bengal Asiatic Society". *Asiatic Researches* 3: 463–68.

JONGHE, D. DE (1949) *Les formes d'asservissement dans les sociétés indigènes du Congo Belge* . . . Brussels.

JUNOD, H. A. (1908) "The BaLemba of the Zoutpansberg". *Folklore* 19: 276–87.

JUNOD, H. A. (1913) *The Life of a South African Tribe*. Neuchatel.

KAPLAN, M. (1974) "Twilight of the Arab Dhow: *National Geographic* 146 (September): 330–51.

KAY, G. (1970) *Rhodesia: A Human Geography*. London.

KENDREW, W. G. (1960) (6th Ed.) *The Climates of the Continents*. Oxford.

KENT, R. K. (1970) *Early Kingdoms in Madagascar, 1500–1700*. New York.

KIGHTLY, C. (1979) *Strongholds of the Realm:*

Defences in Britain from Pre-history to the Twentieth Century. London.

KING, W. (1875) "Preliminary Note on the Goldfields of South-East Wynad. Madras Presidency". *Records of the Geological Survey of India,* part 2 (May): 30–45.

KIRBY, P. R. (1966) *The Indonesian Origin of Certain African Musical Instruments.* Johannesburg.

KONCZACKI, S. A. & KONCZACKI, J. M. (1977) *An Economic History of Tropical Africa, vol. 1: The Pre-Colonial Period.* London.

KORAN, The (Qur'an) 1928 Trans. E. H. Palmer. The World's Classics. London.

KRIGE, E. J. (1980) "African Techniques of Domination and State Formation: Their Relevance Today". 16th Raymond Dart Lecture. Johannesburg.

LABOURET, H. (1925) "L'Or du Lobi". *Bulletin du Comité de l'Afrique Française, Renseignements Coloniaux,* no. 3: 69–73.

LAROUSSE (1960) *Grand Larousse Encyclopaedique.* 11 vols. Paris.

LAVEDAN, P. (1926) *Histoire de l'Urbanisme, Antiquité-Moyen Age.* Paris (for Baghdad, see pp. 276–280).

LAWRENCE, P. & MEGGIT, M. J. (1965) *Gods, Ghosts, and Men in Melanesia: Some Religions of Australian New Guinea and the New Hebrides.* Melbourne and Oxford.

LAWRENCE, T. E. (1939) *Seven Pillars of Wisdom.* London.

LEES, G. M. & FALCON, N. L. (1975) "The Geographical History of the Mesopotamian Plains". *The Geographical Journal* 18 (March): 24–39.

LESTRADE, G. P. (1927) "Some Notes on the Ethnic History of BaVenda and Their Rhodesia Affinities". *South African Journal of Science* 24 (December): 486–95.

LE STRANGE, G. (1905) *The Lands of the Eastern Caliphate.* Cambridge.

LE STRANGE, G. (1924) *Baghdad during the Abbasid Caliphate.* Oxford.

LEWANDOWSKI, S. (1980) "The Hindu Temple in South India." In *Buildings and Society. . . .* Ed. A. D. King, pp. 123–50. London.

LEWIS, D. (1972) *We, the Navigators: The Ancient Art of Land Finding in the Pacific.* Canberra.

LEWIS, D. (1978) *The Voyaging Stars.* Sydney.

LOEWE, M. (1966) *Imperial China: The Historical Background to the Modern Age.* London.

LOMBARD, M. (1975) *The Golden Age of Islam.* Trans. J. Spencer. Amsterdam.

LORCH, F. B. (1951) "Zimbabwe". *Africana Notes and News* 8 (September): 107–18.

LONGRIGG, S. H. & STOKES, F. (1958) *Iraq.* New York.

MACKAY, E. (1948) *Early Indus Civilisations.* London.

MACLAREN, J. M. (1906) "Notes on Some Auriferous Tracts in Southern India". *Records of the Geological Survey of India* 34: 96–131.

MAGGS, T. M. O'C. (1976) *Iron Age Communities of the Southern Highveld.* Council Natal Museum, Occasional Publication no. 2. Pietermaritzburg.

MAITLAND, A. (1971) *Speke.* London.

MAJOR, R. H. (1857) *India in the Fifteenth Century.* Hakluyt Society: London.

MAJUMDAR, D. N. (1961) (4th Ed.) *Races and Cultures of India.* Bombay.

MAJUMDAR, R. C. & PUSALKER, A. D., eds. (1953–54) *The History and Culture of the Indian People.* 10 vols. Bombay.

MALCOLM, H. (1846) *Travels in Hindustan and China.* Edinburgh.

MALINOWSKI, B. (1922) *Argonauts of the Western Pacific.* London.

MALLOWS, E.W.N. (1963) "Pre-European Settlement Patterns in Africa South of the Sahara". *Institute for the Study of Man in Africa,* paper no. 13. Johannesburg.

MARAIS, E. N. (1970) *The Soul of the White Ant.* Cape Town.

MARCO POLO (1908) *The Travels of Marco Polo the Venetian.* (Everyman Ed.) London.

MARTIN, E. B. (1973) *The History of Malindi.* Nairobi.

MANIKU, A. et al. (1977) *Discover Maldives.* Male.

MANIKU, H. A. (1977) *The Maldive Islands . . . A Profile.* Male.

MANIKU, H. A. (1980) "Republic of Maldives". Paper presented to Seminar on Academic Studies. Peking. June. Male.

MASON, J. A. (1957) *The Ancient Civilisation of Peru.* Harmondsworth.

MASON, R. J. (1962) *The Pre-history of the Transvaal.* Johannesburg.

MASON, R. J. (1968a) "Transvaal and Natal Iron Age Settlement Revealed by Aerial Photography and Excavation". *African Studies* 27(4): 1–14.

MASON, R. J. (1968b) "South African Iron Age and Present-Day Venda Architecture and Pottery from the Northern Transavaal South Africa". *African Studies* 27(4): 15–22.

MASON, R. J. (1973a) Report of lecture, University of Witwatersrand *Rand Daily Mail*, 16 October 1973, p. 3, and 17 October 1973, p. 19.

MASON, R. J. (1973*b*) "Early Iron Age Settlement of Southern Africa". *South African Journal of Science* 69:324–326.

MASUDI, A. al- (1861–77) *Les Prairies d'or*. . . . Trans. C. B. de Maynard and P. de Courteille. 9 vols. Paris.

MATHEW, G. (1961) *The Dawn of African History*. Oxford.

MATHEW, G. (1975) "The Dating and Significance of the Periplus of the Erythraean Sea". In H. N. Chittick and R. I. Rotberg (1975), pp. 147–163.

MAUCH, C. (1969) *The Journals of Karl Mauch: His Travels in the Transvaal and Rhodesia, 1869–1872*. Trans. F. O. Bernard. Ed. E. E. Burke. Salisbury.

MAUCH, C. (1971) *Karl Mauch, African Explorer*. Ed. and trans. F. O. Bernard. Cape Town.

MAUNY, R. (1958) "Notes sur le Problème Zimbabwe-Sofala". *Studia*: 176–83.

MAUNY, R. (1961) *Tableau Géographique de l'Ouest Africain au Moyen Âge*. Dakar.

McCRINDLE, J. W. (1882) *The Commerce and Navigation of the Erythraean Sea* (the "Periplus") *and Ancient India as Described by Ktesias the Indian*, Calcutta. (Reprint 1973 Amsterdam.)

McEWAN, P.J.M., ed. (1968) *Africa from Early Times to 1800*. London.

McGEE, T. G. (1967) *The South-East Asian City*. London.

MIERS, S. & KOPTYOFF, I. (1977) *Slavery in Africa: Historical and Anthropoligical Perspectives*. Madison.

MILLER, R. (1952) "Cultivation Terraces in Nigeria". Letter to *The Geographical Journal*, 4 December 1951: 110–11.

MIQUEL, A. (1973) (2nd Ed.) *La Géographie Humaine du Monde musulman Jusqu'au Milieu du 11e Siècle*. Paris.

MOOKERJI, R. K. (1957) (2nd Ed. Rev.) *Indian Shipping: A History of the Sea-borne Trade and Activity of the Indians from the Earliest Times*. Bombay.

MORELAND, W. H., ed. (1931) *Relations of Golconda in the Early Seventeenth Century*. London.

MORELAND, W. H. (1944) *A Short History of India*. London.

MULLAN, J. E. (n.d.) *The Arab Builders of Zimbabwe*. Salisbury.

MUNN, L. (1934) "Ancient Gold Mining Activity (of the Western Portion of the Raichur Doab)". *Journal of the Hyderabad Geological Survey* 2: 77–104.

MUNN, L. (1936) "Observations and Notes on the Method of Ancient Gold Mining in Southern India with Special Reference to the Raichur and Shorapur Districts of Hyderabad State". *Transactions of the Mining and Geological Institute of India*: 103–16.

MURDOCK, G. P. (1959) *Africa—Its Peoples and Their Culture History*. New York.

MELTZER, M. (1972) *Slavery: From the Rise of Western Civilisation to Today*. New York.

MSIKI [A. A. Campbell] (1972) *Mlimo: The Rise and Fall of the Matabele*. Bulawayo.

NEOGI, P. (1914) *Iron in Ancient India*. Calcutta.

NIEBOER, H. J. (1910) *Slavery as an Industrial System*. The Hague.

NIEL, F. (1961) *Dolmens et Menhirs*. Paris.

NOLDEKE, T. (1963) *Sketches from Eastern History*. Trans. J. S. Black, rev. by author. Beirut. (Reprint 1892 ed.)

NORTH-COOMBES, A. (1971) *The Island of Rodrigues*. Port Louis, Mauritius.

O'FLAHERTY, W. D. (1975) *Hindu Myths: A Sourcebook*. . . . Harmondsworth.

OLIVER, R. & MATHEW, G. (1963) *History of East Africa*, vol. 1. Oxford.

OLIVER, R., ed. (1968) (2nd Ed.) *The Dawn of African History*. London.

OLIVER, R. & FAGAN, B. M. (1975) *Africa in the Iron Age c. 500 B.C. to A.D. 1400*. Cambridge.

OPPENHEIM, A. L. (1954) "The Seafaring Merchants of Ur". *American Oriental Society Journal* 74: 6–17.

OSBORN, R. D. (1878) *Islam under the Khalifs of Baghdad*. London.

OWEN, W.F.W. (1833) *Narrative of Voyages to Explore the Shores of Africa, Arabia and Madagascar*. 2 vols. London.

PAINTER, K. S. (1977) "Wealth of the Roman World: Gold and Silver, A.D. 300–700". *Mining Survey* 7: 2–9. Johannesburg.

PACHAI, B., ed. (1972) *The Early History of Malawi*. London.

PALGRAVE, K. C. et al. (1977) *Trees of South Africa*. Cape Town.

PARKER, E. H. (1924)(2nd Ed.) *A Thousand Years of the Tartars*. London.

PARKER, H.M.D. (1958) *The Roman Legions*. Cambridge.

PARMENTIER, H. (1948) *L'Art Architectural Hindou dans l'Inde et en Extrême Orient*. Paris.

PAVER, B. G. (1950) *Zimbabwe Cavalcade: Rhodesia's Romance*. Johannesburg.

PERRIN, G. de BRICHAMBAUT, & WALLEN, C. C. (1963) "A Study of Agroclimatology in Semi-arid and Arid Zones of the Near East". Technical Note 56. World Meteorological Organization. Geneva.

PETERS, C. (1902) *The Eldorado of the Ancients*. London.

PETTIGREW, J. (1959) *Robber Noblemen: A Study of the Political System of the Sikh Jats*. London.

PHILLIPS, J. (1959) *Agriculture and Ecology in Africa*. London.

PHILLIPS, W. (1967) *Oman: A history*. London.

PHILLIPSON, D. W. (1970) "Notes on the Later Prehistoric Radio-Carbon Chronology of Eastern and Southern Africa". *Journal of African History* 11(1):1–15.

PHILLIPSON, D. W. (1976) *The Pre-history of Eastern Zambia*. Memoir 6. *British Institute in East Africa*. Nairobi.

PHILLIPSON, D. W. (1977) *The Later Prehistory of Eastern and Southern Africa*. London.

PIGGOT, S. (1952) *Prehistoric India*. Harmondsworth.

PILLAI, M.S.P. (1963) *Tamil India*. Madras.

PILLAI, V. K. (1904) *The Tamils Eighteen Hundred Years Ago*. Madras.

POIDEBARD, A. (1939) *Un Grand Port Disparu: Tyr*. 2 vols. Paris.

POIDEBARD, A. & LAUFFRAY, J. (1951) *Sidon: Améngagements Antiques du Port de Saida*. Beyrouth.

POPE, G. V. (1911) (7th Ed.) *A Handbook of the Ordinary Dialect of the Tamil Language*. Oxford.

PHILBY, H. St. J. B. (1949) "Two Notes from Central Arabia". *The Geographical Journal* 113: 86–93.

PHILBY, H. St. J. B. (1950) "Motor Tracks and Sabaean Inscriptions". *Njed. The Geographical Journal* 116: 211–15.

POSTGATE, N. (1978) *The First Empires*. London.

POSSELT, F.W.T. (1927) *A Survey of the Native Tribes of Southern Rhodesia* [with map]. Salisbury.

POUJADE, J. (1946) *La Route des Indes et ses Navires*. Paris.

PRINSEP, J. (1836) "Notes on the Nautical Instruments of the Arabs". In G. Ferrand, 1921–1928, pp. 1–24.

PRITCHARD, J. B., ed. (1974) *Solomon and Sheba*. London.

PROUST, F. (1969) "Zimbabwe ou le Tombeau Sacré des Chefs". *Archéologia* 29 (July/August):23–29.

PURCELL, V. (1965) (2nd Ed.) *The Chinese in Southeast Asia*. London.

PYM, C. (1968) *The Ancient Civilisation of Angkor*. New York.

PRENDERGAST, M. D. (1979) "Iron Age Settlement and Economy on Part of the Southern Zambesian Highveld". *South African Archaeological Bulletin* 34(130): 111–19.

QUARITCH-WALES, H. G. (1961) (2nd Ed.) *The Making of Greater India*. London.

QUIGGIN, A. H. (1949) *A Survey of Primitive Money: The Beginnings of Currency*. London.

RANDALL-MacIVER, D. (1906) *Medieval Rhodesia*. London.

RAO, S. R. (1969) "Lothal: le Port de l'Empire de l'Indus". *Archéologia* 29 (July/August): 64–73.

RAPSON, E. J. (1935) *The Puranas*. *Cambridge History of India*, vol. 1, pp. 296–318.

RAVENSTEIN, E. G., ed. (1898) *A Journal of the First Voyage of Vasco da Gama, 1497–1499*. London.

RAWLINSON, H. G. (1952) *India: A Short Cultural History*. London.

RECLUS, E. (1883) *L'Inde (Nouvelle Géographie Universelle* VIII). Paris.

REICKE, B. O. (1968) *The New Testament Era*. London.

REINAUD, J. (1845) *Fragments Arabes et Persanes Inédits*. Amsterdam: Oriental Press (reprint 1974).

REPIQUET, J. (1901) *Le Sultanat d'Anjouan (Iles Comores)*. Paris.

REYNOLDS, B. (1968) *The Material Culture of the Peoples of the Gwembe Valley*. New York.

Rhodesia Publicity Bureau (1930) *The Great Zimbabwe Ruins*. Bulawayo.

RICHARD, W. J. (1908) *The Indian Christians of St. Thomas*. Bemrose.

RICHARD, S.C. & PLACE, J. (1960) *East African Explorers*. London.

RICHARDSON, J. (1885) *A new Malagasy-English Dictionary*. Antanarivo (reprint 1967).

RICHMOND, I. A. (1955) *Roman Britain*. Hardmondsworth.

RIVERS, W.H.R. (1914) *The History of Melanesian Society*. 2 vols. Cambridge.

ROCHLIN, S. A. (1958) "Early Arab Knowledge of the Cape of Good Hope". *Africana Notes and News* 13 (March): 32–57.

ROGERS, J. M. (1970) "Samarra, a Study in Medieval Town Planning". In *The Islamic City*, ed. A.H. Hourani and S. M. Stern, pp. 119–55. Oxford.

ROUX, G. (1966) *Ancient Iraq*. Harmondsworth.

RUSSELL, C.E.B. (1935) *General Rigby, Zanzibar and the Slave Trade*. London.

SANDERSON, J. (1860) *Memoranda of a Trading Trip into the Orange River (Sovereignty) Free State, and the Country of the Transvaal Boers, 1851–1852. Royal Geographical Society Journal* 30: 233–255.

SARASWATI, S. K. (1953) "Architecture". In R.C. Majumdar & A. D. Pulsaker (1953–54), vol. 2, chapter 20A.

SARASWATI, S. K. (1954) "Architecture". In R.C. Majumdar & A. D. Pulsaker (1953–54), vol. 3, chapter 19.

SASTRI, K.A.N. (1949) *Takuapa and its Tamil Inscriptions. Journal of the Royal Asiatic Society of Great Britain*, Malayan Branch, vol. 22, 25–30.

SASTRI, K.A.N. (1966) (3rd Ed.) *A History of South India*. London.

SAUSSURE, L. DE (1923) "L'Origine de la rose des vents et l'invention de la boussole". In G. Ferrand (1928), pp. 31–127.

SAUSSURE, L. DE (n.d.) *Commentaire des Instructions Nautiques de Ibn Majid et Sulayman al-Mahri*. In G. Ferrand (1928), pp. 129–255.

SCHAFER, E. H. (1951) *Iranian Merchants in Tang Dynasty Tales*. University of California Publications in Semitic Philology 11, pp. 403–22.

SCHERER, A. (1974) (3rd Ed.) *Histoire de la Reunion*. Paris.

SCHLICHTER, H. (1893) "Historical Evidence as to the Zimbabwe Ruins". *The Geographical Journal* 11 (July): 44–52.

SCHLICHTER, H. (1899) "Travels and Researches in Rhodesia". *The Geographical Journal* 12 (April): 376–96 (with discussions by Selous et al.: 391–96).

SCHNITGER, F. M. (1964) *Forgotten Kingdoms in Sumatra*. Leiden.

SCHOFF, W. H., trans. (1912) *The Periplus of the Erythraean Sea*. New York.

SCHOFIELD, J. E. (1926) "Zimbabwe: A Critical Examination of the Building Methods Employed". *South African Journal of Science* 23 (December): 971–86.

SELIGMAN, C. G. (1910) *The Melanesians of New Guinea*. Cambridge.

SELIGMAN, C. G. & BRENDA, Z. (1911) *The Veddas*. Cambridge.

SELOUS, F. C. (1893) *Travel and Adventure in South-East Africa*. London.

SELOUS, F. C. et al. (1970) (Reprint) *A Hunter's Wanderings in Africa*. Bulawayo.

SELOUS, F. C. et al. (1899). Discussion on paper by H. Schlichter. See H. Schlichter (1899).

SEVERIN, T. (1982) *The Sinbad Voyage*. London.

SEWELL, R. (1900) *A Forgotten Empire (Vijayanager): A Contribution to the History of India*. London.

SHABAN, M. A. (1970) *The Abbasid Revolution*. Cambridge.

SHABAN, M. A. (1971) *Islamic History*, A.D. 600–750: A New Interpretation. Cambridge.

SHINNIE, P. L., ed. (1971) *The African Iron Age*. Oxford.

SICARD, H. von (1963) "Lemba Initiation Chants". *Ethnos*, parts 2–4. Stockholm.

SICARD, H. von (1963a) "The Ancient Sabi—Zimbabwe Trade Route". *Native Affairs Department Annual:* 60–67.

SIGNATURE (1975) "There's Gold in them thar termite hills". July. Johannesburg.

SILBERBERG, H. K. (1978) *Zimbabwe Ruins: A Mystery Solved. Arts Rhodesia* no. 1, pp. 51–62.

SILLERY, A. (1974) *Botswana: A Short Political History*. London.

SIMMONDS, N. W. (1966) (2nd Ed.) *Bananas*. London.

SINGER, C. (1954) "Some Early Gold Work" *Endeavour* 13 (April): 86–93.

SITWELL, S. (1957) *Arabesque and Honeycomb*. London.

SKEAT, W. W. & BLAGDEN, G. O. (1906) Pagan Races of the Malay Peninsula. London.

SKELTON, R. A. (1970) *Explorers Maps*. London.

SMITH, V. A. (1924) (4th Ed.) *The Early History of India from 600 B.C. to the Mohummadan Conquest*. Revised by S. M. Edwards. Oxford.

SMITH, T. V., ed. (1956) *From Aristotle to Plotinus*. Chicago.

SOPHER, D. E. (1965) *The Sea Nomads: A Study Based on the Literature of the Maritime Boat People of Southeast Asia*. Memoirs of the National Museum no. 5. Singapore.

SOUTH AFRICA SUGAR ASSOCIATION EXPERIMENTAL STATION (1977) *Irrigation of Sugar Cane*. Bulletin no. 7 (rev. April). Mount Edgecombe.

SPATE, O.H.K., Learmonth, A.T.A., & FARMER, B. H. (1967) *India, Pakistan and Ceylon: The Regions*. London.

STAMP, L. D. (1953) *Africa: A Study in Tropical Development*. New York,

STARK, F. (1936) *The Southern Gates of Arabia: A Journey in the Hadhramaut*. London.

STAYT, H. A. (1931a) *The BaVenda*. London.

STAYT, H. A. (1931b) "Notes on the BaLemba". *Journal of the Royal Anthropological Institute* 61: 231–38 and plate 29.

STEINGASS, F. (1930) *A Comprehensive Persian-English Dictionary*. London.

STRABO 1917) *The Geography*. Trans. H. L. Jones. London: Loeb Classical Library. 8 vols.

STEVENS, C. G. (1931) "The Zimbabwe Temple". *Journal of the Royal Anthropological Institute* 61: 181–86.

STOW, G. W. (1905) *The Native Races of South Africa*. London.

SULIVAN, C.G.L. (1873) *Dhow Chasing in Zanzibar Waters*. London.

SUMMERS, R. (1958) *Inyanga: Prehistoric Settlements in Southern Rhodesia*. Cambridge.

SUMMERS, R. (1955) "The Dating of the Zimbabwe Ruins". *Antiquity* 29:107–110.

SUMMERS, R. et al. (1961) "Zimbabwe Excavations 1958". Occasional Papers, National Museum of Southern Rhodesia 3, no. 23A.

SUMMERS, R. (1963) "The Riddle of Zimbabwe". In *Vanished Civilisations: Forgotten Peoples of the Ancient World*", ed. E. Bacon, pp. 43–54. London.

SUMMERS, R. (1964) *Zimbabwe, A Rhodesian Mystery*. Johannesburg.

SUMMERS, R. (1969) *Ancient Mining in Rhodesia and Adjacent Areas: Salisbury*. Trustees of the National Museums of Rhodesia (Museum Memoir no. 3).

SUMMERS, R. (1971) *Ancient Ruins and Vanished Civilisations of Southern Africa*. Cape Town.

SYKES, P. M. (1930) (3rd Ed.) *A History of Persia*. London.

TARN, W. W. (1938) *The Greeks in Bactria and India*. Cambridge.

TARN, W. W. & GRIFFITHS, G. T. (1952) (3rd Ed.) *Hellenistic Civilisation*. London.

TAYLOR, E.R.G. (1971) *The Haven-finding Art*. London.

THAPAR, R. (1966) *A History of India*, vol. 1. Harmondsworth.

THEAL, G. M. (1898–1903) *Records of South-Eastern Africa*. 9 vols. Cape Town.

THESIGER, W. (1967) *The Marsh Arabs*. Harmondsworth.

THURSTON, E. (1906) "Slavery." In *Ethnographic Notes in Southern India*. Government Press: Madras.

THURSTON, E. (1909) *Castes and Tribes of Southern India*. Madras.

TIBBETTS, G. R. (1956) "Pre-Islamic Arabia and S. E. Asia". *Journal of the Malayan Branch of the Royal Asiatic Society* 29 (3): 182–208.

TIBBETTS, G. R. (1961) "Arab Navigation in the Red Sea". *The Geographical Journal* 127(September): 322–34.

TIBBETTS, G. R. (1971) *Arab Navigation in the Indian Ocean before the Coming of the Portuguese*. Royal Asiatic Society of Great Britain and Ireland. Oriental Trans. Fund New Series 42. London.

TOMASCHEK, W. & BITTNER, M. (1897) *Die Topographischen Capitel des Mohit*. Vienna.

TOMLINSON, R. W. (1974) "Preliminary Biogeographical Studies on the Inyanga Mountains Rhodesia". *The South African Geographical Journal* 56 (April): 15–26.

TOUSSAINT, A. (1961) *Histoire de l'Océan Indien*. Paris.

TOUSSAINT, A. (1974) *Histoire de l'Île Maurice*. Paris.

TOY, S. (1957) *The Strongholds of India*. London.

TOY, S. (1965) *The Fortified Cities of India*. London.

TOYNBEE, A. J. (1939) *A Study of History*. 13 vols. London.

UNITED KINGDOM, HYDROGRAPHER OF THE NAVY (1961) *West Coast of India Pilot* (N.P. 38). London. 10th ed.

UNITED KINGDOM, HYDROGRAPHER OF THE NAVY (1967a) *African Pilot No. 3* (N.P. 3). London. 12th ed.

UNITED KINGDOM, HYDROGRAPHER OF THE NAVY (1967b) *Persian Gulf Pilot* (N.P. 63). London. 11th ed.

UNITED KINGDOM, HYDROGRAPHER OF THE NAVY (1967c) *Red Sea and Gulf of Aden Pilot* (N.P. 64). London. 11th ed.

UNITED KINGDOM, HYDROGRAPHER OF THE NAVY (1971) *South Indian Ocean Pilot* (N.P. 39). Taunton.

UNITED KINGDOM, HYDROGRAPHER OF THE NAVY (1973) (3rd Ed.) *Ocean Passages for the World*. Taunton.

VADDAS (1907) (No Author) Ethnographical Survey of Mysore. Prelim. Issue 11, pp. 1–16. Bangalore.

VAN DER SLEEN, W.G.N. (1957) "On the Origin of Some Zimbabwe Beads". Item 59 in Proceedings of the 3rd Pan African Congress on Pre-history, Livingstone 1955. Ed. D. Clark and S. Cole. London.

VAN OORDT, J. F. (1907) *The Origins of the Bantu*. Cape Town.

VAN OORDT, J. F. (1909) *Who Were the Builders of the Great Zimbabwe?* Cape Town.

VAN WARMELO, N. J., ed. (1940) *The Copper Miners of Musina and the Early History of the Zoutpansberg*. Ethnological Publications, vol. 8 Pretoria.

VAN WARMELO, N. J. & PHOPHI, W.W.D. (1948) *Venda Law Parts 1–4*. Ethnological Publications no. 23. Pretoria.

VENTER, A. J. (1975) *Africa Today*. Johannesburg.

VERIN, P. (1969) "Les Origines Malgaches: Indices Culturels et Archéologiques". *Archéologia* 29 (July/August): 38–44.

VILLIERS, A. J. (1952) *The Indian Ocean*. London.

VILLIERS, A. J. (1969) *Sons of Sinbad*. New York.

VON HAGEN, V. W. (1957) *Realm of the Incas*. New York.

WAINWRIGHT, G. A. (1949) *Founders of Zimbabwe Civilisation*. Man 49 (June): 62 ff.

WALTON J. (1956) *African Village*. Pretoria.

WALTON, J. (1957) "Some Features of the Monomotapa Culture". Item 51 in Proceedings of the 3rd Pan-African Congress on Prehistory, Livingston 1955. Ed. D. Clark and S. Cole. London.

WALTON, J. (1965) *Early Ghoya Settlement in the OFS*. Bloemfontein National Museum. Memoir No. 2.

WARMINGTON, B. H. (1928) *The Commerce between the Roman Empire and India*. Cambridge.

WARREN, B. A. (1966) "Medieval Arab References to the Seasonally Reversing Currents of the North Indian Ocean". *Deep Sea Research* 13: 167–71.

WATKINS, T. (Ed.) (1975) *Radiocarbon: Calibration and Prehistory*. Edinburgh.

WATSON, F. (1974) *A Concise History of India*. London.

WENTZEL, V. (1964) "Moçambique. . . ." *National Geographic* 126 (August): 197–231).

WESTERMANN, W. L. (1942) "Industrial Slavery in Roman Italy". *Journal of Economic History* 2: 149–63.

WESTERMANN, W. L. (1955) *The Slave Systems of Greek and Roman Antiquity*. American Philosophical Society, vol. 40. Philadelphia.

WHEATLEY, P. (1961) *The Golden Khersonese*. Kuala Lampur.

WHEELER, J. H. et al. (1955) *Regional Geography of the World*. New York.

WHEELER, M. (1954) *Rome beyond the Imperial Frontiers*. London.

WHEELER, M. (1966) *Civilisations of the Indus Valley and Beyond*. London.

WHEELER, R.E.M. & WHEELER, T. V. (1936) *Verulamium: A Belgic and Two Roman Cities*. Oxford.

WHEELWRIGHT, C. A. (1905) "Native Circumcision Lodge in the Zoutpansberg District". *Journal of the Royal Anthropological Institute* 35: 251–55.

WHITE F. (1905) "Notes on the Great Zimbabwe Elliptical Ruin". *Journal of the Royal Anthropological Institute* 35: 39–47.

WHITTY, A. (1957) The Origins of the Stone Architecture of Zimbabwe. Item 53 in Proceedings of the 3rd Pan African Congress on Prehistory, Livingston 1955. Ed. D. Clark and S. Cole. London 366–377.

WILES, J. (1974) *Delhi Is Far Away: A Journey through India*. London.

WILFORD, F. (1799) *On Egypt and other Countries Adjacent to the Cali River, or Nile of Ethiopia, from the Ancient Books of the Hindus*. Asiatic Researches vol. 3, pp. 295–462.

WILLOUGHBY, J. C. (1893) *A Narrative of Further Excavations at Zimbabwe (Mashonaland)*. London.

WILLCOX, A. R. (1976) *Southern Land*. Cape Town.

WILLET, F. (1971) *African Art: An Introduction*. New York.

WILLS, A. J. (1964) *An Introduction to the History of Central Africa*. London.

WILLS, C. J. (1883) *In the Land of the Lion and Sun*. London.

WILMOT, F. (1971) *Monomotapa (Rhodesia): Its Monuments and Its History from the Most Ancient Times to the Present Century*. London.

WILSON, M. (1970) "The Thousand Years before Van Riebeeck". 6th Raymond Dart Lecture. Johannesburg.

WILSON, M. & THOMPSON, L., eds. (1969) *The Oxford History of South Africa*, vol. 1. Oxford.

WITTFOGEL, K. A.: (1957) *Oriental Despotism*. New Haven.

WOLTERS, O. W. (1967) *Early Indonesian Commerce: A Study of the Origins of Srivijaya.* Ithaca.

WOOLEY, L. (1954) *Excavations at Ur.* London.

WOOLEY, L. (1965) *The Sumerians.* New York.

YOUNG, G. (1977) *Return to the Marshes.* London.

ZAEHNER, R. C. (1961) *The Dawn and Twilight of Zoroastrianism.* London.

ZURCHER, E. (1959) *The Buddhist Conquest of China.*

Index

Page numbers in **boldface** refer to illustrations.